50% OFF Online TSI (TSIA2) Prep Course!

Dear Customer,

We consider it an honor and a privilege that you chose our TSI Study Guide. As a way of showing our appreciation and to help us better serve you, we have partnered with Mometrix Test Preparation to offer you **50% off their online TSI Prep Course**. Many TSI courses are needlessly expensive and don't deliver enough value. With their course, you get access to the best TSI prep material, and **you only pay half price**.

Mometrix has structured their online course to perfectly complement your printed study guide. The TSI Prep Course contains **in-depth lessons** that cover all the most important topics, **220+ video reviews** that explain difficult concepts, **over 1,150 practice questions** to ensure you feel prepared, and more than **300 digital flashcards**, so you can study while you're on the go.

Online TSI Assessment 2.0 Prep Course

Topics Covered:

- Mathematics
  - Quantitative Reasoning
  - Algebraic Reasoning
  - Geometric and Spatial Reasoning
  - Probabilistic and Statistical Reasoning
- Reading
  - Literary and Informational Text Analysis
  - Inferences in a Text or Texts
  - Argumentation and Vocabulary
  - Author's Craft
- Writing
  - Conventions of Grammar and Usage
  - Conventions of Punctuation and Spelling
  - Essay and Revision and Editing

Course Features:

- TSI Study Guide
  - Get content that complements our best-selling study guide.
- 8 Full-Length Practice Tests
  - With over 1,150 practice questions, you can test yourself again and again.
- Mobile Friendly
  - If you need to study on the go, the course is easily accessible from your mobile device.
- TSI Flashcards
  - Their course includes a flashcard mode consisting of over 300 content cards to help you study.

To receive this discount, simply head to their website: mometrix.com/university/tsi or simply scan this QR code with your smartphone. At the checkout page, enter the discount code: **APEXTSI50**

If you have any questions or concerns, please contact Mometrix at support@mometrix.com.

Sincerely,

in partnership with

Free Study Tips Videos/DVD

In addition to this guide, we have created a FREE set of videos with helpful study tips. **These FREE videos provide you with top-notch tips to conquer your exam and reach your goals.**

Our simple request is that you give us feedback about the book in exchange for these strategy-packed videos. We would love to hear what you thought about the book, whether positive, negative, or neutral. It is our #1 goal to provide you with quality products and customer service.

To receive your **FREE Study Tips Videos**, scan the QR code or email freevideos@apexprep.com. Please put "FREE Videos" in the subject line and include the following in the email:

a. The title of the book

b. Your rating of the book on a scale of 1-5, with 5 being the highest score

c. Any thoughts or feedback about the book

Thank you!

TSI Study Guide 2024-2025
3 Practice Tests and TSI Prep Book for the Texas Assessment
[7th Edition]

J. M. Lefort

Written and edited by APEX Publishing.

ISBN 13: 9781637759080

For additional information or for bulk orders, contact info@apexprep.com.

Table of Contents

Welcome

Dear Customer,

Congratulations on taking the next step in your educational journey, and thank you for choosing APEX to help you prepare! We are delighted to be by your side, equipping you with the knowledge and skills needed to make this move forward. Your APEX study guide contains helpful tips and quality study material that will contribute to your success. This study guide has been tailored to assist you in passing your chosen exam, but it also includes strategies to conquer any test with ease. Whether your goal is personal growth or acing that big exam to move up in your career, our goal is to leave you with the confidence and ability to reach the top!

We love to hear success stories, so please let us know how you do on your exam. Since we are continually making improvements to our products, we welcome feedback of any sort. Your achievements as well as criticisms can be emailed to info@apexprep.com.

Sincerely,
APEX Team

FREE Videos/DVD OFFER

Achieving a high score on your exam depends on both understanding the content and applying your knowledge. **Because your success is our primary goal, we offer FREE Study Tips Videos, which provide top-notch test taking strategies to help optimize your testing experience.**

Our simple request is that you email us feedback about our book in exchange for the strategy-packed videos.

To receive your **FREE Study Tips Videos**, scan the QR code or email freevideos@apexprep.com. Please put "FREE Videos" in the subject line and include the following in the email:

a. The title of the book
b. Your rating of the book on a scale of 1-5, with 5 being the highest score
c. Any thoughts or feedback about the book

Thank you!

Test Taking Strategies

1. Reading the Whole Question

A popular assumption in Western culture is the idea that we don't have enough time for anything. We speed while driving to work, we want to read an assignment for class as quickly as possible, or we want the line in the supermarket to dwindle faster. However, speeding through such events robs us from being able to thoroughly appreciate and understand what's happening around us. While taking a timed test, the feeling one might have while reading a question is to find the correct answer as quickly as possible. Although pace is important, don't let it deter you from reading the whole question. Test writers know how to subtly change a test question toward the end in various ways, such as adding a negative or changing focus. If the question has a passage, carefully read the whole passage as well before moving on to the questions. This will help you process the information in the passage rather than worrying about the questions you've just read and where to find them. A thorough understanding of the passage or question is an important way for test takers to be able to succeed on an exam.

2. Examining Every Answer Choice

Let's say we're at the market buying apples. The first apple we see on top of the heap may *look* like the best apple, but if we turn it over, we can see bruising on the skin. We must examine several apples before deciding which apple is the best. Finding the correct answer choice is like finding the best apple. Although it's tempting to choose an answer that seems correct at first without reading the others, it's important to read each answer choice thoroughly before making a final decision on the answer. The aim of a test writer might be to get as close as possible to the correct answer, so watch out for subtle words that may indicate an answer is incorrect. Once the correct answer choice is selected, read the question again and the answer in response to make sure all your bases are covered.

3. Eliminating Wrong Answer Choices

Sometimes we become paralyzed when we are confronted with too many choices. Which frozen yogurt flavor is the tastiest? Which pair of shoes look the best with this outfit? What type of car will fill my needs as a consumer? If you are unsure of which answer would be the best to choose, it may help to use process of elimination. We use "filtering" all the time on sites such as eBay® or Craigslist® to eliminate the ads that are not right for us. We can do the same thing on an exam. Process of elimination is crossing out the answer choices we know for sure are wrong and leaving the ones that might be correct. It may help to cover up the incorrect answer choice. Covering incorrect choices is a psychological act that alleviates stress due to the brain being exposed to a smaller amount of information. Choosing between two answer choices is much easier than choosing between all of them, and you have a better chance of selecting the correct answer if you have less to focus on.

4. Sticking to the World of the Question

When we are attempting to answer questions, our minds will often wander away from the question and what it is asking. We begin to see answer choices that are true in the real world instead of true in the world of the question. It may be helpful to think of each test question as its own little world. This world may be different from ours. This world may know as a truth that the chicken came before the egg or may assert that two plus two equals five. Remember that, no matter what hypothetical nonsense may be in the question, assume it to be true. If the question states that the chicken came before the egg, then choose

your answer based on that truth. Sticking to the world of the question means placing all of our biases and assumptions aside and relying on the question to guide us to the correct answer. If we are simply looking for answers that are correct based on our own judgment, then we may choose incorrectly. Remember an answer that is true does not necessarily answer the question.

5. Key Words

If you come across a complex test question that you have to read over and over again, try pulling out some key words from the question in order to understand what exactly it is asking. Key words may be words that surround the question, such as *main idea, analogous, parallel, resembles, structured,* or *defines.* The question may be asking for the main idea, or it may be asking you to define something. Deconstructing the sentence may also be helpful in making the question simpler before trying to answer it. This means taking the sentence apart and obtaining meaning in pieces, or separating the question from the foundation of the question. For example, let's look at this question:

> Given the author's description of the content of paleontology in the first paragraph, which of the following is most parallel to what it taught?

The question asks which one of the answers most *parallels* the following information: The *description* of paleontology in the first paragraph. The first step would be to see *how* paleontology is described in the first paragraph. Then, we would find an answer choice that parallels that description. The question seems complex at first, but after we deconstruct it, the answer becomes much more attainable.

6. Subtle Negatives

Negative words in question stems will be words such as *not, but, neither,* or *except.* Test writers often use these words in order to trick unsuspecting test takers into selecting the wrong answer—or, at least, to test their reading comprehension of the question. Many exams will feature the negative words in all caps (*which of the following is NOT an example*), but some questions will add the negative word seamlessly into the sentence. The following is an example of a subtle negative used in a question stem:

> According to the passage, which of the following is *not* considered to be an example of paleontology?

If we rush through the exam, we might skip that tiny word, *not,* inside the question, and choose an answer that is opposite of the correct choice. Again, it's important to read the question fully, and double check for any words that may negate the statement in any way.

7. Spotting the Hedges

The word "hedging" refers to language that remains vague or avoids absolute terminology. Absolute terminology consists of words like *always, never, all, every, just, only, none,* and *must.* Hedging refers to words like *seem, tend, might, most, some, sometimes, perhaps, possibly, probability,* and *often.* In some cases, we want to choose answer choices that use hedging and avoid answer choices that use absolute terminology. It's important to pay attention to what subject you are on and adjust your response accordingly.

8. Restating to Understand

Every now and then we come across questions that we don't understand. The language may be too complex, or the question is structured in a way that is meant to confuse the test taker. When you come across a question like this, it may be worth your time to rewrite or restate the question in your own words in order to understand it better. For example, let's look at the following complicated question:

> Which of the following words, if substituted for the word *parochial* in the first paragraph, would LEAST change the meaning of the sentence?

Let's restate the question in order to understand it better. We know that they want the word *parochial* replaced. We also know that this new word would "least" or "not" change the meaning of the sentence. Now let's try the sentence again:

> Which word could we replace with *parochial*, and it would not change the meaning?

Restating it this way, we see that the question is asking for a synonym. Now, let's restate the question so we can answer it better:

> Which word is a synonym for the word *parochial*?

Before we even look at the answer choices, we have a simpler, restated version of a complicated question.

9. Predicting the Answer

After you read the question, try predicting the answer *before* reading the answer choices. By formulating an answer in your mind, you will be less likely to be distracted by any wrong answer choices. Using predictions will also help you feel more confident in the answer choice you select. Once you've chosen your answer, go back and reread the question and answer choices to make sure you have the best fit. If you have no idea what the answer may be for a particular question, forego using this strategy.

10. Avoiding Patterns

One popular myth in grade school relating to standardized testing is that test writers will often put multiple-choice answers in patterns. A runoff example of this kind of thinking is that the most common answer choice is "C," with "B" following close behind. Or, some will advocate certain made-up word patterns that simply do not exist. Test writers do not arrange their correct answer choices in any kind of pattern; their choices are randomized. There may even be times where the correct answer choice will be the same letter for two or three questions in a row, but we have no way of knowing when or if this might happen. Instead of trying to figure out what choice the test writer probably set as being correct, focus on what the *best answer choice* would be out of the answers you are presented with. Use the tips above, general knowledge, and reading comprehension skills in order to best answer the question, rather than looking for patterns that do not exist.

Introduction to the TSI Assessment

Function of the Test

The Texas Success Initiative Assessment (TSI Assessment) is an assessment required by Texas universities in order to determine if students are prepared for college-level course work. The assessment includes Mathematics and English Language Arts and Reading sections. Exemptions for the exam are available depending on scores from the ACT, SAT, TAKS, or transfer work from another university. Those who perform well on the TSI may be enrolled into a college-level course. Those who do not perform well may be placed into a developmental course to ensure preparation for college-level coursework in the future.

Test Administration

For most Texas universities, the rules for taking the TSI assessment are similar. Students must first complete an application for admission into the university. Next, they will be assigned a TCC ID number. After, students must take a mandatory pre-assessment activity before they take the TSI. This activity is given at the same university where students are admitted to take the TSI exam. The pre-assessment activity contains an explanation on the significance of the TSI assessment, developmental education, practice questions, and information of educational resources on campus. Visit your university's website in order to find test dates and times for the pre-assessment activity as well as for the TSI assessment.

Again, those who do not meet the requirements of the TSI assessment in one or more subject areas may be placed in a developmental course or intervention to improve knowledge in that area. Note that the diagnostic test is used for students who score lower than the college readiness benchmark. Students who are not satisfied with their scores may retake the TSI at any time, but it is recommended that time be set aside for studying. Further information about retesting must be obtained through the university students wish to attend.

Test Format

The content areas of the TSI assessment include Mathematics and English Language Arts and Reading. The content areas in Mathematics include the following:

- Quantitative Reasoning
- Algebraic Reasoning
- Geometric and Spatial Reasoning
- Probabilistic and Statistical Reasoning

The content areas in English Language Arts and Reading include the following:

- Literary Text Analysis
- Informational Text Analysis and Synthesis
- Essay Revision and Editing
- Sentence Revision, Editing, and Completion

Mathematics contains 20 multiple-choice questions, and English Language Arts and Reading involves 30 multiple-choice questions and a five-paragraph persuasive essay of 300 to 600 words.

Scoring

Students will have immediate access to their scores once they finish the TSI assessment. A college-ready score in Mathematics involves a passing score on the standard test or an EFL of 6 on the diagnostic test. A college-ready score in English Language Arts and Reading involves a passing score on the standard test or an EFL of at least a 5 on the diagnostic test and essay.

Study Prep Plan for the TSI Assessment

Reducing stress is key when preparing for your test.

Create a study plan to help you stay on track.

Stick with your study plan. You've got this!

1 Week Study Plan

Day 1	Day 2	Day 3	Day 4	Day 5	Day 6	Day 7
Math	Algebraic Reasoning	Probabilistic and Statistical Reasoning	English Language Arts and Reading	Writing: Essay Revision and Editing	Practice Test	Take Your Exam!

2 Week Study Plan

Day 1	Day 2	Day 3	Day 4	Day 5	Day 6	Day 7
Math	Algebraic Expressions and Equations	Algebraic Reasoning	Geometric and Spatial Reasoning	Transformations and Symmetry	Probabilistic and Statistical Reasoning	Probabilistic Reasoning

Day 8	Day 9	Day 10	Day 11	Day 12	Day 13	Day 14
English Language Arts and Reading	Identifying an Authors Purpose, Tone, and Organization or Rhetorical...	Writing: Essay Revision and Editing	Subordination and Coordination	Practice Test	Answer Explanations	Take Your Exam!

30 Day Study Plan

Day 1	Day 2	Day 3	Day 4	Day 5	Day 6	Day 7
Math	Algebraic Expressions and Equations	Word Problems and Applications	Algebraic Reasoning	Expressions, Equations and Functions Involving Powers, Roots, and Radicals	Rational and Exponential Expressions, Equations, and Functions	Geometric and Spatial Reasoning

Day 8	Day 9	Day 10	Day 11	Day 12	Day 13	Day 14
Transformations and Symmetry	Linear, Area, and Three-Dimensional Measurements	Probabilistic and Statistical Reasoning	Statistical Measures	Probabilistic Reasoning	Practice Quiz	Take a Break!

Day 15	Day 16	Day 17	Day 18	Day 19	Day 20	Day 21
English Language Arts and Reading	Synthesizing Ideas by Making a Connection or Comparison Between Two Passages	Determining the Meaning of Words in Context	Take a Break!	Use of Evidence	Adjectives	Fragments and Parallelism

Day 22	Day 23	Day 24	Day 25	Day 26	Day 27	Day 28
Analyzing Word Parts	Practice Quiz	Take a Break!	Mathematics Practice Test	Mathematics Answer Explanations	English Language Arts and Reading Practice Test	English Language Arts and Reading Answer Explanations

Day 29	Day 30
Writing Prompt Test	Take Your Exam!

Math

Quantitative Reasoning

Linear Equations, Inequalities, and Systems

Linear Equations

An **equation in one variable** is a mathematical statement where two algebraic expressions in one variable, usually x, are set equal. To solve the equation, the variable must be isolated on one side of the equals sign. The addition and multiplication principles of equality are used to isolate the variable. The **addition principle of equality** states that the same number can be added to or subtracted from both sides of an equation. Because the same value is being used on both sides of the equals sign, equality is maintained. For example, the equation $2x - 3 = 5x$ is equivalent to both:

$$2x - 3 + 2 = 5x + 2$$

and

$$2x - 3 - 5 = 5x - 5$$

This principle can be used to solve the following equation:

$$x + 5 = 4$$

The variable x must be isolated, so to move the 5 from the left side, subtract 5 from both sides of the equals sign. Therefore,

$$x + 5 - 5 = 4 - 5$$

So, the solution is $x = -1$. This process illustrates the idea of an **additive inverse** because subtracting 5 is the same as adding -5. Basically, add the opposite of the number that must be removed to both sides of the equals sign. The multiplication principle of equality states that equality is maintained when both sides of an equation are multiplied or divided by the same number.

For example, $4x = 5$ is equivalent to both $16x = 20$ and $x = \frac{5}{4}$. Multiplying both sides times 4 and dividing both sides by 4 maintains equality. Solve the equation:

$$6x - 18 = 5$$

This requires the use of both principles. First, apply the addition principle to add 18 to both sides of the equals sign, which results in:

$$6x = 23$$

Then use the multiplication principle to divide both sides by 6, giving the solution:

$$x = \frac{23}{6}$$

Using the multiplication principle in the solving process is the same as involving a multiplicative inverse. A **multiplicative inverse** is a value that, when multiplied by a given number, results in 1. Dividing by 6 is the same as multiplying by $\frac{1}{6}$, which is both the reciprocal and multiplicative inverse of 6.

When solving linear equations, check the answer by plugging the solution back into the original equation. If the result is a false statement, something was done incorrectly during the solution procedure. Checking the example above gives the following:

$$6 \times \frac{23}{6} - 18 = 23 - 18 = 5$$

Therefore, the solution is correct.

Some equations in one variable involve fractions or the use of the distributive property. In either case, the goal is to obtain only one variable term and then use the addition and multiplication principles to isolate that variable. Consider the equation:

$$\frac{2}{3}x = 6$$

To solve for x, multiply each side of the equation by the reciprocal of $\frac{2}{3}$, which is $\frac{3}{2}$. This step results in:

$$\frac{3}{2} \times \frac{2}{3}x = \frac{3}{2} \times 6$$

This simplifies into the solution $x = 9$. Now consider the equation:

$$3(x + 2) - 5x = 4x + 1$$

Use the distributive property to clear the parentheses. Therefore, multiply each term inside the parentheses by 3. This step results in:

$$3x + 6 - 5x = 4x + 1$$

Next, collect like terms on the left-hand side. **Like terms** are terms with the same variable or variables raised to the same exponent(s). Only like terms can be combined through addition or subtraction. After collecting like terms, the equation is:

$$-2x + 6 = 4x + 1$$

Finally, apply the addition and multiplication principles. Add $2x$ to both sides to obtain:

$$6 = 6x + 1$$

Then, subtract 1 from both sides to obtain $5 = 6x$. Finally, divide both sides by 6 to obtain the solution $\frac{5}{6} = x$.

Two other types of solutions can be obtained when solving an equation in one variable. There could be no solution, or the solution set could contain all real numbers. Consider the equation:

$$4x = 6x + 5 - 2x$$

First, the like terms can be combined on the right to obtain:

$$4x = 4x + 5$$

Next, subtract $4x$ from both sides. This step results in the false statement $0 = 5$. There is no value that can be plugged into x that will ever make this equation true. Therefore, there is no solution. The solution procedure contained correct steps, but the result of a false statement means that no value satisfies the equation. The symbolic way to denote that no solution exists is $\emptyset$.

Next, consider the equation:

$$5x + 4 + 2x = 9 + 7x - 5$$

Combining the like terms on both sides results in:

$$7x + 4 = 7x + 4$$

The left-hand side is exactly the same as the right-hand side. Using the addition principle to move terms, the result is $0 = 0$, which is always true. Therefore, the original equation is true for any number, and the solution set is all real numbers. The symbolic way to denote such a solution set is $\mathbb{R}$, or in interval notation, $(-\infty, \infty)$.

The Connection Between Proportional Relationships and Linear Equations

Linear growth involves a quantity, the **dependent variable**, increasing or decreasing at a constant rate as another quantity, the **independent variable**, increases as well. The graph of linear growth is a straight line. Linear growth is represented as the following equation:

$$y = mx + b$$

m is the **slope** of the line, also known as the **rate of change**, and b is the **y-intercept**. If the y-intercept is 0, then the linear growth is actually known as **direct variation**. If the slope is positive, the dependent variable increases as the independent variable increases, and if the slope is negative, the dependent variable decreases as the independent variable increases.

A linear equation that models a linear relationship between two quantities is of the form $y = mx + b$, or in function form:

$$f(x) = mx + b$$

In a linear function, the value of y depends on the value of x, and y increases or decreases at a constant rate as x increases. Therefore, the independent variable is x, and the dependent variable is y. The graph of a linear function is a line, and the constant rate can be seen by looking at the steepness, or **slope**, of the line. If the line increases from left to right, the slope is positive. If the line slopes downward from left to right, the slope is negative. In the function, m represents slope. Each point on the line is an **ordered pair** (x, y), where x represents the x-coordinate of the point and y represents the y-coordinate of the point. The point where $x = 0$ is known as the y-intercept, and it is the place where the line crosses the y-axis. If $x = 0$ is plugged into $f(x) = mx + b$, the result is $f(0) = b$, so therefore, the point $(0, b)$ is the y-intercept of the line. The derivative of a linear function is its slope.

Consider the following situation. A taxicab driver charges a flat fee of $2 per ride and $3 a mile. This statement can be modeled by the function:

$$f(x) = 3x + 2$$

x represents the number of miles and $f(x) = y$ represents the total cost of the ride. The total cost increases at a constant rate of $2 per mile, and that is why this situation is a linear relationship. The slope $m = 3$ is equivalent to this rate of change. The flat fee of $2 is the y-intercept. It is the place where the graph crosses the x-axis, and it represents the cost when $x = 0$, or when no miles have been traveled in the cab. The y-intercept in this situation represents the flat fee.

Linear Inequalities

A **linear equation in x** can be written in the form $ax + b = 0$. A **linear inequality** is very similar, although the equals sign is replaced by an inequality symbol such as $<$, $>$, $\leq$, or $\geq$. In any case, a can never be 0. Some examples of linear inequalities in one variable are:

$$2x + 3 < 0$$

and

$$4x - 2 \leq 0$$

Solving an inequality involves finding the set of numbers that when plugged into the variable, make the inequality a true statement. These numbers are known as the **solution set** of the inequality. To solve an inequality, use the same properties that are necessary in solving equations. First, add or subtract variable terms and/or constants to obtain all variable terms on one side of the equals sign and all constant terms on the other side. Then, either multiply or divide both sides by the same number to obtain an inequality that gives the solution set. When multiplying or dividing by a negative number, change the direction of the inequality symbol. The solution set can be graphed on a number line. Consider the linear inequality:

$$-2x - 5 > x + 6$$

First, add 5 to both sides and subtract x from both sides to obtain $-3x > 11$. Then, divide both sides by -3, making sure to change the direction of the inequality symbol. These steps result in the solution $x < -\frac{11}{3}$. Therefore, any number less than $-\frac{11}{3}$ satisfies this inequality.

Algebraically Solving Linear Equations or Inequalities in One Variable

A **linear equation in one variable** can be solved using the following steps:

1. Simplify both sides of the equation by removing all parentheses, using the distributive property, and collecting all like terms.

2. Collect all variable terms on one side of the equation and all constant terms on the other side by adding the same quantity to or subtracting the same quantity from both sides.

3. Isolate the variable by either multiplying or dividing both sides of the equation by the same number.

4. Check the answer.

The only difference between solving linear inequalities versus equations is that when multiplying by a negative number or dividing by a negative number, the direction of the inequality symbol must be reversed.

If an equation contains multiple fractions, it might make sense to clear the equation of fractions first by multiplying all terms by the least common denominator. Also, if an equation contains several decimals, it might make sense to clear the decimals as well by multiplying times a factor of 10. If the equation has decimals in the hundredths place, multiply every term in the equation by 100.

Systems of Linear Equations and Equalities

Systems of Two Linear Equations in Two Variables

An example of a system of two linear equations in two variables is the following:

$$2x + 5y = 8$$

$$5x + 48y = 9$$

A solution to a system of two linear equations is an ordered pair that satisfies both the equations in the system. A system can have one solution, no solution, or infinitely many solutions. The solution can be found through a graphing technique. The solution to a system of equations is actually equal to the point where both lines intersects. If the lines intersect at one point, there is one solution and the system is said to be **consistent**. However, if the two lines are parallel, they will never intersect and there is no solution. In this case, the system is said to be **inconsistent.** Third, if the two lines are actually the same line, there are infinitely many solutions and the solution set is equal to the entire line. The lines are dependent. Here is a summary of the three cases:

Consistent	**Inconsistent**	**Dependent**
One solution	No solution	Infinite number of solutions
Lines intersect	Lines are parallel	Coincide/Same line

Consider the following system of equations:

$$y + x = 3$$

$$y - x = 1$$

To find the solution graphically, graph both lines on the same xy-plane. Graph each line using either a table of ordered pairs, the x- and y-intercepts, or slope and the y-intercept. Then, locate the point of intersection.

The graph is shown here:

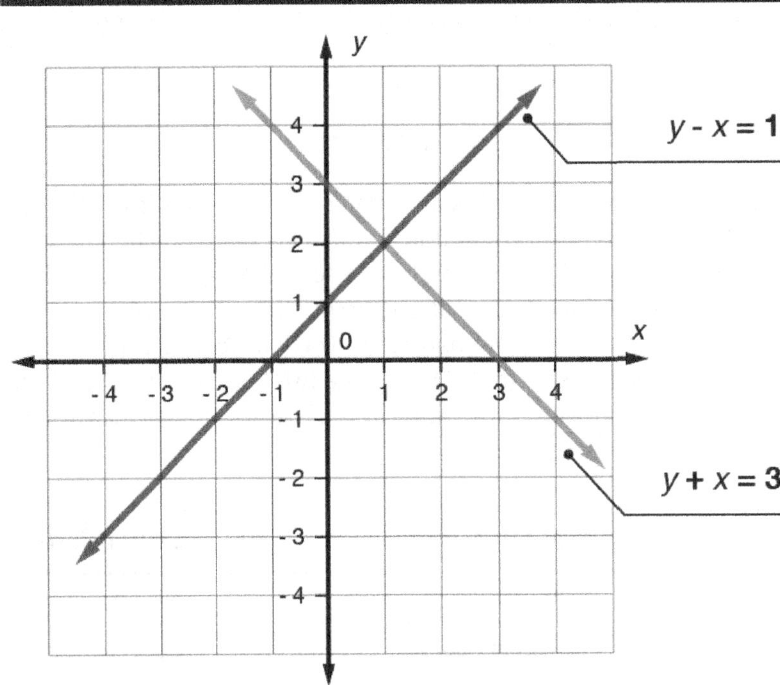

It can be seen that the point of intersection is the ordered pair $(1, 2)$. This solution can be checked by plugging it back into both original equations to make sure it results in true statements. This process results in:

$$2 + 1 = 3$$

$$2 - 1 = 1$$

Both equations are true, so the solution is correct.

The following system has no solution:

$$y = 4x + 1$$

$$y = 4x - 1$$

Both lines have the same slope and different y-intercepts, so they are parallel, meaning that they run alongside each other and never intersect.

Finally, the following solution has infinitely many solutions:

$$2x - 7y = 12$$

$$4x - 14y = 24$$

Note that the second equation is equal to the first equation times 2. Therefore, they are the same line. The solution set can be written in set notation as:

$$\{(x, y)|2x - 7y = 12\}$$

This represents the entire line.

There are two algebraic methods to finding solutions to systems of two linear equations in two variables. The first is substitution. This process is better suited for systems when one of the equations is already solved for one variable, or when solving for one variable is easy to do. The equation that is already solved for is substituted into the other equation for that variable, and this process results in a linear equation in one variable. This equation can be solved for the given variable, and then that solution can be plugged into one of the original equations, which can then be solved for the other variable. This last step is known as **back-substitution**, and the end result is an ordered pair.

The following is an example of a system that is suited for substitution:

$$y = 4x + 2$$

$$2x + 3y = 9$$

The other method is known as **elimination,** or the **addition method**. This is better suited when the equations are in standard form:

$$Ax + By = C$$

The goal in this method is to multiply one or both equations times numbers that result in opposite coefficients. Then, add the equations together to obtain an equation in one variable. Solve for the given variable, then take that value and back-substitute to obtain the other part of the ordered pair solution.

The following is an example of a system that is suited for elimination:

$$2x + 3y = 8$$

$$4x - 2y = 10$$

Note that in order to check an answer when solving a system of equations, the solution must be checked in both original equations to show that it solves not only one of the equations, but both of them.

If either solution results in an untrue statement when inserted into the original equation, then there is no solution to the system. Finally, if throughout either solution procedure the process results in the variables dropping out, which gives a statement that is always true, there are infinitely many solutions.

Systems of Linear Inequalities in Two Variables

A system of linear inequalities in two variables consists of two inequalities in two variables, x and y. For example, the following is a system of linear inequalities in two variables:

$$\begin{cases} 4x + 2y < 1 \\ 2x - y \leq 0 \end{cases}$$

The curly brace on the left side shows that the two inequalities are grouped together. A solution of a single inequality in two variables is an ordered pair that satisfies the inequality. For example, $(1, 3)$ is a solution of the linear inequality:

$$y \geq x + 1$$

because when plugged in, it results in a true statement. The graph of an inequality in two variables consists of all ordered pairs that make the solution true. Therefore, the entire solution set of a single inequality contains many ordered pairs, and the set can be graphed by using a half plane. A **half plane** consists of the set of all points on one side of a line. If the inequality consists of $>$ or $<$, the line is dashed because no solutions actually exist on the line shown. If the inequality consists of $\geq$ or $\leq$, the line is solid and solutions are on the line shown. To graph a linear inequality, graph the corresponding equation found by replacing the inequality symbol with an equals sign. Then pick a test point that exists on either side of the line. If that point results in a true statement when plugged into the original inequality, shade in the side containing the test point. If it results in a false statement, shade in the opposite side.

Solving a system of linear inequalities must be done graphically. Follow the process as described above for both given inequalities. The solution set to the entire system is the region that is in common to every graph in the system.

For example, here is the solution to the following system:

$$\begin{cases} y \geq 3 - x \\ y \leq -3 - x \end{cases}$$

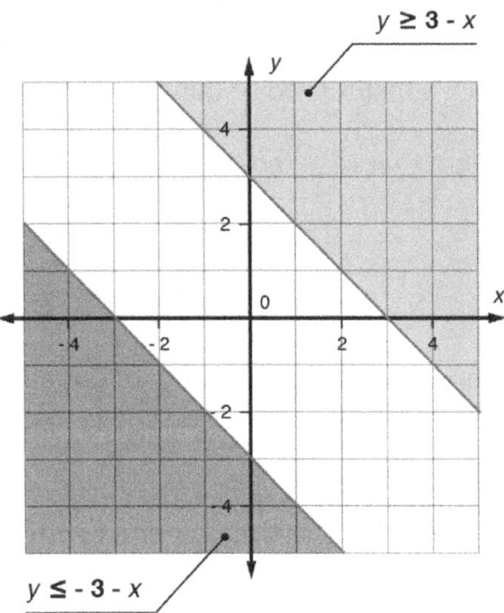

Note that there is no region in common, so this system has no solution.

Algebraic Expressions and Equations

An **algebraic expression** is a mathematical phrase that may contain numbers, variables, and mathematical operations. An expression represents a single quantity. For example, $3x + 2$ is an algebraic expression.

An **algebraic equation** is a mathematical sentence with two expressions that are equal to each other. That is, an equation must contain an equals sign, as in:

$$3x + 2 = 17$$

This statement says that the value of the expression on the left side of the equals sign is equivalent to the value of the expression on the right side. In an expression, there are not two sides because there is no equals sign. The equals sign (=) is the difference between an expression and an equation.

To distinguish an expression from an equation, just look for the equals sign.

Example: Determine whether each of these is an expression or an equation.

- $16 + 4x = 9x - 7$ Solution: Equation
- $-27x - 42 + 19y$ Solution: Expression
- $4 = x + 3$ Solution: Equation

Adding and Subtracting Linear Algebraic Expressions

To add and subtract linear algebraic expressions, you must combine like terms. Like terms are terms that have the same variable with the same exponent. In the following example, the x-terms can be added because the variable and exponent are the same. These terms add to be $9x$. Terms without a variable component are called constants. These terms will add to be nine.

Example: Add	$(3x - 5) + (6x + 14)$	
	$3x - 5 + 6x + 14$	Rewrite without parentheses
	$3x + 6x - 5 + 14$	Commutative property of addition
	$9x + 9$	Combine like terms

When subtracting linear expressions, be careful to add the opposite when combining like terms. Do this by distributing -1, which is multiplying each term inside the second parenthesis by negative one. Remember that distributing -1 changes the sign of each term.

Example: Subtract	$(17x + 3) - (27x - 8)$	
	$17x + 3 - 27x + 8$	Distributive Property
	$17x - 27x + 3 + 8$	Commutative property of addition
	$-10x + 11$	Combine like terms

Example: Simplify by adding or subtracting:

$$(6m + 28z - 9) + (14m + 13) - (-4z + 8m + 12)$$

$6m + 28z - 9 + 14m + 13 + 4z - 8m - 12$	Distributive Property
$6m + 14m - 8m + 28z + 4z - 9 + 13 - 12$	Commutative Property of Addition
$12m + 32z - 8$	Combine like terms

Using the Distributive Property to Generate Equivalent Linear Algebraic Expressions

The Distributive Property:

$$a(b + c) = ab + ac$$

The **distributive property** is a way of taking a factor and multiplying it through a given expression in parentheses. Each term inside the parentheses is multiplied by the outside factor, eliminating the parentheses. The following example shows how to distribute the number 3 to all the terms inside the parentheses.

Example: Use the distributive property to write an equivalent algebraic expression:

$$3(2x + 7y + 6)$$

$3(2x) + 3(7y) + 3(6)$	Distributive property
$6x + 21y + 18$	Simplify

Because $a - b$ can be written $a + (-b)$, the distributive property can be applied in the example below.

Example: Use the distributive property to write an equivalent algebraic expression.

$$7(5m - 8)$$

$7[5m + (-8)]$	Rewrite subtraction as addition of -8
$7(5m) + 7(-8)$	Distributive property
$35m - 56$	Simplify

In the following example, note that the factor of 2 is written to the right of the parentheses but is still distributed as before.

Example: Use the distributive property to write an equivalent algebraic expression:

$(3m + 4x - 10)2$

$(3m)2 + (4x)2 + (-10)2$ Distributive property

$6m + 8x - 20$ Simplify

Example: $-(-2m + 6x)$

In this example, the negative sign in front of the parentheses can be interpreted as:

$-1(-2m + 6x)$

$-1(-2m) + (-1)(6x)$ Distributive property

$2m - 6x$ Simplify

Evaluating Simple Algebraic Expressions for Given Values of Variables

To evaluate an algebra expression for a given value of a variable, replace the variable with the given value. Then perform the given operations to simplify the expression.

Example: Evaluate $12 + x$ for $x = 9$

$12 + (9)$ Replace x with the value of 9 as given in the problem. It is a good idea to always use parentheses when substituting this value. This will be particularly important in the following examples.

21 Add

Now see that when x is 9, the value of the given expression is 21.

Example: Evaluate $4x + 7$ for $x = 3$

$4(3) + 7$ Replace the x in the expression with 3

$12 + 7$ Multiply (remember order of operations)

19 Add

Therefore, when x is 3, the value of the given expression is 19.

Example: Evaluate $-7m - 3r - 18$ for $m = 2$ and $r = -1$

$-7(2) - 3(-1) - 18$ Replace m with 2 and r with -1

$-14 + 3 - 18$ Multiply

-29 Add

So, when m is 2 and r is -1, the value of the given expression is -29.

Using Mathematical Terms to Identify Parts of Expressions and Describe Expressions

A **variable** is a symbol used to represent a number. Letters, like x, y, and z, are often used as variables in algebra.

A **constant** is a number that cannot change its value. For example, 18 is a constant.

A **term** is a constant, variable, or the product of constants and variables. In an expression, terms are separated by $+$ and $-$ signs. Examples of terms are $24x$, -32, and $15xyz$.

Like terms are terms that contain the same variables. For example, $6z$ and $-8z$ are like terms, and $9xy$ and $17xy$ are like terms. Constants, like 23 and 51, are like terms as well.

A **factor** is something that is multiplied by something else. A factor may be a constant, a variable, or a sum of constants or variables.

A **coefficient** is the numerical factor in a term that has a variable. In the term $16x$, the coefficient is 16.

Example: Given the expression, $6x - 12y + 18$, answer the following questions.

How many terms are in the expression?
Solution: 3

Name the terms.
Solution: $6x$, $-12y$, and 18 (Notice that the minus sign preceding the 12 is interpreted to represent negative 12)

Name the factors.
Solution: $6, x, -12, y$

What are the coefficients in this expression?
Solution: 6 and -12

What is the constant in this expression?
Solution: 18

Simplifying Rational Algebraic Expressions

When given a problem, it is necessary to determine the best form of an expression or equation to use, given the context. Usually this involves some algebraic manipulation. If an equation is given, the simplest form of the equation is best. Simplifying involves using the distributive property, collecting like terms, etc. If an equation is needed to be solved, properties involving performing the same operation on both sides of the equation must be used. For example, if a number is added to one side of the equals sign, it must be added to the other side as well. This maintains a true equation.

If an expression is given, simplifying can only involve properties allowing to rewrite the expression as an equivalent form. If there is no equals sign, mathematical operations cannot be performed on the expression, unless it is a rational expression. A **rational expression** can be written in the form of a fraction, in which the numerator and denominator are both polynomials and the denominator is not equal to zero. Rational expressions can always be multiplied by a form of 1. For example, consider the following rational expression involving radicals: $\frac{2}{\sqrt{2}}$

It is incorrect to write a fraction with a root in the denominator, and therefore the expression must be rationalized. Multiply the fraction times $\frac{\sqrt{2}}{\sqrt{2}}$, a form of 1. This results in:

$$\frac{2}{\sqrt{2}} \times \frac{\sqrt{2}}{\sqrt{2}} = \frac{2\sqrt{2}}{\sqrt{4}} = \frac{2\sqrt{2}}{2} = \sqrt{2}$$

This is the most suitable form of the expression.

Creating an Equivalent Form of an Algebraic Expression

Two algebraic expressions are equivalent if they represent the same value, even if they look different. To obtain an equivalent form of an algebraic expression, follow the laws of algebra. For instance, addition and multiplication are both commutative and associative. Therefore, terms in an algebraic expression can be added in any order and multiplied in any order. For example,

$$4x + 2y \text{ is equivalent to } 2y + 4x$$

and

$$y \times 2 + x \times 4$$

Also, the distributive law allows a number to be distributed throughout parentheses, as in the following:

$$a(b + c) = ab + ac$$

The expressions on both sides of the equals sign are equivalent. Collecting like terms is also important when working with equivalent forms because the simplest version of an expression is always the easiest one to work with.

Note that an expression is not an equation, and therefore expressions cannot be multiplied times numbers, divided by numbers, or have numbers added to them or subtracted from them and still have equivalent expressions. These processes can only happen in equations when the same step is performed on both sides of the equals sign.

Factoring Expressions

A factorization of an algebraic expression can be found. Throughout the process, a more complicated expression can be decomposed into products of simpler expressions. To factor a polynomial, first determine if there is a greatest common factor. If there is, factor it out. For example,

$$2x^2 + 8x$$

This has a greatest common factor of $2x$ and can be written as:

$$2x(x + 4)$$

After this, determine if the remaining polynomial follows a factoring pattern. If the polynomial has two terms, it could be a difference of squares, a sum of cubes, or a difference of cubes. If it falls into one of these categories, use the following rules:

$$a^2 - b^2 = (a + b)(a - b)$$

$$a^3 + b^3 = (a + b)(a^2 - ab + b^2)$$

$$a^3 - b^3 = (a - b)(a^2 + ab + b^2)$$

If there are three terms, and if the trinomial is a perfect square trinomial, it can be factored into the following:

$$a^2 + 2ab + b^2 = (a + b)^2$$

$$a^2 - 2ab + b^2 = (a - b)^2$$

If not, try factoring into a product of two binomials in the form of:

$$(x + p)(x + q)$$

For example, to factor:

$$x^2 + 6x + 8$$

determine what two numbers have a product of 8 and a sum of 6. Those numbers are 4 and 2, so the trinomial factors into $(x + 2)(x + 4)$.

Finally, if there are four terms, try factoring by grouping. First, group terms together that have a common monomial factor. Then, factor out the common monomial factor from the first two terms. Next, look to see if a common factor can be factored out of the second set of two terms that results in a common binomial factor. Finally, factor out the common binomial factor of each expression, for example:

$$xy - x + 5y - 5$$

$$x(y - 1) + 5(y - 1)$$

$$(y - 1)(x + 5)$$

After the expression is completely factored, check the factorization by multiplying it out; if this results in the original expression, then the factoring is correct. Factorizations are helpful in solving equations that consist of a polynomial set equal to 0. If the product of two algebraic expressions equals 0, then at least one of the factors is equal to 0. Therefore, factor the polynomial within the equation, set each factor equal to 0, and solve. For example,

$$x^2 + 7x - 18 = 0$$

This can be solved by factoring into:

$$(x + 9)(x - 2) = 0$$

Set each factor equal to 0, and solve to obtain $x = -9$ and $x = 2$.

Word Problems and Applications

Translating Phrases and Sentences into Expressions, Equations, and Inequalities

When presented with a real-world problem, the first step is to determine what unknown quantity must be solved for. Use a **variable**, such as x or t, to represent that unknown quantity. Sometimes there can be two or more unknown quantities. In this case, either choose an additional variable, or if a relationship exists between the unknown quantities, express the other quantities in terms of the original variable. After choosing the variables, form algebraic expressions and/or equations that represent the verbal statement in the problem. The following table shows examples of vocabulary used to represent the different operations:

Addition	Sum, plus, total, increase, more than, combined, in all
Subtraction	Difference, less than, subtract, reduce, decrease, fewer, remain
Multiplication	Product, multiply, times, part of, twice, triple
Division	Quotient, divide, split, each, equal parts, per, average, shared

The combination of operations and variables form both mathematical expression and equations. The differences between expressions and equations are that there is no equals sign in an expression, and that expressions are evaluated to find an unknown quantity, while equations are solved to find an unknown quantity. Also, inequalities can exist within verbal mathematical statements. Instead of a statement of equality, expressions state quantities are *less than*, *less than or equal to*, *greater than*, or *greater than or equal to*. Another type of inequality is when a quantity is said to be not equal to another quantity ($\neq$).

The steps for solving inequalities in one variable are the same steps for solving equations in one variable. The addition and multiplication principles are used. However, to maintain a true statement when using the $<$, $\leq$, $>$, and $\geq$ symbols, if a negative number is either multiplied times both sides of an inequality or divided from both sides of an inequality, the sign must be flipped. For instance, consider the following inequality:

$$3 - 5x \leq 8$$

First, 3 is subtracted from each side to obtain:

$$-5x \leq 5$$

Then, both sides are divided by -5, while flipping the sign, to obtain $x \geq -1$. Therefore, any real number greater than or equal to -1 satisfies the original inequality.

Solving Real-World One- or Multi-Step Problems with Rational Numbers

One-step problems take only one mathematical step to solve. For example, solve the equation:

$$5x = 45$$

This is a one-step problem because the one step of dividing both sides of the equation by 5 is the only step necessary to obtain the solution $x = 9$. The multiplication principle of equality is the one step used to isolate the variable. The equation is of the form $ax = b$, where a and b are rational numbers. Similarly, the addition principle of equality could be the one step needed to solve a problem. In this case, the equation would be of the form:

$$x + a = b$$

or

$$x - a = b \text{ for real numbers } a \text{ and } b.$$

A multi-step problem involves more than one step to find the solution, or it could consist of solving more than one equation. An equation that involves both the addition principle and the multiplication principle is a two-step problem, and an example of such an equation is:

$$2x - 4 = 5$$

To solve, add 4 to both sides and then divide both sides by 2. An example of a two-step problem involving two separate equations is:

$$y = 3x$$

$$2x + y = 4$$

The two equations form a system that must be solved together in two variables. The system can be solved by the substitution method. Since y is already solved for in terms of x, replace y with $3x$ in the equation $2x + y = 4$, resulting in $2x + 3x = 4$. Therefore, $5x = 4$ and $x = \frac{4}{5}$. Because there are two variables, the solution consists of a value for both x and for y. Substitute $x = \frac{4}{5}$ into either original equation to find y. The easiest choice is $y = 3x$. Therefore:

$$y = 3 \times \frac{4}{5} = \frac{12}{5}$$

The solution can be written as the ordered pair $\left(\frac{4}{5}, \frac{12}{5}\right)$.

Real-world problems can be translated into both one-step and multi-step problems. In either case, the word problem must be translated from the verbal form into mathematical expressions and equations that can be solved using algebra. An example of a one-step real-world problem is the following: A cat weighs half as much as a dog living in the same house. If the dog weighs 14.5 pounds, how much does the cat weigh? To solve this problem, an equation can be used. In any word problem, the first step must be defining variables that represent the unknown quantities. For this problem, let x be equal to the unknown weight of the cat. Because two times the weight of the cat equals 14.5 pounds, the equation to be solved is:

$$2x = 14.5$$

Use the multiplication principle to divide both sides by 2. Therefore,

$$x = 7.25$$

The cat weighs 7.25 pounds.

Most of the time, real-world problems require multiple steps. The following is an example of a multi-step problem: The sum of two consecutive page numbers is equal to 437. What are those page numbers? First, define the unknown quantities. If x is equal to the first page number, then $x + 1$ is equal to the next page number because they are consecutive integers. The sum is equal to 437. Putting this information together results in the equation:

$$x + x + 1 = 437$$

To solve, first collect like terms to obtain:

$$2x + 1 = 437$$

Then, subtract 1 from both sides and then divide by 2. The solution to the equation is $x = 218$. Therefore, the two consecutive page numbers that satisfy the problem are 218 and 219. It is always important to make sure that answers to real-world problems make sense. For instance, it should be a red flag if the solution to this same problem resulted in decimals, which would indicate the need to check the work. Page numbers are whole numbers; therefore, if decimals are found to be answers, the solution process should be double-checked for mistakes.

To solve problems, follow these steps: Identify the variables that are known, decide which equation should be used, substitute the numbers, and solve. To solve an equation for the amount of time that has elapsed since an event, use the equation $T = L - E$ where T represents the elapsed time, L represents the later time, and E represents the earlier time. For example, the Minnesota Vikings have not appeared in the Super Bowl since 1976. If the year is now 2023, how long has it been since the Vikings were in the Super Bowl? The later time, L, is 2021, $E = 1976$ and the unknown is T. Substituting these numbers, the equation is $T = 2021 - 1976$, and so $T = 45$. It has been 45 years since the Vikings have appeared in the Super Bowl. Questions involving total cost can be solved using the formula, $C = I + T$ where C represents the total cost, I represents the cost of the item purchased, and T represents the tax amount. To find the length of a rectangle given the area is 32 square inches and the width is 8 inches, the formula $A = L \times W$ can be used.

Substitute 32 for A and substitute 8 for W, giving the equation $32 = L \times 8$. This equation is solved by dividing both sides by 8 to find that the length of the rectangle is 4. The formula for volume of a rectangular prism is given by the equation $V = L \times W \times H$. If the length of a rectangular juice box is 4 centimeters, the width is 2 centimeters, and the height is 8 centimeters, what is the volume of this box? Substituting in the formula we find $V = 4 \times 2 \times 8$, so the volume is 64 cubic centimeters. In a similar fashion as those previously shown, the mass of an object can be calculated given the formula, $Mass = Density \times Volume$.

Solving Real-World Problems Involving Percentages

Percentages are defined as parts per one hundred. To convert a decimal to a percentage, move the decimal point two units to the right and place the percent sign after the number. Percentages appear in many scenarios in the real world. It is important to make sure the statement containing the percentage is translated to a correct mathematical expression. Be aware that it is extremely common to make a mistake when working with percentages within word problems.

An example of a word problem containing a percentage is the following: 35% of people speed when driving to work. In a group of 5,600 commuters, how many would be expected to speed on the way to their place of employment? The answer to this problem is found by finding 35% of 5,600. First, change the percentage to the decimal 0.35. Then compute the product:

$$0.35 \times 5{,}600 = 1{,}960$$

Therefore, it would be expected that 1,960 of those commuters would speed on their way to work based on the data given. In this situation, the word "of" signals to use multiplication to find the answer. Another way percentages are used is in the following problem: Teachers work 8 months out of the year. What percent of the year do they work? To answer this problem, find what percent of 12 the number 8 is, because there are 12 months in a year. Therefore, divide 8 by 12, and convert that number to a percentage:

$$\frac{8}{12} = \frac{2}{3} = 0.66\bar{6}$$

The percentage rounded to the nearest tenth place tells us that teachers work 66.7% of the year. Percentage problems can also find missing quantities like in the following question: 60% of what number is 75? To find the missing quantity, turn the question into an equation. Let x be equal to the missing quantity. Therefore,

$$0.60x = 75.$$

Divide each side by 0.60 to obtain 125. Therefore, 60% of 125 is equal to 75.

Sales tax is an important application relating to percentages because tax rates are usually given as percentages. For example, a city might have an 8% sales tax rate. Therefore, when an item is purchased with that tax rate, the real cost to the customer is 1.08 times the price in the store. For example, a $25 pair of jeans costs the customer:

$$\$25 \times 1.08 = \$27$$

If the sales tax rates is unknown, it can be determined after an item is purchased. If a customer visits a store and purchases an item for $21.44, but the price in the store was $19, they can find the tax rate by first subtracting $\$21.44 - \$19$ to obtain $2.44, the sales tax amount. The sales tax is a percentage of the in-store price. Therefore, the tax rate is:

$$\frac{2.44}{19} = 0.128$$

This has been rounded to the nearest thousandths place. In this scenario, the actual sales tax rate given as a percentage is 12.8%.

Solving Real-World Problems Involving Proportions

Fractions appear in everyday situations, and in many scenarios, they appear in the real-world as ratios and in proportions. A **ratio** is formed when two different quantities are compared. For example, in a group of 50 people, if there are 33 females and 17 males, the ratio of females to males is 33 to 17. This expression can be written in the fraction form as $\frac{33}{50}$, where the denominator is the sum of females and males, or by using the ratio symbol, $33 : 17$. The order of the number matters when forming ratios. In the same setting, the ratio of males to females is 17 to 33, which is equivalent to $\frac{17}{50}$ or $17 : 33$. A **proportion** is an equation involving two ratios. The equation $\frac{a}{b} = \frac{c}{d}$, or $a: b = c: d$ is a proportion, for real numbers a, b, c, and d. Usually, in one ratio, one of the quantities is unknown, and cross-multiplication is used to solve for the unknown. Consider:

$$\frac{1}{4} = \frac{x}{5}$$

To solve for x, cross-multiply to obtain:

$$5 = 4x$$

Divide each side by 4 to obtain the solution $x = \frac{5}{4}$. It is also true that percentages are ratios in which the second term is 100 minus the first term. For example, 65% is 65:35 or $\frac{65}{100}$. Therefore, when working with percentages, one is also working with ratios.

Real-world problems frequently involve proportions. For example, consider the following problem: If 2 out of 50 pizzas are usually delivered late from a local Italian restaurant, how many would be late out of 235 orders? The following proportion would be solved with x as the unknown quantity of late pizzas:

$$\frac{2}{50} = \frac{x}{235}$$

Cross multiplying results in $470 = 50x$. Divide both sides by 50 to obtain $x = \frac{470}{50}$, which in lowest terms is equal to $\frac{47}{5}$. In decimal form, this improper fraction is equal to 9.4. Because it does not make sense to answer this question with decimals (portions of pizzas do not get delivered) the answer must be rounded. Traditional rounding rules would say that 9 pizzas would be expected to be delivered late. However, to be safe, rounding up to 10 pizzas out of 235 would probably make more sense.

Solving Real-World Problems Involving Ratios and Rates of Change

Recall that a **ratio** is the comparison of two different quantities. Comparing 2 apples to 3 oranges results in the ratio $2 : 3$, which can be expressed as the fraction $\frac{2}{5}$. Note that order is important when discussing ratios. The number mentioned first is the antecedent, and the number mentioned second is the consequent. Note that the consequent of the ratio and the denominator of the fraction are *not* the same. When there are 2 apples to 3 oranges, there are five fruit total; two fifths of the fruit are apples, while three fifths are oranges. The ratio $2 : 3$ represents a different relationship that the ratio $3 : 2$. Also, it is important to make sure that when discussing ratios that have units attached to them, the two quantities use the same units. For example, to compare 8 feet to 4 yards, Therefore, the ratio would be 8 feet to 12 feet, which can be expressed as the fraction $\frac{8}{20}$. Also, note that it is proper to refer to ratios in lowest terms. Therefore, the ratio of 8 feet to 4 yards is equivalent to the fraction $\frac{2}{5}$.

Many real-world problems involve ratios. Often, problems with ratios involve proportions, as when two ratios are set equal to find the missing amount. However, some problems involve deciphering single ratios. For example, consider an amusement park that sold 345 tickets last Saturday. If 145 tickets were sold to adults and the rest of the tickets were sold to children, what would the ratio of the number of adult tickets to children's tickets be? A common mistake would be to say the ratio is $145 : 345$. However, 345 is the total number of tickets sold, not the number of children's tickets. There were $345 - 145 = 200$ tickets sold to children. The correct ratio of adult to children's tickets is $145 : 200$. As a fraction, this expression is written as $\frac{145}{345}$, which can be reduced to $\frac{29}{69}$.

While a ratio compares two measurements using the same units, rates compare two measurements with different units. Examples of rates would be \$200 for 8 hours of work, or 500 miles traveled per 20 gallons. Because the units are different, it is important to always include the units when discussing rates. Key words in rate problems include for, per, on, from, and in. Just as with ratios, it is important to write rates in lowest terms. A common rate in real-life situations is cost per unit, which describes how much one item/unit costs. When evaluating the cost of an item that comes in several sizes, the cost per unit rate can help buyers determine the best deal. For example, if 2 quarts of soup was sold for \$3.50 and 3 quarts was sold for \$4.60, to determine the best buy, the cost per quart should be found:

$$\frac{\$3.50}{2\text{ qt}} = \$1.75 \text{ per quart and } \frac{\$4.60}{3\text{ qt}} = \$1.53 \text{ per quart.}$$

Therefore, the better deal would be the 3-quart option.

Rate of change problems involve calculating a quantity per some unit of measurement. Usually the unit of measurement is time. For example, meters per second is a common rate of change. To calculate this measurement, find the amount traveled in meters and divide by total time traveled. The result is the average speed over the entire time interval. Another common rate of change used in the real world is miles per hour. Consider the following problem that involves calculating an average rate of change in temperature. Last Saturday, the temperature at 1:00 a.m. was 34 degrees Fahrenheit, and at noon, the temperature had increased to 75 degrees Fahrenheit. What was the average rate of change over that time interval? The average rate of change is calculated by finding the change in temperature and dividing by the total hours elapsed. Therefore, the rate of change was equal to:

$$\frac{75-34}{12-1} = \frac{41}{11} \text{ degrees per hour}$$

This quantity rounded to two decimal places is equal to 3.73 degrees per hour.

A common rate of change that appears in algebra is the slope calculation. Given a linear equation in one variable, $y = mx + b$, the *slope*, m, is equal to $\frac{rise}{run}$ or $\frac{change\ in\ y}{change\ in\ x}$. In other words, slope is equivalent to the ratio of the vertical and horizontal changes between any two points on a line. The vertical change is known as the *rise*, and the horizontal change is known as the *run*. Given any two points on a line (x_1, y_1) and (x_2, y_2), slope can be calculated with the formula:

$$m = \frac{y_2 - y_1}{x_2 - x_1} = \frac{\Delta y}{\Delta x}$$

Common real-world applications of slope include determining how steep a staircase should be, calculating how steep a road is, and determining how to build a wheelchair ramp.

Many times, problems involving rates and ratios involve proportions. A proportion states that two ratios (or rates) are equal. The property of cross products can be used to determine if a proportion is true, meaning both ratios are equivalent. If $\frac{a}{b} = \frac{c}{d}$, then to clear the fractions, multiply both sides by the least common denominator, bd. This results in $ad = bc$, which is equal to the result of multiplying along both diagonals. For example,

$$\frac{4}{40} = \frac{1}{10}$$

This grants the cross product:

$$4 \times 10 = 40 \times 1$$

This is equivalent to $40 = 40$ and shows that this proportion is true. Cross products are used when proportions are involved in real-world problems. Consider the following: If 3 pounds of fertilizer will cover 75 square feet of grass, how many pounds are needed for 375 square feet? To solve this problem, set up a proportion using two ratios. Let x equal the unknown quantity, pounds needed for 375 feet. Setting the two ratios equal to one another yields the equation:

$$\frac{3}{75} = \frac{x}{375}$$

Cross-multiplication gives:

$$3 \times 375 = 75x$$

Therefore, $1{,}125 = 75x$. Divide both sides by 75 to get $x = 15$. Therefore, 15 pounds of fertilizer are needed to cover 375 square feet of grass.

Another application of proportions involves similar triangles. If two triangles have corresponding angles with the same measurements and corresponding sides with proportional measurements, the triangles are said to be similar. If two angles are the same, the third pair of angles are equal as well because the sum of all angles in a triangle is equal to 180 degrees. Each pair of equivalent angles are known as **corresponding angles. Corresponding sides** face the corresponding angles, and it is true that corresponding sides are in proportion. For example, consider the following set of similar triangles:

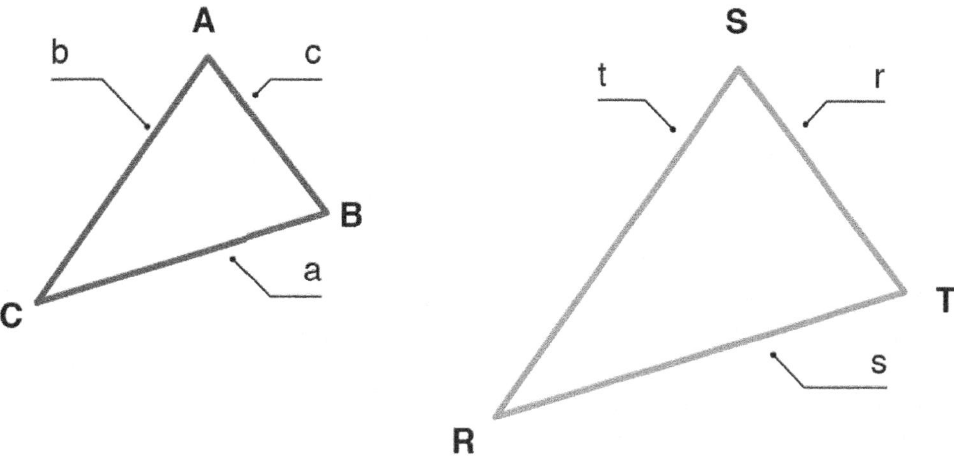

Angles A and S have the same measurement, angles C and R have the same measurement, and angles B and T have the same measurement. Therefore, the following proportion can be set up from the sides:

$$\frac{c}{r} = \frac{a}{s} = \frac{b}{t}$$

This proportion can be helpful in finding missing lengths in pairs of similar triangles. For example, if the following triangles are similar, a proportion can be used to find the missing side lengths, a and b.

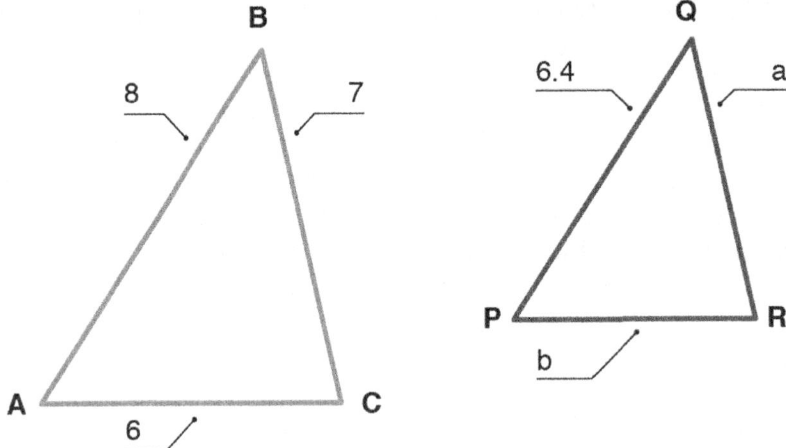

The proportions $\frac{8}{6.4} = \frac{6}{b}$ and $\frac{8}{6.4} = \frac{7}{a}$ can both be cross multiplied and solved to obtain $a = 5.6$ and $b = 4.8$.

A real-life situation that uses similar triangles involves measuring shadows to find heights of unknown objects. Consider the following problem: A building casts a shadow that is 120 feet long, and at the same time, another building that is 80 feet high casts a shadow that is 60 feet long. How tall is the first building? Each building, together with the sun rays and shadows casted on the ground, forms a triangle. They are similar because each building forms a right angle with the ground, and the sun rays form equivalent angles. Therefore, these two pairs of angles are both equal. Because all angles in a triangle add up to 180 degrees, the third angles are equal as well. Both shadows form corresponding sides of the triangle, the buildings form corresponding sides, and the sun rays form corresponding sides. Therefore, the triangles are similar, and the following proportion can be used to find the missing building length:

$$\frac{120}{x} = \frac{60}{80}$$

Cross-multiply to obtain the equation $9{,}600 = 60x$. Then, divide both sides by 60 to obtain $x = 160$. This means that the first building is 160 feet high.

Applying Estimation Strategies and Rounding Rules to Real-World Problems

Sometimes it is helpful to find an estimated answer to a problem rather than working out an exact answer. An estimation might be much quicker to find, and it might be all that is required given the scenario. For example, if Aria goes grocery shopping and has only a $100 bill to cover all of her purchases, it might be appropriate for her to estimate the total of the items she is purchasing to determine if she has enough money to cover them. Also, an estimation can help determine if an answer makes sense. For example, if an answer in the 100s is expected, but the result is a fraction less than 1, something is wrong in the calculation.

The first type of estimation involves rounding. **Rounding** consists of expressing a number in terms of the nearest decimal place like the tenth, hundredth, or thousandth place, or in terms of the nearest whole number unit like tens, hundreds, or thousands place. When rounding to a specific place value, look at the

digit to the right of the place. If it is 5 or higher, round the number to its left up to the next value, and if it is 4 or lower, keep that number at the same value. For instance, 1,654.2674 rounded to the nearest thousand is 2,000, and the same number rounded to the nearest thousandth is 1,654.267. Rounding can make it easier to estimate totals at the store. Items can be rounded to the nearest dollar. For example, a can of corn that costs $0.79 can be rounded to $1.00, and then all other items can be rounded in a similar manner and added together.

When working with larger numbers, it might make more sense to round to higher place values. For example, when estimating the total value of a dealership's car inventory, it would make sense to round the car values to the nearest thousands place. The price of a car that is on sale for $15,654 can be estimated at $16,000. All other cars on the lot could be rounded in the same manner and then added together. Depending on the situation, it might make sense to calculate an over-estimate. For example, to make sure Aria has enough money at the grocery store, rounding up for each item would ensure that she will have enough money when it comes time to pay. A $0.40 item rounded up to $1.00 would ensure that there is a dollar to cover that item. Traditional rounding rules would round $0.40 to $0, which does not make sense in this particular real-world setting. Aria might not have a dollar available at checkout to pay for that item if she uses traditional rounding. It is up to the customer to decide the best approach when estimating.

Estimating is also very helpful when working with measurements. Bryan is updating his kitchen and wants to retile the floor. Again, an over-measurement might be useful. Also, rounding to nearest half-unit might be helpful. For instance, one side of the kitchen might have an exact measurement of 14.32 feet, and the most useful measurement needed to buy tile could be estimating this quantity to be 14.5 feet. If the kitchen was rectangular and the other side measured 10.9 feet, Bryan might round the other side to 11 feet. Therefore, Bryan would find the total tile necessary according to the following area calculation:

$$14.5 \times 11 = 159.5 \text{ square feet}$$

To make sure he purchases enough tile, Bryan would probably want to purchase at least 160 square feet of tile. This is a scenario in which an estimation might be more useful than an exact calculation. Having more tile than necessary is better than having an exact amount, in case any tiles are broken or otherwise unusable.

Finally, estimation is helpful when exact answers are necessary. Consider a situation in which Sabina has many operations to perform on numbers with decimals, and she is allowed a calculator to find the result. Even though an exact result can be obtained with a calculator, there is always a possibility that Sabina could make an error while inputting the data. For example, she could miss a decimal place, or misuse a parenthesis, causing a problem with the actual order of operations. A quick estimation at the beginning could help ensure that her final answer is within the correct range.

Sabina has to find the exact total of 10 cars listed for sale at the dealership. Each price has two decimal places included to account for both dollars and cents. If one car is listed at $21,234.43 but Sabina incorrectly inputs into the calculator the price of $2,123.443, this error would throw off the final sum by almost $20,000. A quick estimation at the beginning, by rounding each price to the nearest thousands place and finding the sum of the prices, would give Sabina an amount to compare the exact amount to. This comparison would let Sabina see if an error was made in her exact calculation.

Algebraic Reasoning

Quadratic and Other Polynomial Expressions, Equations, and Functions

In math, a **relation** is a relationship between two sets of numbers. By using a rule, it takes a number from the first set and matches it to a number in the second set. A relation consists of a set of inputs, known as the **domain,** and a set of outputs, known as the **range.** A **function** is a relation in which each member of the domain is paired to only one other member of the range. In other words, each input has only one output.

Here is an example of a relation that is not a function:

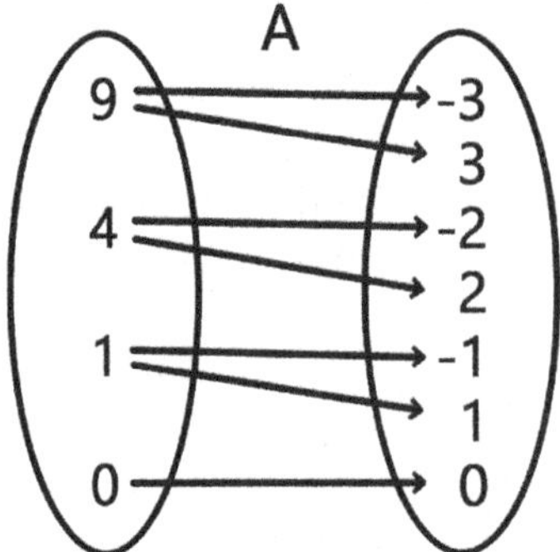

Every member of the first set, the domain, is mapped to two members of the second set, the range. Therefore, this relation is not a function.

A function can also be represented by a table of ordered pairs, a graph of ordered pairs (a scatterplot), or a set of ordered pairs as shown in the following:

Mapping

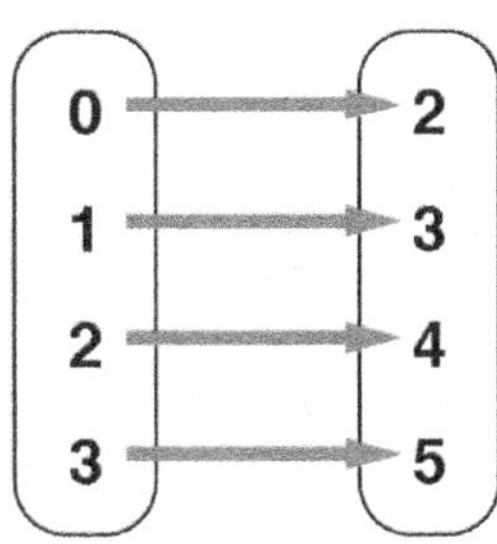

Table

x	y
0	2
1	3
2	4
3	5

Graph

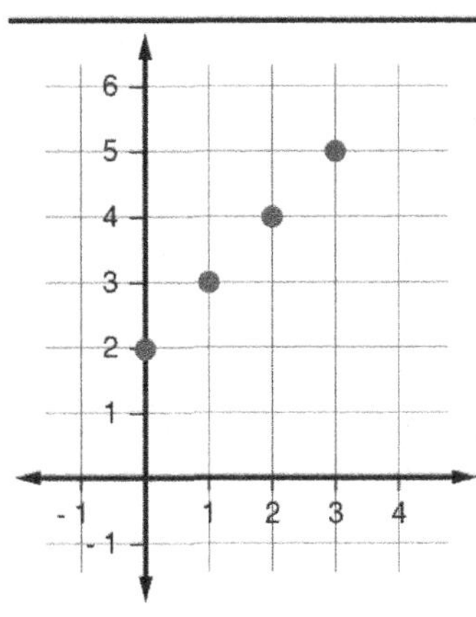

Ordered Pairs

{(0,2),(1,3),(2,4),(3,5)}

Note that this relation is a function because every member of the domain is mapped to exactly one member of the range.

An **equation** occurs when two algebraic expressions are set equal to one another. Functions can be represented in equation form. Given an equation in two variables, x and y, it can be expressed in function form if solved for y. For example, the linear equation:

$$2x + y = 5$$

This can be solved for y to obtain:

$$y = -2x + 5$$

otherwise known as **slope-intercept** form. To place the equation in function form, replace y with $f(x)$, which is read "f of x." Therefore:

$$f(x) = -2x + 5$$

This notation clarifies the input–output relationship of the function. The function f is a function of x, so an x value can be plugged into the function to obtain an output. For example,

$$f(2) = -2 \times 2 + 5 = 1$$

Therefore, an input of 2 corresponds to an output of 1.

A function can be graphed by plotting ordered pairs in the xy-plane in the same way that the equation form is graphed. The graph of a function always passes the **Vertical Line Test.** Basically, for any graph, if a vertical line can be drawn through any part of the graph and it hits the graph in more than one place, the graph is not a function. For example, the graph of a circle is not a function. The Vertical Line Test shows that with these relationships, the same x-value has more than one y-value, which goes against the definition of a function.

Inequalities look like equations, but instead of an equals sign, $<$, $>$, $\leq$, $\geq$, or $\neq$ are used. Here are some examples of inequalities:

$$2x + 7 < y$$

$$3x^2 \geq 5$$

and

$$x \neq 4$$

Inequalities show relationships between algebraic expressions when the quantities are different. Inequalities can also be expressed in function form if they are solved for y. For instance, the first inequality listed above can be written as:

$$2x + y < f(x)$$

Even and Odd Functions

A function is considered **even** when $f(x) = f(-x)$ for all values of x. This relationship means that the graph of an even function is perfectly symmetrical about the y-axis. In other words, the graph is reflected over the y-axis. The term "even" describes these functions because functions like x^2, x^4, x^6, and so on display this characteristic. That said, there are some functions that are even that don't involve x raised to an even exponent. For example, the graph of $f(x) = cos(x)$ is also symmetrical over the y-axis. There are also functions that *do* have an even exponent that are *not* even functions; although $f(x) = x^2 + 3$ *is* an even function, $f(x) = (x + 3)^2$ is *not* because $f(x) \neq f(-x)$ for all values of x.

A function is considered **odd** when $-f(x) = f(-x)$ for all values of x. This relationship means that the graph of an odd function is perfectly symmetrical about the origin. The term "odd" describes these functions because functions like x, x^3, x^5, x^7, and so on display this characteristic. As with even functions, exceptions to these exponential values exist. For example, the graph of $f(x) = sin(x)$, also has origin symmetry. There are also function that *do* have an odd exponent that are *not* odd functions; while $f(x) = x^3 - 3x$ is an odd function. $f(x) = x^3 - 1$ is not because $-f(x) \neq f(-x)$ for all values of x.

The majority of functions do not display these unique relationships and are thus neither even nor odd. Essentially, to algebraically determine if a function is even, odd, or neither, various values need to be plugged in for $f(x)$ and $f(-x)$. If all values of x yield the same output for $f(x)$ and $f(-x)$, the function is even. If all values of x yield the same output for $-f(x)$ and $f(-x)$, the function is odd. Any other situation indicates the function is neither even nor odd. To graphically determine if a function is even, odd, or neither, symmetry needs to be evaluated. If the function is perfectly symmetrical across the y-axis, it is an even function. If it is symmetrical about the origin, the function is odd. Any other situation indicates that the function is neither even nor odd.

It should be noted that there is one function that is both even *and* odd: $f(x) = 0$.

Quadratic Functions

When given data in ordered pairs, choosing an appropriate function or equation to model the data is important. Besides linear relationships, other common relationships that exist are quadratic and exponential. A helpful way to determine what type of function to use is to find the difference between consecutive dependent variables. Basically, find pairs of ordered pairs where the x-values increase by 1, and take the difference of the y-values. If the differences in the y-values are always the same value, then the function is **linear**. If the differences in the y-values when the x-values increase by 1 are not the same, the function could be quadratic or exponential. If the differences are not the same, find differences of those differences. If consecutive differences are the same, then the function is **quadratic**. If consecutive differences are not the same, try taking ratios of consecutive y-values. If the ratios are the same, the data have an exponential relationship and an exponential function should be used.

For example, the ordered pairs $(1, 4)$, $(2, 6)$, $(3, 8)$, and $(4, 10)$ have a linear relationship because the difference in y-values is 2 for every increase in x of 1. The ordered pairs $(1, 0)$, $(2, 3)$, $(3, 10)$, and $(4, 21)$ have a nonlinear relationship. The first differences in y-values are 3, 7, and 11; however, consecutive second differences are both 4, which means this is a quadratic relationship. Lastly, the ordered pairs $(1, 10)$, $(2, 30)$, $(3, 90)$, and $(4, 270)$ have an exponential relationship. Taking ratios of consecutive y-values leads to a common ratio of 4.

The general form of a **quadratic equation** is:

$$y = ax^2 + bx + c$$

Its vertex form is:

$$y = a(x - h)^2 + k \text{ with vertex } (h, k)$$

If the vertex and one other point are known, the vertex form should be used to solve for a. If three points, not the vertex, are known, the general form should be used. The three points create a system of three equations in three unknowns that can be solved for.

Solving a Quadratic Equation

Given a quadratic equation in standard form:

$$ax^2 + bx + c = 0$$

with constants a, b, and c, such that $c \neq 0$, it can have either two real solutions, one real solution, or two complex solutions of the form $a + bi$ (no real solutions). The number of solutions is determined using its determinant:

$$b^2 - 4ac$$

If the determinant is positive, there are two real solutions. If the determinant is negative, there are no real solutions. If the determinant is equal to 0, there is one real solution. For example, given the quadratic equation:

$$2x^2 - x + 4 = 0$$

Its determinant is:

$$(-1)^2 - 4(2)(4) = 1 - 32 = -31$$

This is less than 0. Therefore, it has two complex solutions.

There are a number of ways to solve a quadratic equation. The first way is through **factoring**. If the equation is in standard form and the polynomial can be factored, set each factor equal to 0 and solve. This can be done because if $ab = 0$, either $a = 0$, $b = 0$, or both are equal to 0. For example:

$$x^2 - 7x + 10 = (x - 5)(x - 2)$$

Therefore, the solutions of $x^2 - 7x + 10 = 0$ are those that satisfy both $x - 5 = 0$ and $x - 2 = 0$, or $x = 5$ and 2. This is the simplest method to solve quadratic equations; however, not all quadratic polynomials can be factored, so this method does not work for all quadratic equations.

Another method is through **completing the square**. The polynomial $x^2 + 10x - 9$ cannot be factored, so complete the square in the equation $x^2 + 10x - 9 = 0$ to find its solutions. First, add 9 to both sides, resulting in:

$$x^2 + 10x = 9$$

Then, divide the x-coefficient by 2, square it, and add it to both sides of the equation. In this example, $\left(\frac{10}{2}\right)^2 = 25$ is added to both sides of the equation to obtain:

$$x^2 + 10x + 25 = 9 + 25 = 34$$

The polynomial, which is now a perfect square trinomial, can then be factored into:

$$(x + 5)^2 = 34$$

Finally, solving for x involves first taking the square root of both sides and then subtracting 5 from both sides. This process leads to the two solutions:

$$x = \pm\sqrt{34} - 5$$

This method always works for any quadratic equation.

The final method of solving a quadratic equation is to use the **quadratic formula**. Given a quadratic equation in standard form:

$$ax^2 + bx + c = 0$$

Its solutions always can be found using the formula:

$$x = \frac{-b \pm \sqrt{b^2 - 4ac}}{2a}$$

This method, like completing the square, can always be used.

Polynomial Functions

A **polynomial function** is a function containing a polynomial expression, which is an expression containing constants and variables combined using the four mathematical operations. The degree of a polynomial depends on the largest exponent in the expression. Typical polynomial functions are **quartic,** with a degree of 4, **cubic,** with a degree of 3, and **quadratic,** with a degree of 2. Note that the exponents on the variables can only be nonnegative integers. The domain of any polynomial function is all real numbers because any number plugged into a polynomial expression grants a real number output. An example of a quartic polynomial equation is:

$$y = x^4 + 3x^3 - 2x + 1$$

The zeros of a polynomial function are the points where its graph crosses the y-axis. In order to find the number of real zeros of a polynomial function, use **Descartes' Rule of Signs**, which states that the number of possible positive real zeros is equal to the number of sign changes in the coefficients. If there is only one sign change, there is only one positive real zero. In the example above, the signs of the coefficients are positive, positive, negative, and positive. The sign changes twice; therefore, there are at most two positive real zeros. The number of possible negative real zeros is equal to the number of sign changes in the coefficients when plugging $-x$ into the equation. Again, if there is only one sign change, there is only one negative real zero. The polynomial result when plugging -x into the equation is:

$$y = (-x)^4 + 3(-x)^3 - 2(-x) + 1$$

$$y = x^4 - 3x^3 + 2x + 1$$

The sign changes two times, so there are at most two negative real zeros. Another polynomial equation this rule can be applied to is:

$$y = x^3 + 2x - x - 5$$

There is only one sign change in the terms of the polynomial, so there is exactly one real zero. When plugging $-x$ into the equation, the polynomial result is:

$$-x^3 - 2x - x - 5$$

There are no sign changes in this polynomial, so there are no possible negative zeros.

Adding, Subtracting, and Multiplying Polynomial Equations

When working with polynomials, **like terms** are terms that contain exactly the same variables with the same powers. For example, x^4y^5 and $9x^4y^5$ are like terms. The coefficients are different, but the same variables are raised to the same powers. When adding polynomials, only terms that are like can be added. When adding two like terms, just add the coefficients and leave the variables alone. This process uses the distributive property. For example,

$$x^4y^5 + 9x^4y^5$$

$$(1+9)x^4y^5$$

$$10x^4y^5$$

Therefore, when adding two polynomials, simply add the like terms together. Unlike terms cannot be combined.

Subtracting polynomials involves adding the opposite of the polynomial being subtracted. Basically, the sign of each term in the polynomial being subtracted is changed, and then the like terms are combined because it is now an addition problem. For example, consider the following:

$$6x^2 - 4x + 2 - (4x^2 - 8x + 1).$$

Add the opposite of the second polynomial to obtain:

$$6x^2 - 4x + 2 + (-4x^2 + 8x - 1)$$

Then, collect like terms to obtain:

$$2x^2 + 4x + 1$$

Multiplying polynomials involves using the product rule for exponents that:

$$b^m b^n = b^{m+n}$$

Basically, when multiplying expressions with the same base, just add the exponents. Multiplying a monomial times a monomial involves multiplying the coefficients together and then multiplying the variables together using the product rule for exponents. For instance,

$$8x^2y \times 4x^4y^2 = 32x^6y^3$$

When multiplying a monomial times a polynomial that is not a monomial, use the distributive property to multiply each term of the polynomial times the monomial.

For example,

$$3x(x^2 + 3x - 4)$$

$$3x^3 + 9x^2 - 12x$$

Finally, multiplying two polynomials when neither one is a monomial involves multiplying each term of the first polynomial times each term of the second polynomial. There are some shortcuts, given certain scenarios.

For instance, a binomial times a binomial can be found by using the **FOIL (Firsts, Outers, Inners, Lasts)** method shown here:

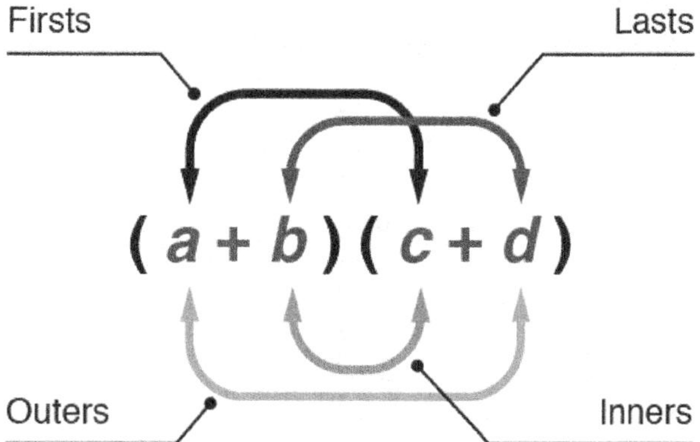

Finding the product of a sum and difference of the same two terms is simple because if it was to be foiled out, the outer and inner terms would cancel out. For instance,

$$(x + y)(x - y) = x^2 + xy - xy - y^2$$

Finally, the square of a binomial can be found using the following formula:

$$(a \pm b)^2 = a^2 \pm 2ab + b^2$$

The Relationship Between Zeros and Factors of Polynomials

A polynomial is a mathematical expression containing addition, subtraction, or multiplication of one or more constants multiplied by variables raised to positive powers. A **polynomial equation** is a polynomial set equal to another polynomial, or in standard form, a polynomial is set equal to zero. A **polynomial function** is a polynomial set equal to y. For instance, $x^2 + 2x - 8$ is a polynomial, $x^2 + 2x - 8 = 0$ is a polynomial equation, and $y = x^2 + 2x - 8$ is the corresponding polynomial function. To solve a polynomial equation, the x-values in which the graph of the corresponding polynomial function crosses the x-axis are sought.

These coordinates are known as the **zeros** of the polynomial function because they are the coordinates in which the y-coordinates are 0. One way to find the zeros of a polynomial is to find its factors, then set each individual factor equal to 0, and solve each equation to find the zeros. A **factor** is a linear expression, and to completely factor a polynomial, the polynomial must be rewritten as a product of individual linear factors. The polynomial listed above can be factored as:

$$(x + 4)(x - 2)$$

Setting each factor equal to zero results in the zeros $x = -4$ and $x = 2$.

Here is the graph of the zeros of the polynomial:

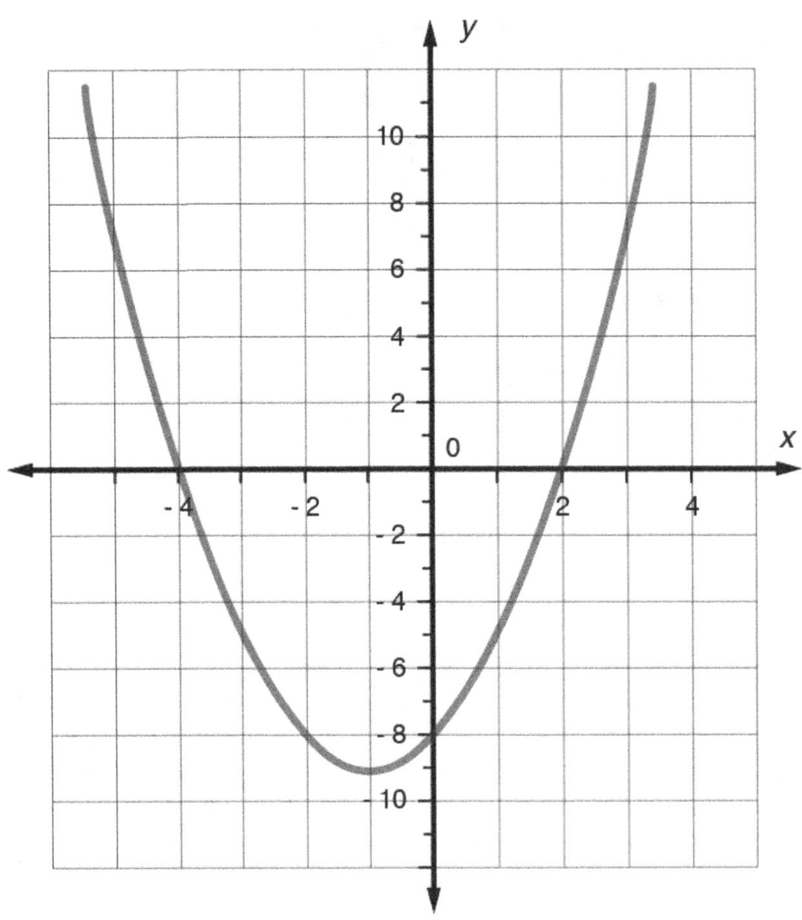

Expressions, Equations and Functions Involving Powers, Roots, and Radicals

Numbers can also be written using exponents. The number 7,000 can be written as:

$$7 \times 1{,}000$$

7 is in the thousands place. It can also be written as:

$$7 \times 10^3$$

because

$$1{,}000 = 10^3$$

Another number that can use this notation is 500. It can be written as:

$$5 \times 100$$

or

$$5 \times 10^2$$

because

$$100 = 10^2$$

The number 30 can be written as 3×10, or 3×10^1, because $10 = 10^1$. Notice that each one of the exponents of 10 is equal to the number of zeros in the number. Seven is in the thousands place, with three zeros, and the exponent on ten is 3. The five is in the hundreds place, with two zeros, and the exponent on the ten is 2. A question may give the number 40,000 and ask for it to be rewritten using exponents with a base of ten. Because the number has a four in the ten-thousands place and four zeros, it can be written using an exponent of four:

$$4 \times 10^4$$

The nth root of a is given as $\sqrt[n]{a}$, which is called a **radical.** Typical values for n are 2 and 3, which represent the square and cube roots. In this form, n represents an integer greater than or equal to 2, and a is a real number. If n is even, a must be nonnegative, and if n is odd, a can be any real number. This radical can be written in exponential form as $a^{\frac{1}{n}}$. Therefore, $\sqrt[4]{15}$ is the same as $15^{\frac{1}{4}}$ and $\sqrt[3]{-5}$ is the same as $(-5)^{\frac{1}{3}}$.

In a similar fashion, the nth root of a can be raised to a power m, which is written as $\left(\sqrt[n]{a}\right)^m$. This expression is the same as $\sqrt[n]{a^m}$. For example,

$$\sqrt[2]{4^3} = \sqrt[2]{64} = 8 = \left(\sqrt[2]{4}\right)^3 = 2^3$$

Because $\sqrt[n]{a} = a^{\frac{1}{n}}$, both sides can be raised to an exponent of m, resulting in:

$$\left(\sqrt[n]{a}\right)^m = \sqrt[n]{a^m} = a^{\frac{m}{n}}$$

This rule allows:

$$\sqrt[2]{4^3} = \left(\sqrt[2]{4}\right)^3 = 4^{\frac{3}{2}} = (2^2)^{\frac{3}{2}} = 2^{\frac{6}{2}} = 2^3 = 8$$

Negative exponents can also be incorporated into these rules. Any time an exponent is negative, the base expression must be flipped to the other side of the fraction bar and rewritten with a positive exponent. For example,

$$2^{-3} = \frac{1}{2^3} = \frac{1}{8}$$

Therefore, two more relationships between radical and exponential expressions are:

$$a^{-\frac{1}{n}} = \frac{1}{\sqrt[n]{a}}$$

$$a^{-\frac{m}{n}} = \frac{1}{\sqrt[n]{a^m}} = \frac{1}{\left(\sqrt[n]{a}\right)^m}$$

Thus,

$$8^{-\frac{1}{3}} = \frac{1}{\sqrt[3]{8}} = \frac{1}{2}$$

All of these relationships are very useful when simplifying complicated radical and exponential expressions. If an expression contains both forms, use one of these rules to change the expression to contain either all radicals or all exponential expressions. This process makes the entire expression much easier to work with, especially if the expressions are contained within equations.

Consider the following example:

$$\sqrt{x} \times \sqrt[4]{x}$$

It is written in radical form; however, it can be simplified into one radical by using exponential expressions first. The expression can be written as:

$$x^{\frac{1}{2}} \times x^{\frac{1}{4}}$$

It can be combined into one base by adding the exponents as:

$$x^{\frac{1}{2}+\frac{1}{4}} = x^{\frac{3}{4}}$$

Writing this back in radical form, the result is $\sqrt[4]{x^3}$.

Creating Equivalent Expressions Involving Rational Exponents and Radicals

Re-writing complex radical expressions as equivalent forms with rational exponents can help to simplify them. The rule that helps this conversion is:

$$\sqrt[n]{x^m} = x^{\frac{m}{n}}$$

If $m = 1$, the rule is simply:

$$\sqrt[n]{x} = x^{\frac{1}{n}}$$

For example, consider the following expression:

$$\sqrt[4]{x}\sqrt[2]{y}$$

This can be written as one radical expression, but first it needs to be converted to an equivalent expression. The equivalent expression is $x^{\frac{1}{4}}y^{\frac{1}{2}}$. The goal is to have one radical, which means one index n, so a common denominator of the exponents must be found. The common denominator is 4, so an equivalent expression is $x^{\frac{1}{4}}y^{\frac{2}{4}}$. The exponential rule $a^m b^m = (ab)^m$ can be used to factor $\frac{1}{4}$ out of both variables. This process results in the expression $(xy^2)^{\frac{1}{4}}$, and its equivalent radical form is $\sqrt[4]{xy^2}$. Converting to rational exponents has allowed the entire expression to be written as one radical.

Another type of problem could involve going in the opposite direction: starting with rational exponents and using an equivalent radical form to simplify the expression. For example, $32^{\frac{1}{5}}$ might not appear equal to 2, but putting it in its equivalent radical form $\sqrt[5]{32}$ shows that it is equivalent to the fifth root of 32, which is 2.

Radical Functions

A **radical equation** is an equation that contains a variable in the **radicand,** which is the expression under the root. The radical can be a square root, a cube root, or a higher root. To solve an equation containing a root, arrange the terms so that one radical is by itself on one side of the equals sign. Then raise both sides of the equation to the value of the root. For example, square both sides if the root contains a square root, and cube both sides if the root contains a cube root. Then, solve the resulting equation. If the equation still contains a radical, those steps must be completed again to remove the equation of all radicals. Finally, it is crucial that all solutions are checked in the original equation. Some solutions to this equation, once the radicals are removed, might not be solutions to the original radical equation. Consider the following radical equation:

$$\sqrt{3x+1} - \sqrt{x+4} = 1$$

Add the second radical to both sides, and then square both sides to obtain:

$$3x + 1 = x + 4 + 2\sqrt{x+4} + 1.$$

Next, collect like terms and isolate the radical to obtain:

$$4x^2 - 16x + 16 = 4(x+4)$$

This simplifies into the quadratic equation $4x^2 - 20x$, which can be solved using factoring:

$$4x(x-5) = 0$$

So, it has solutions, $x = 0$ and $x = 5$. Both values must be checked into the original radical equation. because $x = 0$ does not check, it is not a real solution and is called an **extraneous solution**. However, $x = 5$ is a solution.

If an equation contains a variable in the denominator of a fraction, it is known as a **rational equation.** Anything, that when plugged into the equation, contains a zero denominator, cannot be a solution of the equation. To solve a rational equation, multiply both sides of the equation by the LCD (least common denominator) of all of the terms in the equation. Then, solve the resulting equation, making sure that the solutions do not cause any term to have a zero denominator in the original equation. Here is an example of solving the rational equation:

$$\frac{5}{x} - \frac{1}{3} = \frac{1}{x}$$

$$3x \times \left(\frac{5}{x} - \frac{1}{3}\right) = 3x \times \left(\frac{1}{x}\right)$$ Multiply both sides by the LCD

$$3x \times \frac{5}{x} - 3x \times \frac{1}{3} = 3x \times \frac{1}{x}$$ Distribute

$$15 - x = 3$$
$$-x = -12$$
$$x = 12$$
Simplify, and then solve

Both sides of the equation were initially multiplied times the LCD, $3x$. Note that the only number that could cause a problem as a solution would be $x = 0$, because it would create a 0 in the denominator.

Rational and Exponential Expressions, Equations, and Functions

Rational Expressions

A **rational expression** is a fraction or a ratio in which both the numerator and denominator are polynomials that are not equal to zero. A polynomial is a mathematical expression containing addition, subtraction, or multiplication of one or more constants multiplied by variables raised to positive powers. Here are some examples of rational expressions:

$$\frac{2x^2 + 6x}{x}$$

$$\frac{x - 2}{x^2 - 6x + 8}$$

$$\frac{x + 2}{x^3 - 1}$$

Such expressions can be simplified using different forms of division. The first example can be simplified in two ways. Then, cancelling out an x in each numerator and the x in each denominator results in $2x + 6$. It also can be simplified using factoring and then crossing common factors out of the numerator and denominator. For example, it can be written as:

$$\frac{2x(x + 3)}{x} = 2(x + 3) = 2x + 6$$

The second expression above can also be simplified using factoring. It can be written as:

$$\frac{x - 2}{(x - 2)(x - 4)} = \frac{1}{x - 4}$$

Finally, the third example can only be simplified using long division, as there are no common factors in the numerator and denominator. First, divide the first term of the numerator by the first term of the denominator, then write the result in the quotient. Then, multiply the divisor times that number and write it below the dividend. Subtract and continue the process until each term in the divisor is accounted for.

Here is the actual long division:

Simplifying Expressions Using Long Division

$$
\begin{array}{r|rrrr}
 & x^2 & -2x & +4 & \\
\hline
x+2 & x^3 & & & -1 \\
 & x^3 & +2x^2 & & \\
\hline
 & & -2x^2 & & -1 \\
 & & -2x^2 & -4x & \\
\hline
 & & & 4x & -1 \\
 & & & 4x & +8 \\
\hline
 & & & & -9
\end{array}
$$

Exponential Equations

An **exponential equation** is used to model something with exponential growth or decay. If something grows exponentially, such as compound interest, the amount is multiplied times a growth factor for every increase in x. If something decays exponentially, the amount is multiplied times a factor between 0 and 1 for every increase in x. When a population is declining, an exponential decay equation can be used to represent the situation. The general form of an exponential function is:

$$y = b \times a^x$$

a is the base and b is the y-intercept.

Exponential growth involves the dependent variable changing by a common ratio every unit increase. The equation of exponential growth is:

$$y = a^x, \text{ for } a > 0, a \neq 1$$

The value a is known as the **base**. Consider the exponential equation:

$$y = 2^x$$

When x equals 1, y equals 2, and when x equals 2, y equals 4. For every unit increase in x, the value of the output variable doubles. Here is the graph of $y = 2^x$.

Notice that as the dependent variable, y, gets very large, x increases slightly. This characteristic of this graph is why sometimes a quantity is said to be blowing up exponentially.

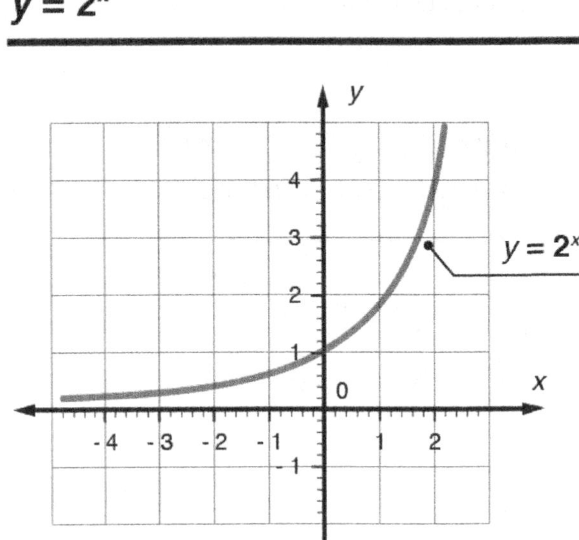

Logarithmic Functions

For $x > 0, b > 0, b \neq 1$, the function $f(x) = \log_b x$ is known as the **logarithmic function** with base b. With $y = \log_b x$ its exponential equivalent is $b^y = x$. In either case, the **exponent** is y and the **base** is b. Therefore, $3 = \log_2 8$ is the same as $2^3 = 8$

So, in order to find the logarithm with base 2 of 8, find the exponent that when 2 is raised to that value results in 8. Similarly,

$$\log_3 243 = 5$$

In order to do this mentally, ask the question, what exponent does 3 need to be raised to so that it results in 243? The answer is 5. Most logarithms do not have whole number results. In this case, a calculator can be used. A calculator typically has buttons with base 10 and base e (Euler's number, the base in the natural log), so the change of base formula can be used to calculate these logs. For instance,

$$\log_3 55 = \frac{\log 55}{\log 3} = 3.64$$

Similarly, the natural logarithm with base e could be used to obtain the same result:

$$\log_3 55 = \frac{\ln 55}{\ln 3} = 3.64$$

The domain of a logarithmic function $f(x) = \log_b x$ is all positive real numbers. This is because the exponent must be a positive number. The range of a logarithmic function $f(x) = \log_b x$ is all real numbers. The graphs of all logarithmic functions of the form $f(x) = \log_b x$ always pass through the point $(1, 0)$ because anything raised to the power of 0 is 1. Therefore, such a function always has an x-intercept at 1. If the base is greater than 1, the graph increases from the left to the right along the x-axis. If the base is between 0 and 1, the graph decreases from the left to the right along the x-axis. In both situations, the y-axis is a vertical asymptote. The graph will never touch the y-axis, but it does approach it closely. Here are the graphs of the two cases of logarithmic functions:

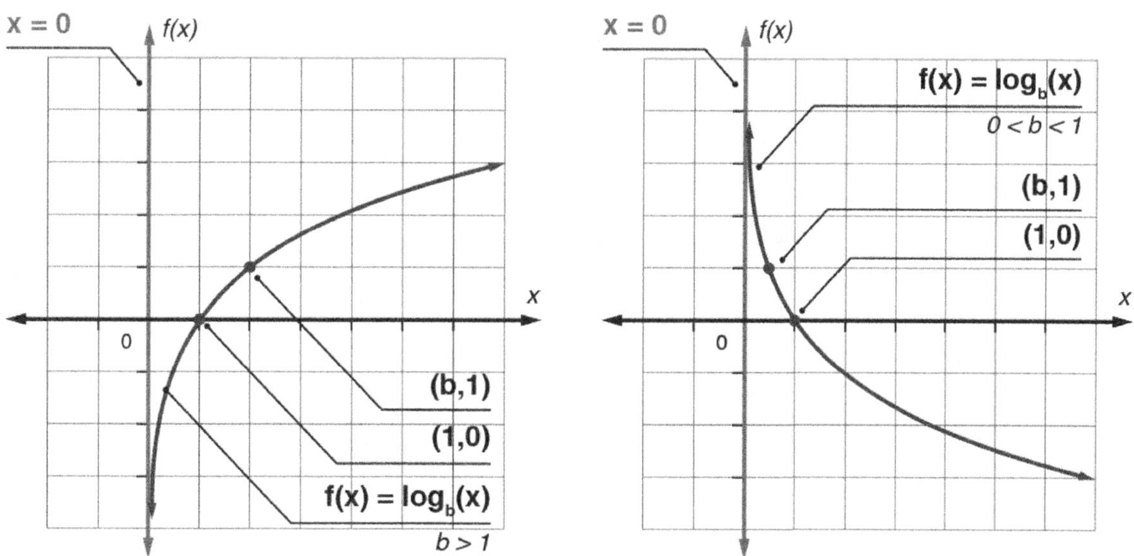

Geometric and Spatial Reasoning

Plane Geometry

Coordinate geometry is the intersection of algebra and geometry. Within this system, the points in a geometric shape are defined using ordered pairs. In the two-dimensional coordinate system, an x- and y-axis form the ***xy*-plane**. The x-axis is a horizontal scale, and the y-axis is a vertical scale. The ordered pair where the axes cross is known as the **origin**. To the right of the origin, the x-values are positive, and to the left of the origin, the x-values are negative. The y-values above the origin are positive, and y-values below the origin are negative. The axes split the plane into four quadrants, and the first quadrant is where both x- and y-values are positive. To plot an ordered pair means to locate the point corresponding to the x- and y-coordinates. For example, plotting $(4, 3)$ means moving to the right 4 units from 0 in the x direction and then moving up 3 units in the y direction.

Here is a picture of the xy-plane, also known as the **rectangular** or **Cartesian coordinate system**:

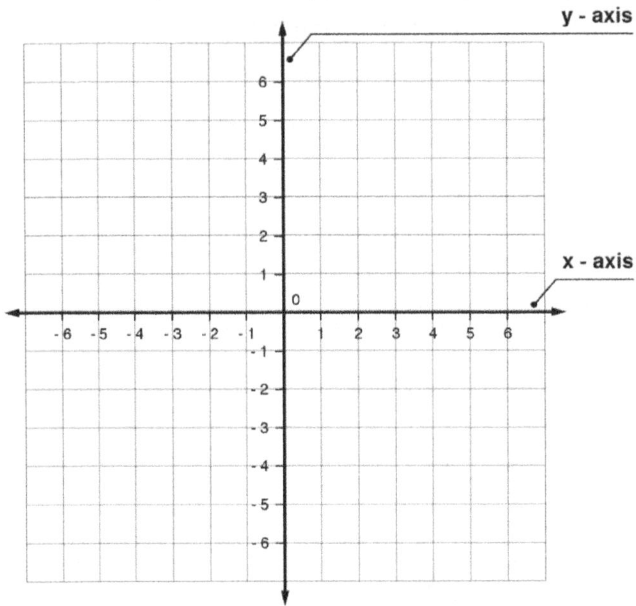

The coordinate system allows us to visualize relationships between equations and geometric figures. For instance, an equation in two variables, x and y, is represented as a straight line on the xy-coordinate plane. A solution of an equation in two variables is an ordered pair that satisfies the equation. A graph of an equation can be found by plotting several ordered pairs that are solutions of the equation and then connecting those points with a straight line or smooth curve. Here is the graph of:

$$4x + y = 8$$

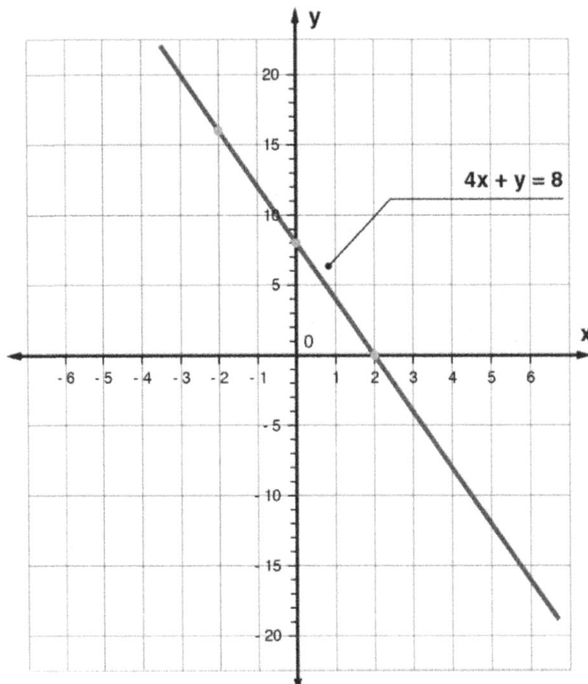

Three ordered pairs that are solutions to the equation were found and plotted. Those points are $(-2, 16)$, $(0, 8)$, and $(2, 0)$. The points were connected using a straight line. Note that the point $(0, 8)$ is where the line crosses the y-axis. This point is known as the **y-intercept**. The y-intercept can always be found by plugging $x = 0$ into the equation. Also, the point $(2, 0)$ is where the line crosses the x-axis. This point is known as the **x-intercept**, and it can always be found for any equation of a line by plugging $y = 0$ into the equation. The equation above is written in standard form:

$$Ax + By = C$$

Often an equation is written in slope-intercept form, $y = mx + b$, where m represents the slope of the line, and b represents the y-intercept. The above equation can be solved for y to obtain:

$$y = -4x + 8$$

This shows a slope of -4 and a y-intercept of 8, meaning the point $(0, 8)$.

The **slope** of a line is the measure of steepness of a line, and it compares the vertical change of the line, the **rise**, to the horizontal change of the line, the **run**. The formula for slope of a line through two distinct points (x_1, y_1) and (x_2, y_2) is:

$$m = \frac{y_2 - y_1}{x_2 - x_1}$$

If the line increases from left to right, the slope is positive, and if the line decreases from left to right, as shown above, the slope is negative. If a line is horizontal, like the line representing the equation $y = 5$, the slope is 0. If a line is vertical, like the line representing the equation $x = 2$, the line has undefined slope.

In order to graph a function, it can be done the same way as equations. The $f(x)$ represents the dependent variable y in the equation, so replace $f(x)$ with y and plot some points. For example, the same graph above would be found for the function:

$$f(x) = -4x + 8$$

Graphs other than straight lines also exist. For example, here are the graphs of $f(x) = x^2$ and $f(x) = x^3$, the squaring and cubic functions.

$f(x) = x^2$

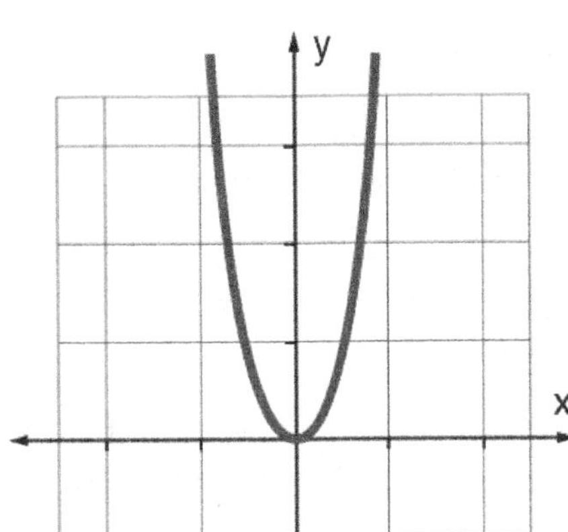

$f(x) = x^4$

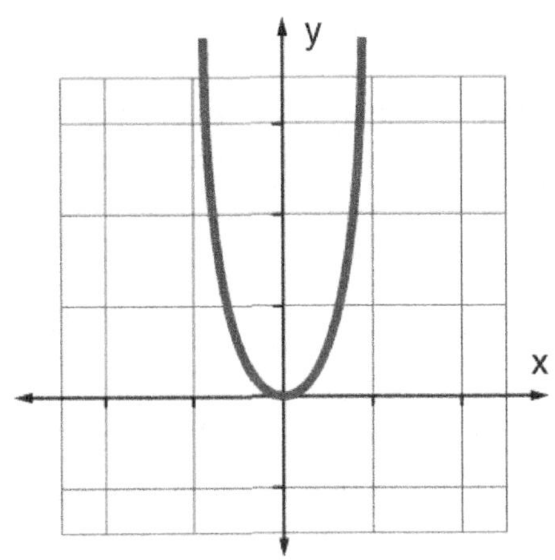

If the equals sign is changed to an inequality symbol such as $<$, $>$, $\leq$, or $\geq$ in an equation, the result is an inequality. If it is changed to a linear equation in two variables, the result is a linear inequality in two variables. A solution of an inequality in two variables is an ordered pair that satisfies the inequality. For example, $(1, 3)$ is a solution of the linear inequality:

$$y \geq x + 1$$

When plugged in, it results in a true statement. The graph of an inequality in two variables consists of all ordered pairs that make the solution true. A half-plane consists of the set of all points on one side of a line in the xy-plane, and the solution to a linear inequality is a half-plane. If the inequality consists of $>$ or $<$, the line is dashed, and no solutions actually exist on the line shown. If the inequality consists of $\geq$ or $\leq$, the line is solid, and solutions do exist on the line shown. In order to graph a linear inequality, graph the corresponding equation found by replacing the inequality symbol with an equals sign.

Then pick a test point on either side of the line. If that point results in a true statement when plugged into the original inequality, shade in the side containing the test point. If it results in a false statement, shade in the opposite side. Here is the graph of the inequality:

$$y < x + 1$$

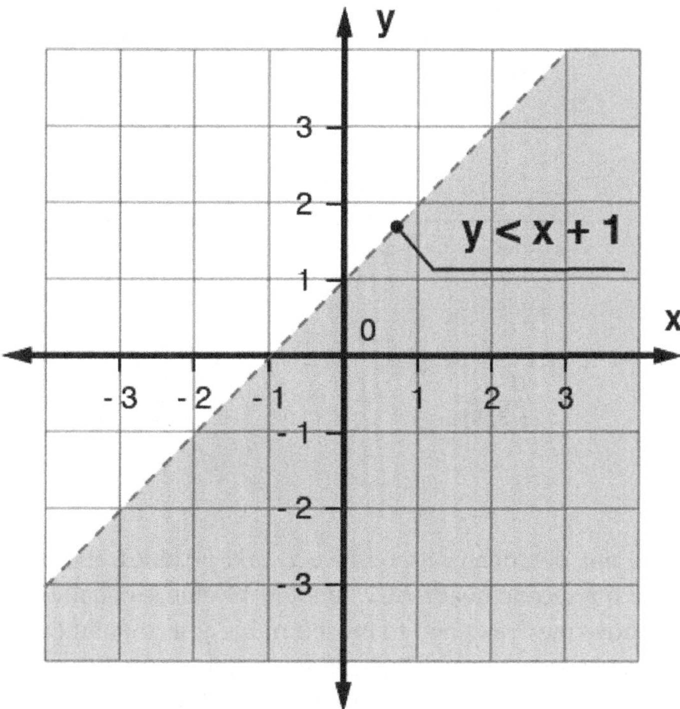

The Coordinate Plane

The coordinate plane is a way of identifying the position of a point in relation to two axes. The coordinate plane is made up of two intersecting lines, the x-axis and the y-axis. These lines intersect at a right angle, and their intersection point is called the origin. The points on the coordinate plane are labeled based on their position in relation to the origin. If a point is found 4 units to the right and 2 units up from the origin, the location is described as $(4, 2)$. These numbers are the x- and y-coordinates, always written in the order (x, y). This point is also described as lying in the first quadrant. Every point in the first quadrant has a location that is positive in the x and y directions.

The following figure shows the coordinate plane with examples of points that lie in each quadrant.

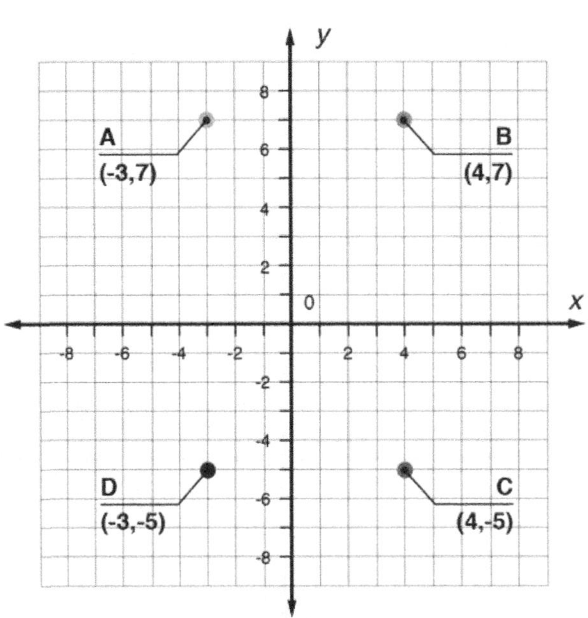

Point B lies in the first quadrant, described with positive x- and y-values, above the x-axis and to the right of the y-axis. Point A lies in the second quadrant, where the x-value is negative and the y-value is positive. This quadrant is above the x-axis and to the left of the y-axis. Point D lies in the third quadrant, where both the x- and y-values are negative. Points in this quadrant are described as being below the x-axis and to the left of the y-axis. Point C is in the fourth quadrant, where the x-value is positive and the y-value is negative.

Straight Lines

Geometric figures can be identified by matching the definition with the object. For example, a line segment is made up of two connected endpoints. A **ray** is made up of one endpoint and one extending side that goes on forever. A line has no endpoints and two sides that extend forever. These three geometric figures are shown below. What happens at A and B determines the name of each figure.

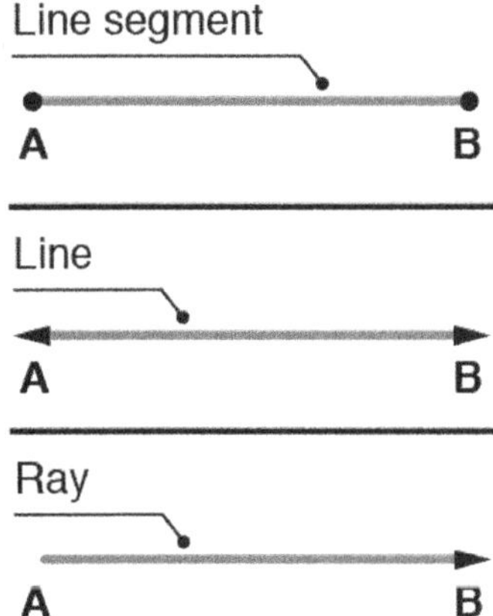

A set of lines can be parallel, perpendicular, or neither, depending on how the two lines interact. Parallel lines run alongside each other but never intersect. **Perpendicular** lines intersect at a 90-degree, or a right, angle. An example of these two sets of lines is shown below. Also shown in the figure are non-examples of these two types of lines. Because the first set of lines, in the top left corner, will eventually intersect if they continue, they are not parallel. In the second set, the lines run in the same direction and will never intersect, making them parallel. The third set, in the bottom left corner, intersect at an angle that is not right, or not 90 degrees. The fourth set is perpendicular because the lines intersect at exactly a right angle.

Lines

Not Parallel | Parallel

Not Perpendicular | Perpendicular

Circles in the Coordinate Plane

Recall that a circle is the set of all points the same distance, known as radius r, from a single point C, known as the center of the circle. The center has coordinates (h, k) and any point on the circle is an ordered pair with coordinates (x, y). A right triangle with hypotenuse r can be formed with these two points as seen here:

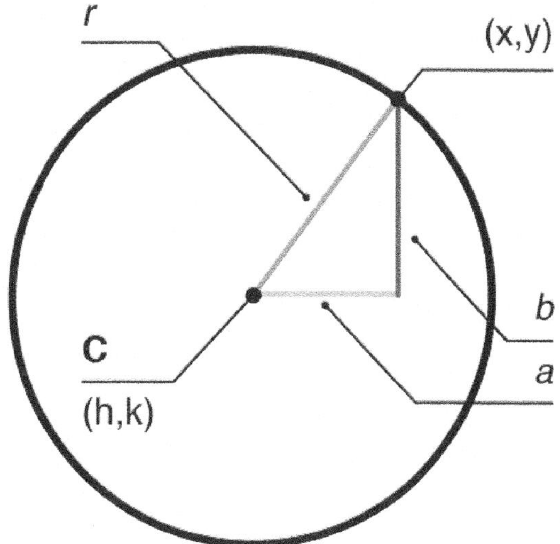

The other side lengths are a and b. The **Pythagorean Theorem** states that:

$$a^2 + b^2 = r^2$$

However, a can be replaced by $|x - h|$ and b can be replaced by $|y - k|$ because the distance between any two coordinates in the coordinate plane is the absolute value of their difference. That substitution gives:

$$(x - h)^2 + (y - k)^2 = r^2$$

This is the formula used to find the equation of any circle with center (h, k) and radius r. Therefore, if any problem gives the coordinates of the center of a circle and its radius length, this is the equation in two variables that allows any other point on the circle to be found.

Oftentimes, the center or the radius of a circle are not easily seen in the given equation of the circle. If the equation is in standard form of a polynomial equation like:

$$ax^2 + ay^2 + cx + dy + e = 0$$

the algebraic technique of completing the square must be used to find the coordinates of the center and the radius. Completing the square must be done within both variables x and y. First, the constant term needs to be subtracted off of both sides of the equation, and then the x and y terms need to be grouped together. Then, the entire equation needs to be divided by a. Then, divide the coefficient of the x term by 2, square it, and add that value to both sides of the equation. This value should be grouped with the x terms. Next, divide the coefficient of the y term by 2, square it, and add it to both sides of the equation, grouping it with the y terms. The trinomial in both x and y are now perfect square trinomials and can be factored into squares of a binomial. This process results in $(x - h)^2 + (y - k)^2 = r^2$, showing the radius and coordinates of the center.

Transformations and Symmetry

Two-dimensional figures can undergo various types of transformations in the plane. They can be shifted horizontally and vertically, reflected, compressed, or stretched.

A shift, also known as a slide or a translation, moves the shape in one direction. Here is a **picture of a shift:**

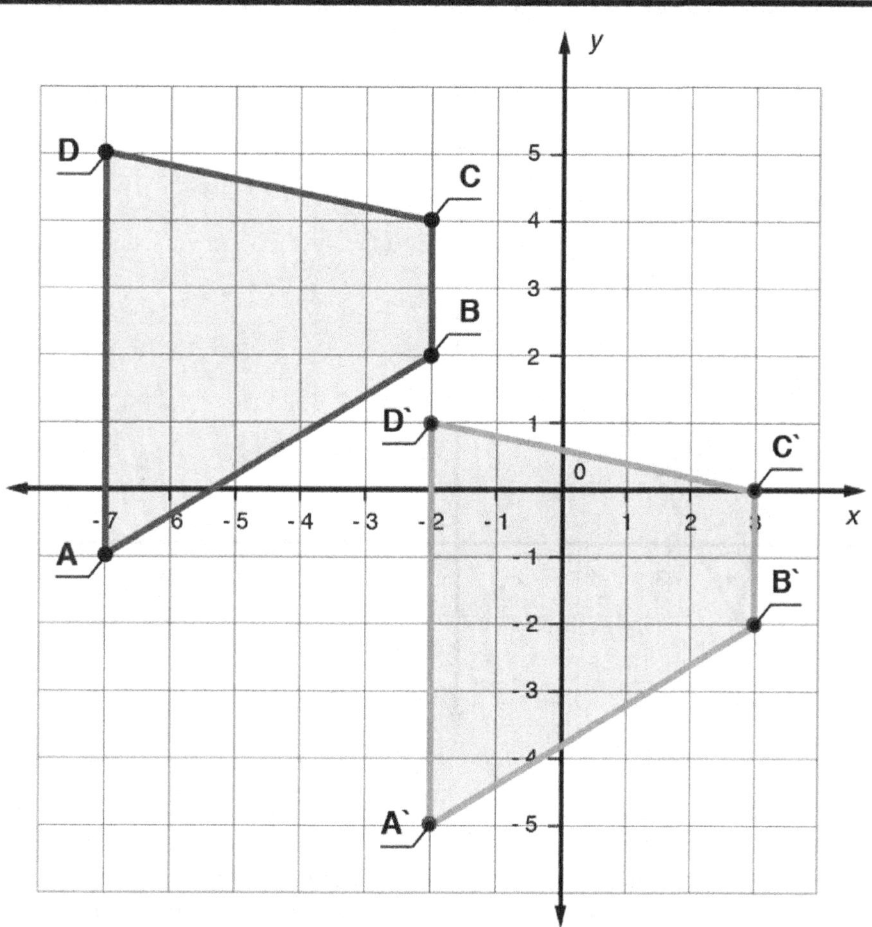

Notice that the size of the original shape has not changed at all. If the shift occurs within a **Cartesian coordinate system**, the standard x- and y-coordinate plane, it can be represented by adding to or subtracting from the x- and y-coordinates of the original shape. All vertices will move the same number of units because the shape and size of the shape do not change.

A figure can also be reflected, or flipped, over a given line known as the **line of reflection**. For example, consider the following picture:

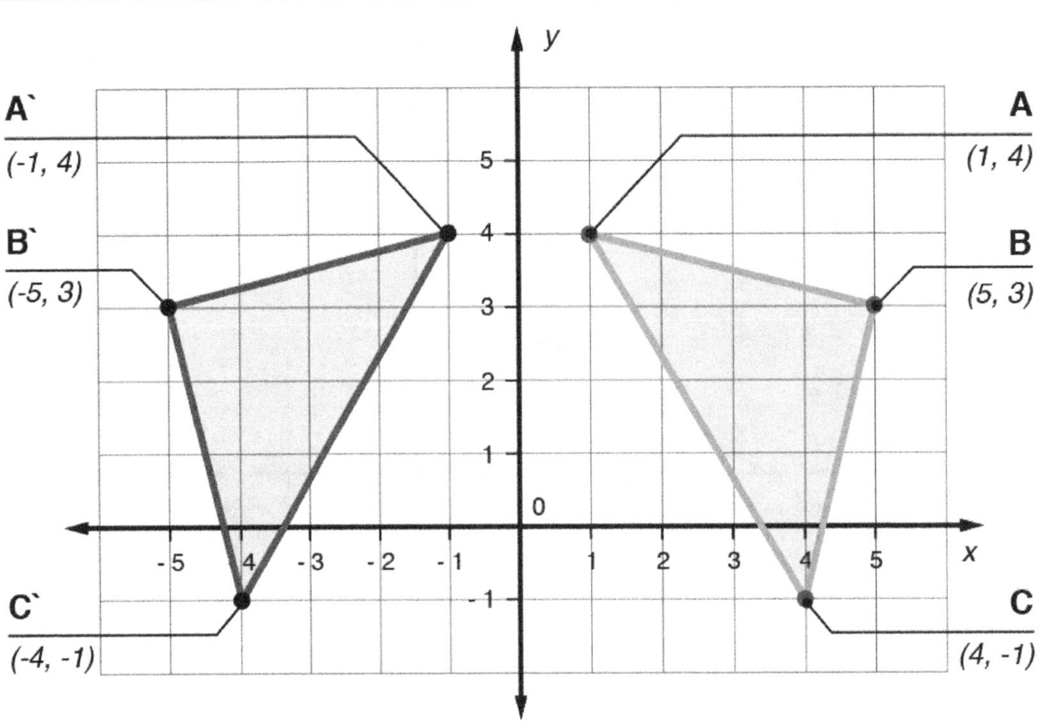

After the reflection, the original shape remains the same size, but the coordinates change. For example, if a shape gets reflected over the y-axis, as above, the y-coordinate stays the same, but the x-coordinates are made negative. For example, the triangle above starts in the first and fourth quadrants, but it is reflected over y-axis to the second and third quadrants. Point A has the initial coordinates of $(1, 4)$, but in the reflection, the point A' becomes $(-1, 4)$.

Similarly, if the shape is reflected over the x-axis, the x-coordinate stays the same, but the y-coordinates are made negative. For instance, in the graphic below, the point C at $(3, 5)$ becomes C' at $(3, -5)$.

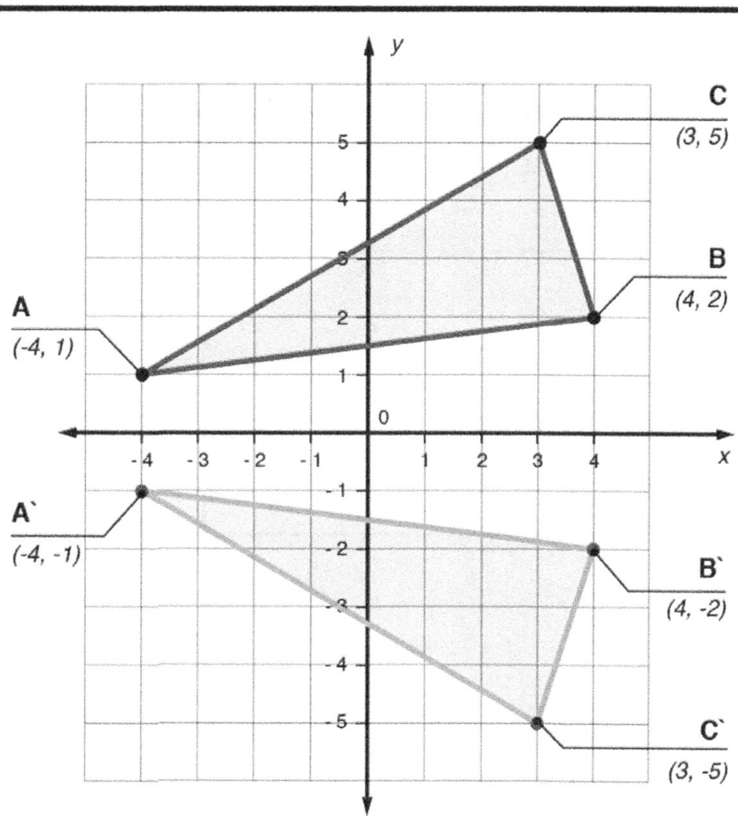

A compression or stretch of a figure involves changing the size of the original figure; both transformations are called **dilations**. A compression shrinks the size of the figure. We can think about this as a multiplication process by multiplying times a value between 0 and 1. A stretch of a figure results in a figure larger than the original shape. If we consider multiplication, the factor would be greater than 1. Here is picture of a dilation that is comprised of a stretch in which the original square doubled in size:

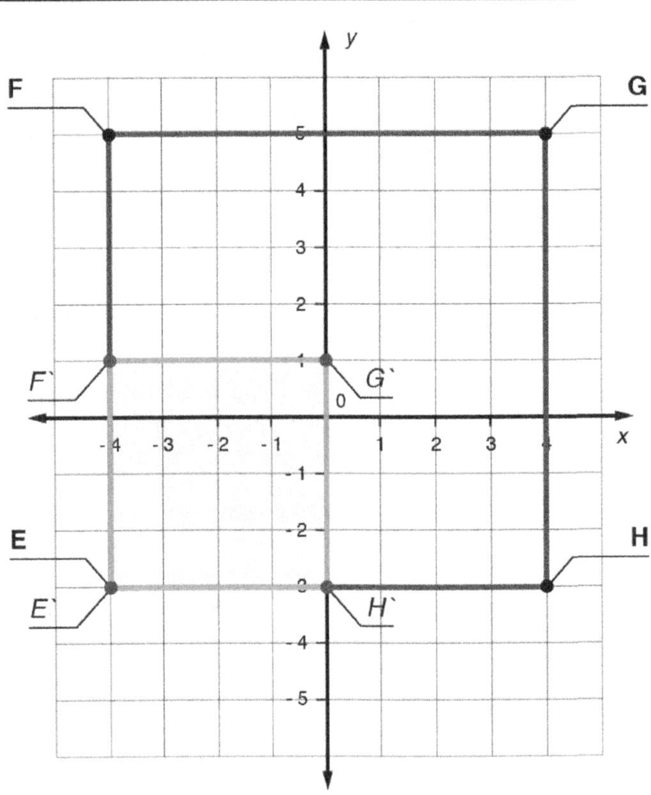

If a shape within the Cartesian coordinate system gets stretched, its coordinates get multiplied by a number greater than 1, and if a shape gets compressed, its coordinates get multiplied by a number between 0 and 1.

A figure can undergo any combination of transformations. For instance, it can be shifted, reflected, and stretched at the same time.

If two figures have the exact same angle measurements and equal side lengths, then they are **congruent**. Two figures are similar if they have the same angle measurements but not side lengths. Basically, angles are congruent in similar triangles and their side lengths are constant multiples of each other. Proving two shapes are similar involves showing that all angles are the same; proving two shapes are congruent involves showing that all angles are the same *and* that all sides are the same. If two pairs of angles are congruent in two triangles, then those triangles are similar because their third angles have to be equal due to the fact that all three angles add up to 180 degrees.

There are five main theorems that are used to prove congruence in triangles. Each theorem involves showing that different combinations of sides and angles are the same in two triangles, which proves the triangles are congruent. The **side-side-side (SSS) theorem** states that if all sides are equal in two triangles, the triangles are congruent. The **side-angle-side (SAS) theorem** states that if two pairs of sides and the included angles are equal in two triangles then the triangles are congruent. Similarly, the **angle-side-angle (ASA) theorem** states that if two pairs of angles and the included side lengths are equal in two triangles, the triangles are similar. The **angle-angle-side (AAS) theorem** states that two triangles are congruent if they have two pairs of congruent angles and a pair of corresponding equal side lengths that are not included. Finally, the **hypotenuse-leg (HL) theorem** states that if two right triangles have equal hypotenuses and an equal pair of shorter sides, the triangles are congruent. An important item to note is that angle-angle-angle (AAA) is not enough information to prove congruence because the three angles could be equal in two triangles, but their sides could be different lengths.

Sets of Points in the Plane

Shapes can be plotted on the coordinate plane to identify the location of each vertex and the length of each side. The original triangle (called the **preimage**) is seen in the figure below in the first quadrant. The reflection of this triangle is in the second quadrant. A reflection across the y-axis can be found by determining each point's distance to the y-axis and moving it that same distance on the opposite side. For example, the point C is located at $(4, 1)$. The reflection of this point moves to $(-4, 1)$ when reflected across the y-axis. The original point A The original point A is located at $(1, 3)$, and the reflection across the y-axis is located at $(-1, 3)$. It is evident that the reflection across the y-axis changes the sign of the x-coordinate. A reflection across the x-axis changes the sign of the y-coordinate instead.

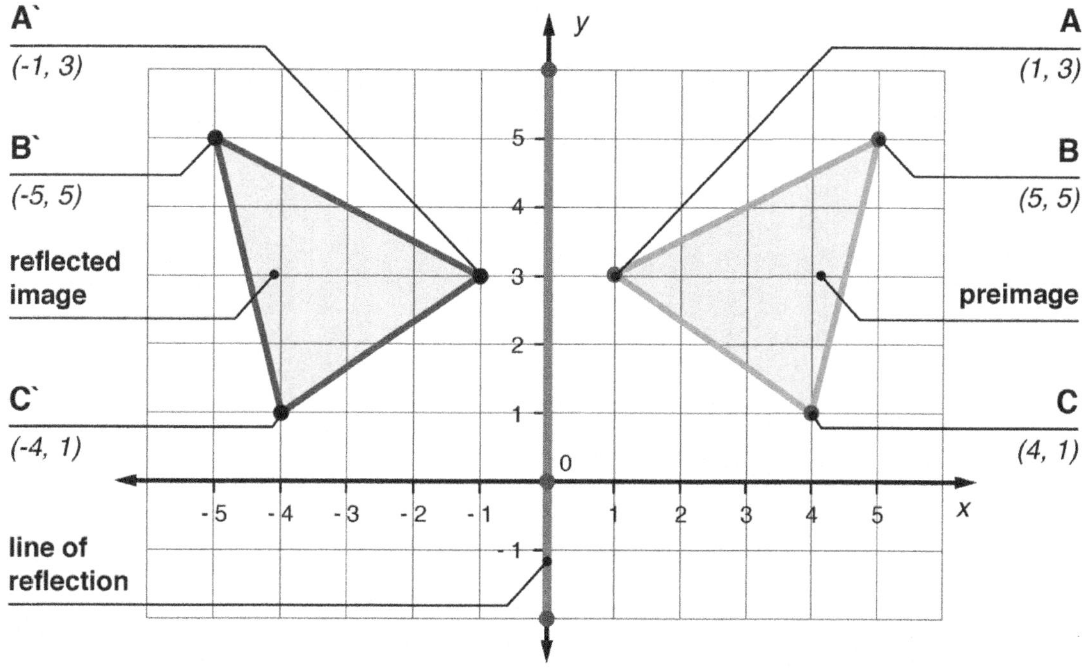

Linear, Area, and Three-Dimensional Measurements

Perimeter

Perimeter is the distance around an object. The perimeter of an object can be found by adding the lengths of all sides. Perimeter may be used in problems dealing with lengths around objects such as fences or borders. It may also be used in finding missing lengths or working backwards. If the perimeter is given, but a length is missing, use subtraction to find the missing length. Given a square with side length s, the formula for perimeter is $P = 4s$. Given a rectangle with length l and width w, the formula for perimeter is:

$$P = 2l + 2w$$

The perimeter of a triangle is found by adding the three side lengths, and the perimeter of a trapezoid is found by adding the four side lengths. The units for perimeter are always the original units of length, such as meters, inches, miles, etc. When discussing a circle, the distance around the object is referred to as its circumference, not perimeter. The formula for the circumference of a circle is $C = 2\pi r$, where r represents the radius of the circle. This formula can also be written as $C = d\pi$, where d represents the diameter of the circle.

Area

Area is the two-dimensional space covered by an object. These problems may include the area of a rectangle, a yard, or a wall to be painted. Finding the area may require a simple formula or multiple formulas used together. The units for area are square units, such as square meters, square inches, and square miles. Given a square with side length s, the formula for its area is $A = s^2$.

Some other formulas for common shapes are shown below.

Shape	Formula	Graphic
Rectangle	$Area = length \times width$	
Triangle	$Area = \frac{1}{2} \times base \times height$	height base
Circle	$Area = \pi \times radius^2$	radius

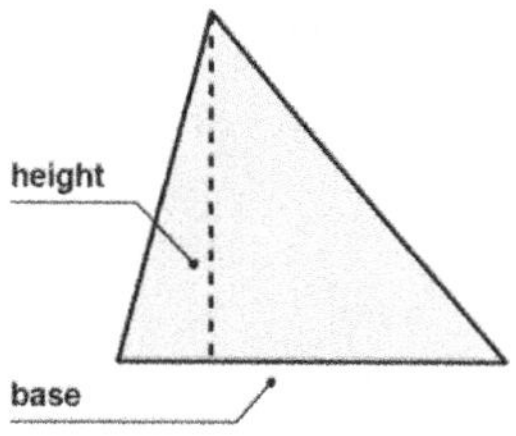

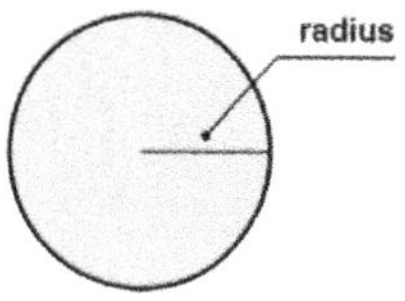

The following formula, not as widely used as those shown above, but very important, is the area of a trapezoid:

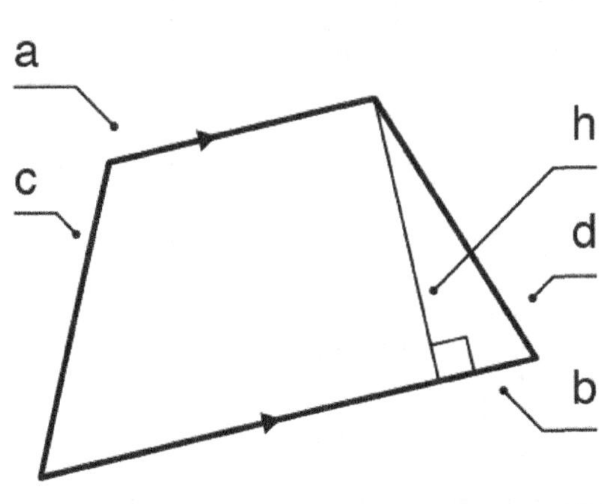

$$A = \frac{1}{2}(a + b)h$$

To find the area of the shapes above, use the given dimensions of the shape in the formula. Complex shapes might require more than one formula. To find the area of the figure below, break the figure into two shapes. The rectangle has dimensions 11 cm by 6 cm. The triangle has dimensions 3 cm by 6 cm. Plug the dimensions into the rectangle formula:

$$A = 11 \times 6$$

Multiplication yields an area of 66 cm^2. The triangle's area can be found using the formula:

$$A = \frac{1}{2} \times 4 \times 6$$

Multiplication yields an area of 12 cm^2. Add the two areas to find the total area of the figure, which is 78 cm^2.

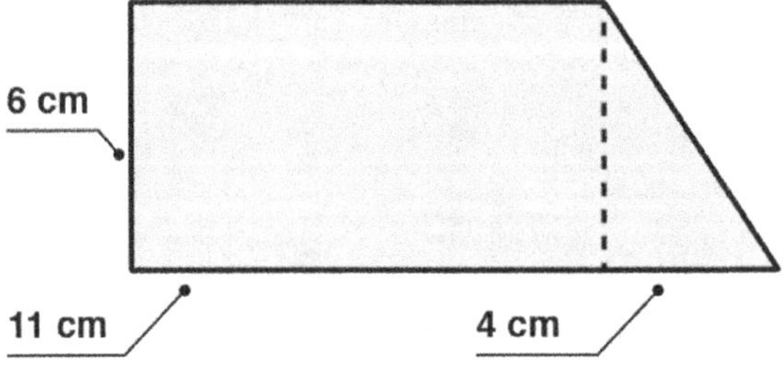

Instead of combining areas, some problems may require subtracting them, or finding the difference.

To find the area of the shaded region in the figure below, determine the area of the whole figure. Then subtract the area of the circle from the whole.

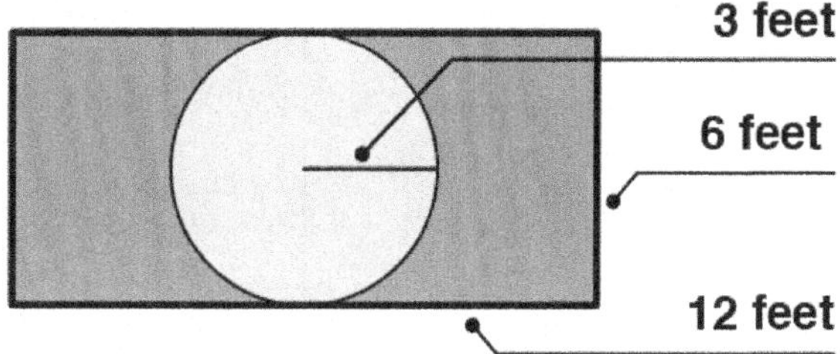

The following formula shows the area of the outside rectangle:

$$A = 12 \times 6 = 72 \text{ ft}^2$$

The area of the inside circle can be found by the following formula:

$$A = \pi(3)^2 = 9\pi = 28.3 \text{ ft}^2$$

As the shaded area is outside the circle, the area for the circle can be subtracted from the area of the rectangle to yield an area of 43.7 ft^2.

Volume

Volume is three-dimensional and describes the amount of space that an object occupies, but it's different from area because it has three dimensions instead of two. The units for volume are cubic units, such as cubic meters, cubic inches, and cubic millimeters. Volume can be found by using formulas for common objects such as cylinders and boxes.

The following chart shows a diagram and formula for the volume of two objects.

Shape	Formula	Diagram
Rectangular Prism (box)	$V = length \times width \times height$	
Cylinder	$V = \pi \times radius^2 \times height$	

Volume formulas of these two objects are derived by finding the area of the bottom two-dimensional shape, such as the circle or rectangle, and then multiplying times the height of the three-dimensional shape. Other volume formulas include the volume of a cube with side length s: $V = s^3$; the volume of a sphere with radius r:

$$V = \frac{4}{3}\pi r^3$$

The volume of a cone with radius r and height h:

$$V = \frac{1}{3}\pi r^2 h$$

If a soda can has a height of 5 inches and a radius on the top of 1.5 inches, the volume can be found using one of the given formulas. A soda can is a cylinder. Knowing the given dimensions, the formula can be completed as follows:

$$V = \pi(radius)^2 \times height$$

$$\pi(1.5 \text{ in})^2 \times 5 \text{ in} = 35.325 \text{ in}^3$$

Notice that the units for volume are inches cubed because it refers to the number of cubic inches required to fill the can.

Surface Area

Surface area is defined as the area of the surface of a figure. A **pyramid** has a surface made up of four triangles and one square. To calculate the surface area of a pyramid, the areas of each individual shape are calculated. Then the areas are added together. This method of decomposing the shape into two-dimensional figures to find area, then adding the areas, can be used to find surface area for any figure. Once these measurements are found, the area is described with square units. For example, the following figure shows a rectangular prism. The figure beside it shows the rectangular prism broken down into two-dimensional shapes, or rectangles. The area of each rectangle can be calculated by multiplying the length by the width. The area for the six rectangles can be represented by the following expression:

$$5 \times 6 + 5 \times 10 + 5 \times 6 + 6 \times 10 + 5 \times 10 + 6 \times 10$$

The total for all these areas added together is $280\ \text{cm}^2$, or 280 centimeters squared. This measurement represents the surface area because it is the area of all six surfaces of the rectangular prism.

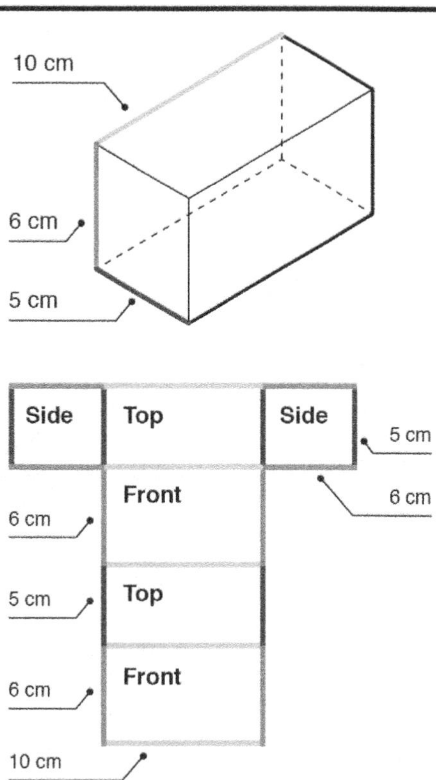

Another shape that has a surface area is a cylinder. The shapes used to make up the **cylinder** are two circles and a rectangle wrapped around between the two circles. A common example of a cylinder is a can. The two circles that make up the bases are obvious shapes. The rectangle can be more difficult to see, but the label on a can will help illustrate it. When the label is removed from a can and laid flat, the shape is a rectangle. When the areas for each shape are needed, there will be two formulas. The first is the area for the circles on the bases. This area is given by the formula $A = \pi r^2$. There will be two of these areas—one for the top and one for the bottom if the can (cylinder) is standing upright on a shelf. Then the area of the rectangle must be determined. The width of the rectangle is equal to the height of the can, h. The length

of the rectangle is equal to the circumference of the base circle, $2\pi r$. The area for the rectangle can be found by using the formula:

$$A = 2\pi r \times h$$

By adding the two areas for the bases and the area of the rectangle, the surface area of the cylinder can be found, described in units squared.

Solving for Missing Values in Triangles, Circles, and Other Figures

Solving for missing values in shapes requires knowledge of the shape and its characteristics. For example, a triangle has three sides and three angles that add up to 180 degrees. If two angle measurements are given, the third can be calculated. For the triangle below, the one given angle has a measure of 55 degrees. The missing angle is x. The third angle is labeled with a square, which indicates a measure of 90 degrees. Because all angles must add up to 180 degrees, the following equation can be used to find the missing x-value:

$$55° + 90° + x = 180°$$

Adding the two given angles and subtracting the total from 180 gives an answer of 35 degrees.

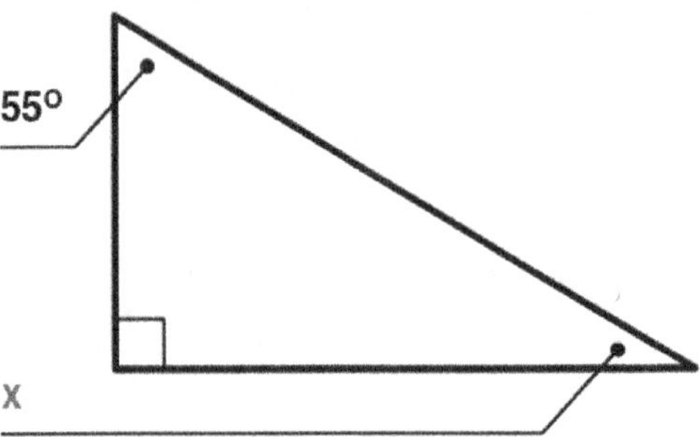

A similar problem can be solved with circles. If the radius is given but the circumference is unknown, the circumference can be calculated based on the formula $C = 2\pi r$. This example can be used in the figure below. The radius can be substituted for r in the formula. Then the circumference can be found as:

$$C = 2\pi \times 8 = 16\pi = 50.24 \text{ cm}$$

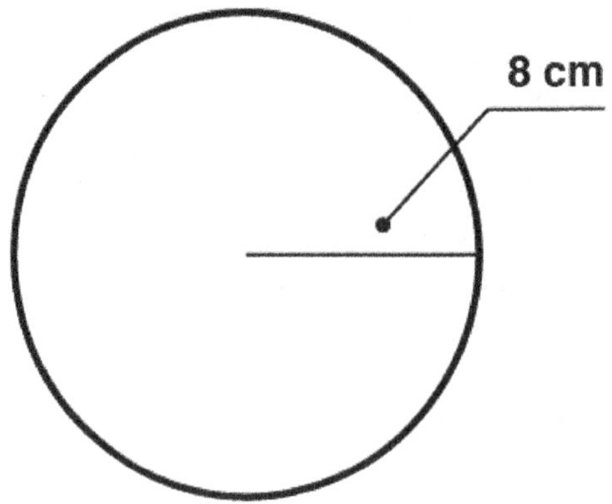

Other figures that may have missing values could be the length of a square, given the area, or the perimeter of a rectangle, given the length and width. All of the missing values can be found by first identifying all the characteristics that are known about the shape, then looking for ways to connect the missing value to the given information.

Probabilistic and Statistical Reasoning

Interpreting Categorical and Quantitative Data

They all organize, categorize, and compare data, and they come in different shapes and sizes. Each type has its own way of showing information, whether through a column, shape, or picture. To answer a question relating to a table, chart, or graph, some steps should be followed. First, the problem should be read thoroughly to determine what is being asked to determine what quantity is unknown. Then, the title of the table, chart, or graph should be read. The title should clarify what data is actually being summarized in the table. Next, look at the key and labels for both the horizontal and vertical axes, if they are given. These items will provide information about how the data is organized. Finally, look to see if there is any more labeling inside the table. Taking the time to get a good idea of what the table is summarizing will be helpful as it is used to interpret information.

Tables are a good way of showing a lot of information in a small space. The information in a table is organized in columns and rows. For example, a table may be used to show the number of votes each candidate received in an election. By interpreting the table, one may observe which candidate won the election and which candidates came in second and third. In using a bar chart to display monthly rainfall amounts in different countries, rainfall can be compared between countries at different times of the year. Graphs are also a useful way to show change in variables over time, as in a line graph, or percentages of a whole, as in a pie graph.

The table below relates the number of items to the total cost. The table shows that one item costs $5. By looking at the table further, five items cost $25, ten items cost $50, and fifty items cost $250. This cost can be extended for any number of items. Since one item costs $5, then two items would cost $10. Though this information is not in the table, the given price can be used to calculate unknown information.

Number of Items	1	5	10	50
Cost ($)	5	25	50	250

A **bar graph** is a graph that summarizes data using bars of different heights. It is useful when comparing two or more items or when seeing how a quantity changes over time. It has both a horizontal and vertical axis. To interpret bar graphs, recognize what each bar represents and connect that to the two variables. The bar graph below shows the scores for six people during three different games. The different colors of the bars distinguish between the three games, and the height of the bar indicates their score for that game. William scored 25 on game 3, and Abigail scored 38 on game 3. By comparing the bars, it is obvious that Williams scored lower than Abigail.

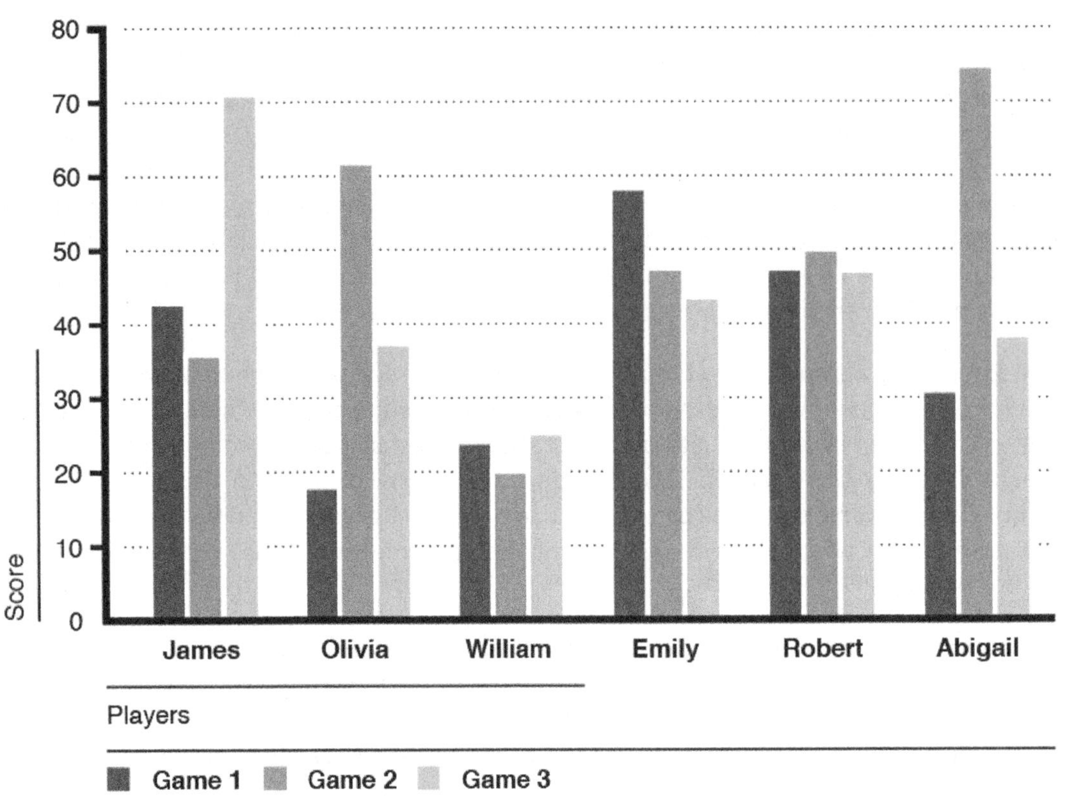

A line graph is a way to compare two variables that are plotted on opposite axes of a graph. The line indicates a continuous change as it rises or falls. The line's rate of change is known as its slope. The horizontal axis often represents a variable of time. Readers can quickly see if an amount has grown or decreased over time. The bottom of the graph, or the x-axis, shows the units for time, such as days, hours, months, etc. If there are multiple lines, a comparison can be made between what the two lines represent.

For example, the following line graph, shown previously, displays the change in temperature over five days. The top line represents the high, and the bottom line represents the low for each day. Looking at the top line alone, the high decreases for a day, then increases on Wednesday. Then it decreases on Thursday and increases again on Friday. The low temperatures have a similar trend, shown in the bottom line. The range in temperatures each day can also be calculated by finding the difference between the top line and bottom line on a particular day. On Wednesday, the range was 14 degrees, from 62 to 76°F.

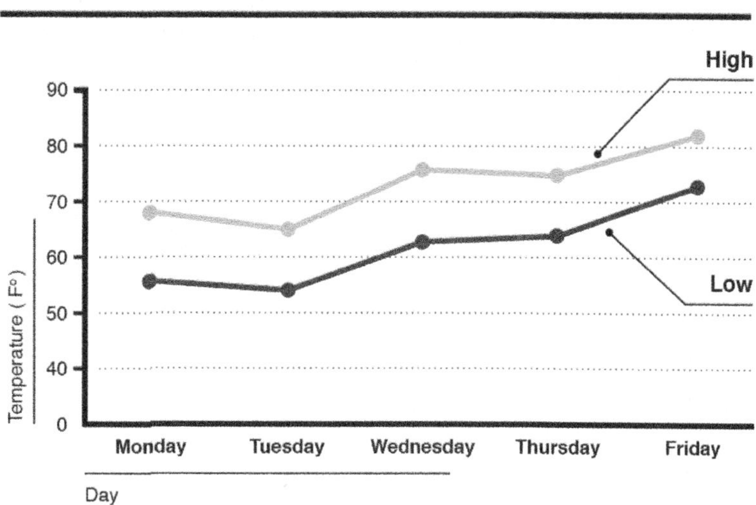

Pie charts show percentages of a whole; they are circular representations of data used to highlight numerical proportions. Each category represents a piece of the pie, and together, all of the pieces make up a whole. The size of each pie slice is proportional to the amount it represents; therefore, a reader can quickly make comparisons by visualizing the sizes of the pieces. They can be useful for comparison between different categories. The following pie chart is a simple example of three different categories shown in comparison to each other.

Light gray represents cats, dark gray represents dogs, and the medium shade of gray represents other pets. These three equal pieces each represent just more than 33 percent, or $\frac{1}{3}$ of the whole. Values 1 and 2 may be combined to represent $\frac{2}{3}$ of the whole. In an example where the total pie represents 75,000 animals, then cats would be equal to $\frac{1}{3}$ of the total, or 25,000. Dogs would equal 25,000 and other pets also equal 25,000.

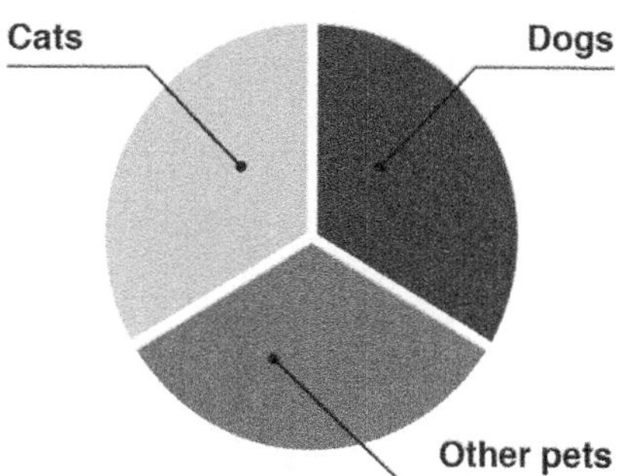

Since circles have 360 degrees, they are used to create pie charts. Because each piece of the pie is a percentage of a whole, that percentage is multiplied times 360 to get the number of degrees each piece represents. In the example above, each piece is $\frac{1}{3}$ of the whole, so each piece is equivalent to 120 degrees. Together, all three pieces add up to 360 degrees.

Stacked bar graphs are also used fairly frequently when comparing multiple variables at one time. They combine some elements of both pie charts and bar graphs, using the organization of bar graphs and the proportionality aspect of pie charts. The following is an example of a stacked bar graph that represents the number of students in a band playing drums, flute, trombone, and clarinet. Each bar graph is broken up further into girls and boys.

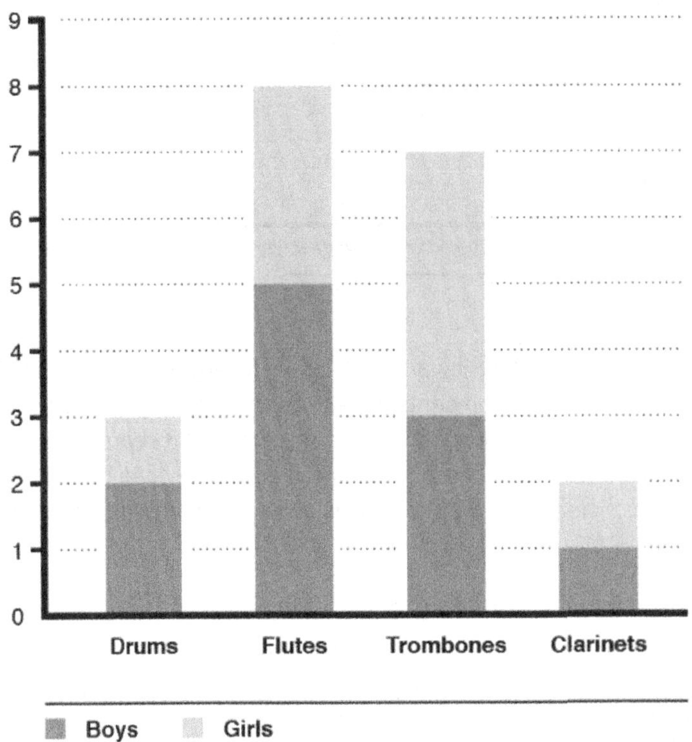

To determine how many boys play trombone, refer to the darker portion of the trombone bar, which indicates three boys.

As mentioned, a **scatterplot** is another way to represent paired data. It uses Cartesian coordinates, like a line graph, meaning it has both a horizontal and vertical axis. Each data point is represented as a dot on the graph. The dots are never connected with a line. For example, the following is a scatterplot showing the connection between people's ages and heights.

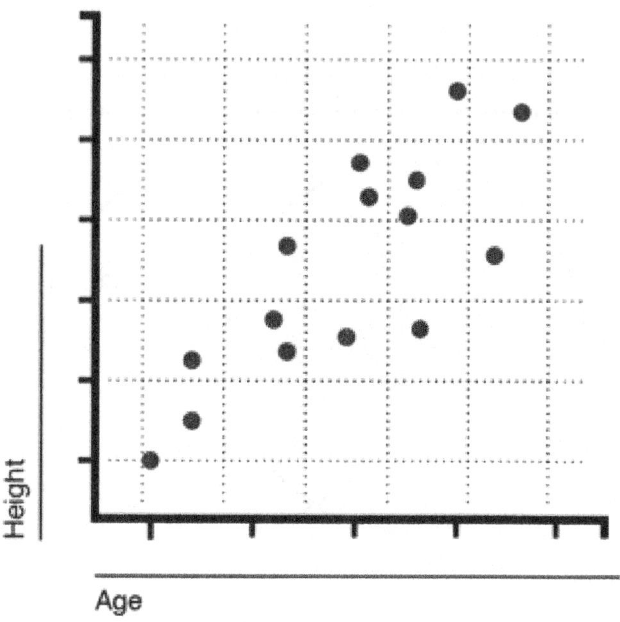

A scatterplot, also known as a **scattergram,** can be used to predict another value and to see if a correlation exists between two variables in a set of data. If the data resembles a straight line, then it is associated, or correlated. The following is an example of a scatterplot in which the data does not seem to have an association:

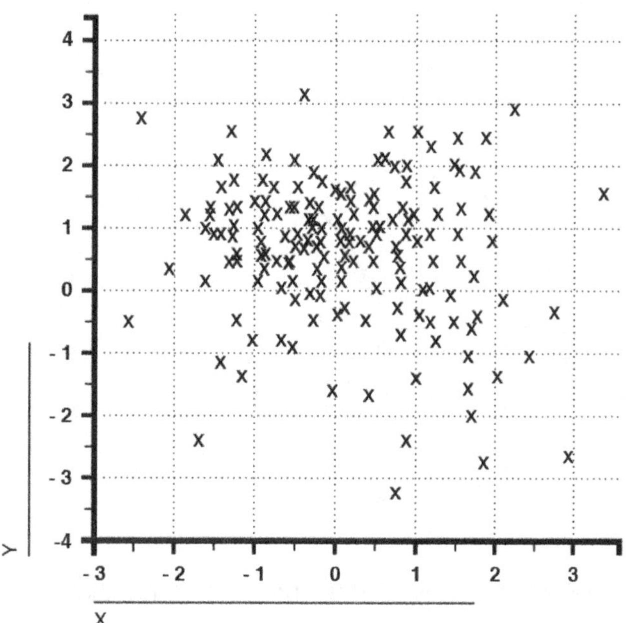

Sets of numbers and other similarly organized data can also be represented graphically. Venn diagrams are a common way to do so. A **Venn diagram** represents each set of data as a circle. The circles overlap, showing that each set of data is overlapping. A Venn diagram is also known as a **logic diagram** because it visualizes all possible logical combinations between two sets. Common elements of two sets are represented by the area of overlap. The following is an example of a Venn diagram of two sets A and B:

Parts of the Venn Diagram

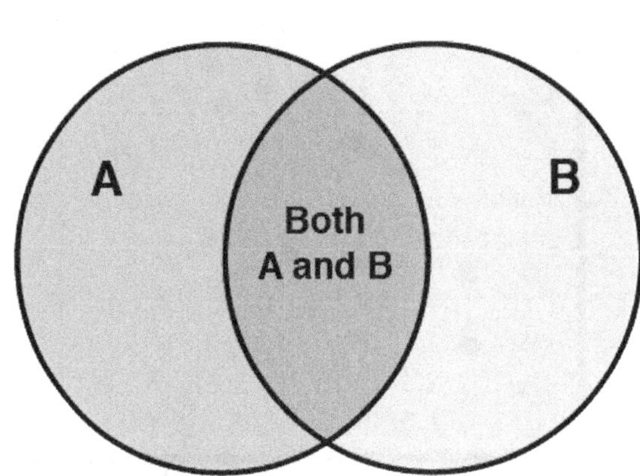

Another name for the area of overlap is the **intersection.** The intersection of A and B, written $A \cap B$, contains all elements that are in both sets A and B. The **union** of A and B, $A \cup B$, contains all elements in both sets A and B. Finally, the **complement** of $A \cup B$ is equal to all elements that are not in either set A or set B. These elements are placed outside of the circles.

The following is an example of a Venn diagram representing 24 students who were surveyed about their siblings. Ten students only had a brother, seven students only had a sister, and five had both a brother and a sister. Therefore, five is the intersection, represented by the section where the circles overlap. Two students did not have a brother or a sister. Therefore, two is the complement and is placed outside of the circles.

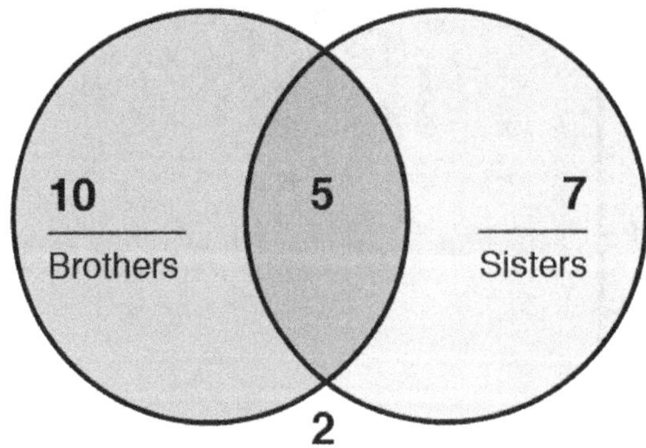

Venn diagrams can have more than two sets of data. The more circles, the more logical combinations are represented by the overlapping. The following is a Venn diagram that represents sock colors worn by a

class of students. There were 30 students surveyed. The innermost region represents those students that had green, pink, and blue on their socks (perhaps in a striped pattern). Therefore, two students had all three colors. In this example, all students had at least one color on their socks, so there is no complement.

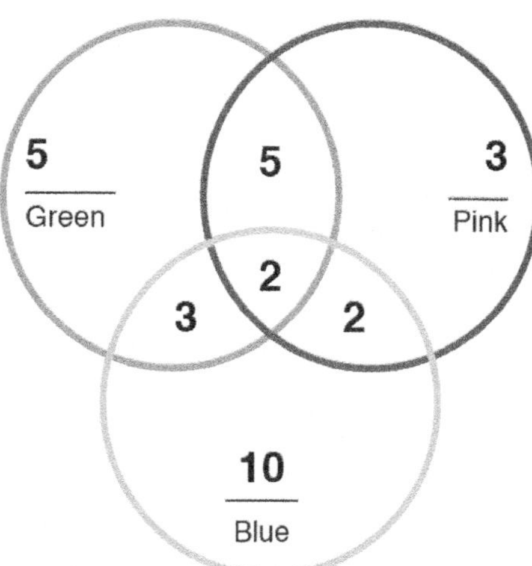

Venn diagrams are typically not drawn to scale; however, if they are, and if each circle's area is proportional to the amount of data it represents, then it is called an area-proportional Venn diagram.

Describing Distributions

One way information can be interpreted from tables, charts, and graphs is through statistics. The three most common calculations for a set of data are the mean, median, and mode. These three are called **measures of central tendency**, which are helpful in comparing two or more different sets of data. The **mean** refers to the average and is found by adding up all values and dividing the total by the number of values. In other words, the mean is equal to the sum of all values divided by the number of data entries. For example, if you bowled a total of 532 points in 4 bowling games, your mean score was:

$$\frac{532}{4} = 133 \text{ points per game}$$

Students can apply the concept of mean to calculate what score they need on a final exam to earn a desired grade in a class.

The **median** is found by lining up values from least to greatest and choosing the middle value. If there is an even number of values, then calculate the mean of the two middle amounts to find the median. For example, the median of the set of dollar amounts $5, $6, $9, $12, and $13 is $9. The median of the set of dollar amounts $1, $5, $6, $8, $9, $10 is $7, which is the mean of $6 and $8. The **mode** is the value that occurs the most. The mode of the data set {1, 3, 1, 5, 5, 8, 10} actually refers to two numbers: 1 and 5. In this case, the data set is **bimodal** because it has two modes. A data set can have no mode if no amount is repeated. Another useful statistic is range. The **range** for a set of data refers to the difference between the highest and lowest value.

In some cases, numbers in a list of data might have weights attached to them. In that case, a **weighted mean** can be calculated. A common application of a weighted mean is GPA. In a semester, each class is assigned a number of credit hours, its weight, and at the end of the semester each student receives a grade. To compute GPA, an A is a 4, a B is a 3, a C is a 2, a D is a 1, and an F is a 0. Consider a student that takes a 4-hour English class, a 3-hour math class, and a 4-hour history class and receives all B's. The weighted mean, GPA, is found by multiplying each grade times its weight, number of credit hours, and dividing by the total number of credit hours. Therefore, the student's GPA is:

$$\frac{3 \times 4 + 3 \times 3 + 3 \times 4}{11} = \frac{33}{11} = 3.0.$$

The following bar chart shows how many students attend a cycle class on each day of the week. To find the mean attendance for the week, add each day's attendance together:

$$10 + 7 + 6 + 9 + 8 + 14 + 4 = 58$$

Then divide the total by the number of days:

$$58 \div 7 = 8.3$$

The mean attendance for the week was 8.3 people. The median attendance can be found by putting the attendance numbers in order from least to greatest: 4, 6, 7, 8, 9, 10, 14, and choosing the middle number: 8 people. This set of data has no mode because no numbers repeat. The range is 10, which is found by finding the difference between the lowest number, 4, and the highest number, 14.

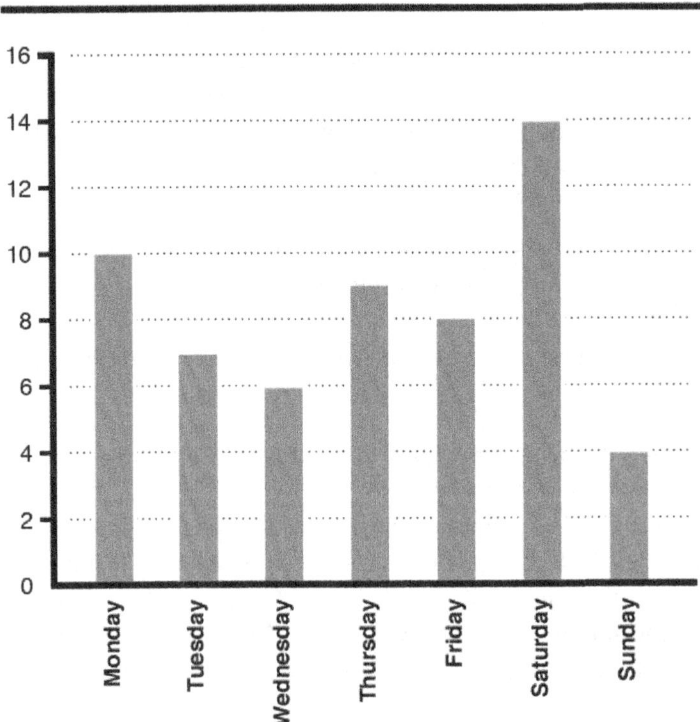

A **histogram** is a bar graph used to group data into "bins" that cover a range on the horizontal, or x-axis. Histograms consist of rectangles whose heights are equal to the frequency of a specific category. The horizontal axis represents the specific categories. Because they cover a range of data, these bins have no gaps between bars, unlike the bar graph above. In a histogram showing the heights of adult golden retrievers, the bottom axis would be groups of heights, and the y-axis would be the number of dogs in each range. Evaluating this histogram would show the height of most golden retrievers as falling within a certain range. It also provides information to find the average height and range for how tall golden retrievers may grow.

The following is a histogram that represents exam grades in a given class. The horizontal axis represents ranges of the number of points scored, and the vertical axis represents the number of students. For example, approximately 33 students scored in the 60 to 70 range.

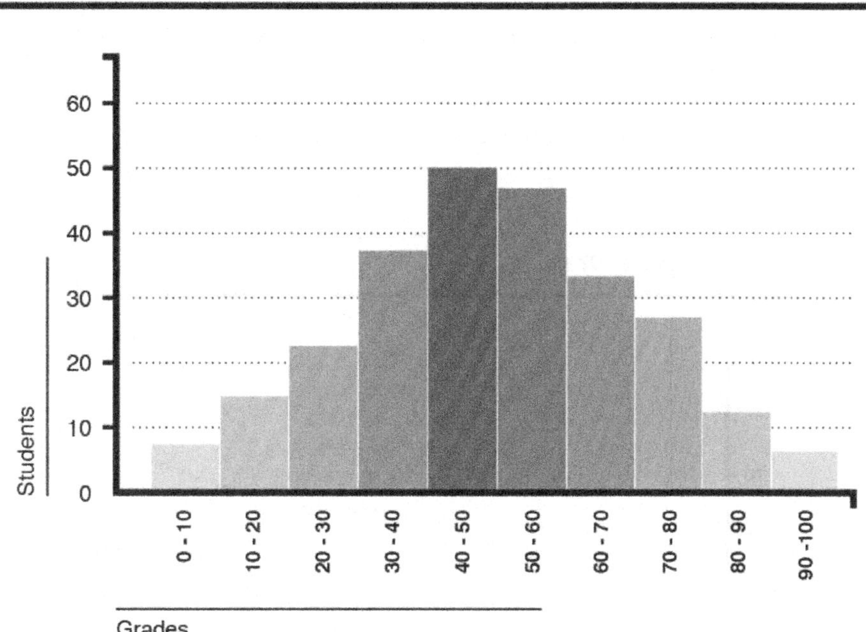

Certain measures of central tendency can be easily visualized with a histogram. If the points scored were shown with individual rectangles, the tallest rectangle would represent the mode. A bimodal set of data would have two peaks of equal height. Histograms can be classified as having data **skewed to the left, skewed to the right**, or **normally distributed**, which is also known as **bell-shaped**.

These three classifications can be seen in the following chart:

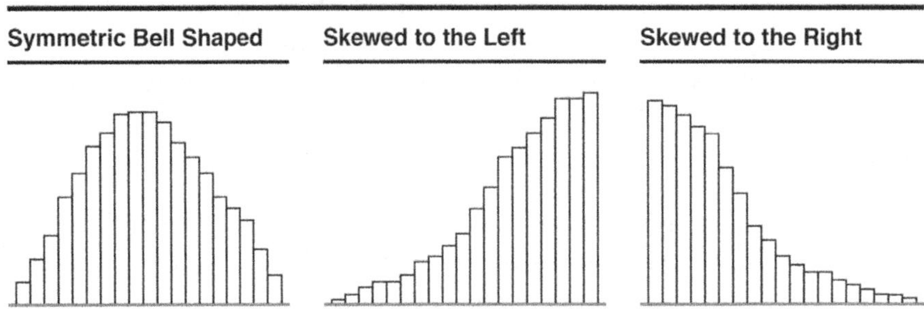

When the data is normal, the mean, median, and mode are very similar because they all represent the most typical value in the data set. In this case, the mean is typically considered the best measure of central tendency because it includes all data points. However, if the data is skewed, the mean becomes less meaningful because it is dragged in the direction of the skew. Therefore, the median becomes the best measure because it is not affected by any outliers.

The measures of central tendency and the range may also be found by evaluating information on a line graph.

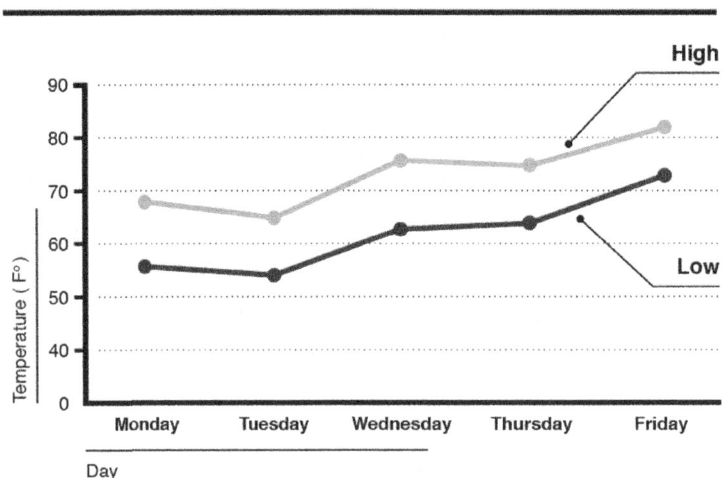

In the line graph above that shows the daily high and low temperatures, the average high temperature can be found by gathering data from each day on the triangle line. The days' highs are 69, 65, 75, 74, and 81. To find the average, add them together to get 364, then divide by 5 (because there are 5 temperatures). The average high for the five days is 72.8. If 72.8 degrees is found on the graph, it will fall in the middle of all the values. The average low temperature can be found in the same way.

Given a set of data, the **correlation coefficient**, r, measures the association between all the data points. If two values are **correlated**, there is an association between them. However, correlation does not necessarily mean causation, or that one value causes the other. There is a common mistake made that assumes correlation implies causation. Average daily temperature and number of sunbathers are both correlated and have causation. If the temperature increases, that change in weather causes more people to want to catch some rays. However, wearing plus-size clothing and having heart disease are two variables that are correlated but do not have causation. The larger someone is, the more likely he or she is to have heart disease. However, being overweight does not cause someone to have the disease.

The value of the correlation coefficient is between -1 and 1, where -1 represents a perfect negative linear relationship, 0 represents no relationship between the two data sets, and 1 represents a perfect positive linear relationship. A negative linear relationship means that as x-values increase, y-values decrease. A positive linear relationship means that as x-values increase, y-values increase. The formula for computing the correlation coefficient is:

$$r = \frac{n\sum xy - (\sum x)(\sum y)}{\sqrt{n(\sum x^2) - (\sum x)^2}\sqrt{n(\sum y^2) - (y)^2}}$$

n is the number of data points. The closer r is to 1 or -1, the stronger the correlation. A correlation can be seen when plotting data. If the graph resembles a straight line, there is a correlation.

Solving Problems Involving Measures of Center and Range

As mentioned, a data set can be described by calculating the mean, median, and mode. These values allow the data to be described with a single value that is representative of the data set.

The most common measure of center is the **mean,** also referred to as the **average.**

To calculate the mean:

1. Add all data values together
2. Divide by the sample size (the number of data points in the set)

The **median** is middle data value, so that half of the data lies below this value and half lies above it.

To calculate the median:

1. Order the data from least to greatest
2. The point in the middle of the set is the median
3. If there is an even number of data points, add the two middle points and divide by 2

The **mode** is the data value that occurs most often.

To calculate the mode:

1. Order the data from least to greatest
2. Find the value that occurs most often

Example: Amelia is a leading scorer on the school's basketball team. The following data set represents the number of points that Amelia has scored in each game this season. Use the mean, median, and mode to describe the data.

16, 12, 26, 14, 28, 14, 12, 15, 25

Solution:

Mean:

$$16 + 12 + 26 + 14 + 28 + 14 + 12 + 15 + 25 = 162$$

$$162 \div 9 = 18$$

Amelia averages 18 points per game.

Median:

12, 12, 14, 14, **15**, 16, 25, 26, 28

Amelia's median score is 15.

Mode:

12, 12, 14, 14, 15, 16, 25, 26, 28

The numbers 12 and 14 each occur twice, so this data set has 2 modes: 12 and 14.

The **range** is the difference between the largest and smallest values in the set. In the example above, the range is $28 - 12 = 16$.

Determining How Changes in Data Affect Measures of Center or Range

An **outlier** is a data point that lies an unusual distance from other points in the data set. Removing an outlier from a data set will change the measures of central tendency. Removing a large outlier (a high number) from a data set will decrease both the mean and the median. Removing a small outlier (a number much lower than most in the data set) from a data set will increase both the mean and the median. For example, in data set {3, 6, 8, 12, 13, 14, 60}, the data point 60, is an outlier because it is unusually far from the other points. In this data set, the mean is 16.6. Notice that this mean number is even larger than all other data points in the set except for 60. Removing the outlier changes the mean to 9.3, and the median goes from 12 to 10. Removing an outlier will also decrease the range. In the data set above, the range is 57 when the outlier is included, but it decreases to 11 when the outlier is removed.

Adding an outlier to a data set will also affect the measures of central tendency. When a larger outlier is added to a data set, the mean and median increase. When a small outlier is added to a data set, the mean and median decrease. Adding an outlier to a data set will increase the range.

This does not seem to provide an appropriate measure of center when considering this data set. What will happen if that outlier is removed? Removing the extremely large data point, 60, is going to reduce the mean to 9.3. The mean decreased dramatically because 60 was much larger than any of the other data values. What would happen with an extremely low value in a data set like this one, {12, 87, 90, 95, 98, 100}? The mean of the given set is 80. When the outlier, 12, is removed, the mean should increase and fit

more closely to the other data points. Removing 12 and recalculating the mean show that this is correct. After removing the outlier, the mean is 94. So, removing a large outlier will decrease the mean while removing a small outlier will increase the mean.

Statistical Measures

Statistics is the branch of mathematics that deals with the collection, organization, and analysis of data. In order to answer a statistical question, one must collect and analyze data. When collecting data, expect variability. For example, "How many pets does Yanni own?" is not a statistical question because it can be answered in one way. "How many pets do the people in a certain neighborhood own?" is a statistical question because, to determine this answer, one would need to collect data from each person in the neighborhood, and it is reasonable to expect the answers to vary.

Identify these as statistical or not statistical:

- How old are you?
- What is the average age of the people in your class?
- How tall are the students in Mrs. Jones' sixth grade class?
- Do you like Brussels sprouts?

The first and last questions are not statistical, but the two middle questions are.

Data collection can be done through surveys, experiments, observations, and interviews. A **census** is a type of survey that is done with a whole population. Because it can be difficult to collect data for an entire population, sometimes a **sample** is used. In this case, one would survey only a fraction of the population and make inferences about the data. Sample surveys are not as accurate as a census, but they are an easier and less expensive method of collecting data. An **experiment** is used when a researcher wants to explain how one variable causes change in another variable. For example, if a researcher wanted to know if a particular drug affects weight loss, he or she would choose a **treatment group** that would take the drug, and another group, the **control group**, that would not take the drug.

Special care must be taken when choosing these groups to ensure that bias is not a factor. **Bias** occurs when an outside factor influences the outcome of the research. In observational studies, the researcher does not try to influence either variable but simply observes the behavior of the subjects. Interviews are sometimes used to collect data as well. The researcher will ask questions that focus on her area of interest in order to gain insight from the participants. When gathering data through observation or interviews, it is important that the researcher is well trained so that he or she does not influence the results and the study remains reliable. A study is reliable if it can be repeated under the same conditions and the same results are received each time.

The Random Processes Underlying Statistical Experiments

For researchers to make valid conclusions about population characteristics and parameters, the sample used to compare must be random. In a **random sample**, every member of the population must have an equal chance of being selected. In this situation, the sample is **unbiased** and is said to be a good representation of the population. If a sample is selected in an inappropriate manner, it is said to be **biased.** A sample can be biased if, for example, some subjects were more likely to be chosen than others. In order to have unbiased samples, the four main sampling methods used tend to be random, systematic, stratified, and cluster sampling.

Random sampling occurs when, given a sample size *n*, all possible samples of that size are equally likely to be chosen. Random numbers from calculators are typically used in this setting. Each member of a population is paired with a number, and then a set of random numbers is generated. Each person paired with one of those random numbers is selected. A **systematic sample** is when every fourth, seventh, tenth, etc., person from a population is selected to be in a sample. A **stratified sample** is when the population is divided into subgroups, or **strata**, using a characteristic, and then members from each stratum are randomly selected. For example, university students could be divided into age groups and then selected from each age group. Finally, a **cluster sample** is when a sample is used from an already selected group, like city block or zip code. These four methods are used most frequently because they are most likely to yield unbiased results.

Once an unbiased sample is obtained, data need to be collected. Common data collection methods include surveys with questions that are unbiased, contain clear language, avoid double negatives, and do not contain compound sentences that ask two questions at once. When formulating these questions, the simpler verbiage, the better.

Using Random Sampling to Draw Inferences About a Population

In statistics, a **population** contains all subjects being studied. For example, a population could be every student at a university or all males in the United States. A **sample** consists of a group of subjects from an entire population. A sample would be 100 students at a university or 100,000 males in the United States. **Inferential statistics** is the process of using a sample to generalize information concerning populations. **Hypothesis testing** is the actual process used when evaluating claims made about a population based on a sample.

A **statistic** is a measure obtained from a sample, and a **parameter** is a measure obtained from a population. For example, the mean SAT score of the 100 students at a university would be a statistic, and the mean SAT score of all university students would be a parameter.

The beginning stages of hypothesis testing starts with formulating a **hypothesis**, a statement made concerning a population parameter. The hypothesis may be true, or it may not be true. The test will answer that question. In each setting, there are two different types of hypotheses: the **null hypothesis**, written as H_0, and the **alternative hypothesis**, written as H_1. The null hypothesis represents verbally when there is not a difference between two parameters, and the alternative hypothesis represents verbally when there is a difference between two parameters.

Consider the following experiment: A researcher wants to see if a new brand of allergy medication has any effect on drowsiness of the patients who take the medication. He wants to know if the average hours spent sleeping per day increases. The mean for the population under study is 8 hours, so $\mu = 8$. In other words, the population parameter is μ, the mean. The null hypothesis is $\mu = 8$ and the alternative hypothesis is $\mu > 8$. When using a smaller sample of a population, the null hypothesis represents the situation when the mean remains unaffected and the alternative hypothesis represents the situation when the mean increases. The chosen statistical test will apply the data from the sample to actually decide whether the null hypothesis should or should not be rejected.

Probabilistic Reasoning

Chance Processes and Probability Models

Probability describes how likely it is that an event will occur. Probabilities are always a number from zero to 1. If an event has a high likelihood of occurrence, it will have a probability close to 1. If there is only a

small chance that an event will occur, the likelihood is close to zero. A fair six-sided die has one of the numbers 1, 2, 3, 4, 5, and 6 on each side. When this die is rolled there is a one in six chance that it will land on 2. This is because there are six possibilities and only one side has a 2 on it.

The probability then is $\frac{1}{6}$ or 0.167. The probability of rolling an even number from this die is three in six, which is $\frac{1}{2}$ or 0.5. This is because there are three sides on the die with even numbers (2, 4, 6), and there are six possible sides. The probability of rolling a number less than 10 is 1; since every side of the die has a number less than 6, it would be impossible to roll a number 10 or higher. On the other hand, the probability of rolling a number larger than 20 is zero. There are no numbers greater than 20 on the die, so it is certain that this will not occur, thus the probability is zero.

If a teacher says that the probability of anyone passing her final exam is 0.2, is it highly likely that anyone will pass? No, the probability of anyone passing her exam is low because 0.2 is closer to zero than to 1. If another teacher is proud that the probability of students passing his class is 0.95, how likely is it that a student will pass? It is highly likely that a student will pass because the probability, 0.95, is very close to 1.

A probability experiment is a repeated action that has a specific set of possible results. The result of such an experiment is known as an **outcome,** and the set of all potential outcomes is known as the **sample space.** An **event** consists of one or more of those outcomes. For example, consider the probability experiment of tossing a coin and rolling a six-sided die. The coin has two possible outcomes—a heads or a tails—and the die has six possible outcomes—rolling each number 1–6. Therefore, the sample space has twelve possible outcomes: a heads or a tails paired with each roll of the die.

A **simple event** is an event that consists of a single outcome. For instance, selecting a queen of hearts from a standard fifty-two-card deck is a simple event; however, selecting a queen is not a simple event because there are four possibilities.

Classical, or **theoretical, probability** is when each outcome in a sample space has the same chance to occur. The probability for an event is equal to the number of outcomes in that event divided by the total number of outcomes in the sample space. For example, consider rolling a six-sided die. The probability of rolling a 2 is $\frac{1}{6}$, and the probability of rolling an even number is $\frac{3}{6}$, or $\frac{1}{2}$, because there are three even numbers on the die. This type of probability is based on what should happen in theory but not what actually happens in real life.

Empirical probability is based on actual experiments or observations. For example, if a die is rolled eight times, and a 1 is rolled two times, the empirical probability of rolling a 1 is $\frac{2}{8} = \frac{1}{4}$, which is higher than the theoretical probability. The Law of Large Numbers states that as an experiment is completed repeatedly, the empirical probability of an event should get closer to the theoretical probability of an event.

The **addition rule** is necessary to find the probability of event A or event B occurring or both occurring at the same time. If events A and B are **mutually exclusive** or **disjoint,** which means they cannot occur at the same time:

$$P(A \text{ or } B) = P(A) + P(B)$$

If events A and B are not mutually exclusive:

$$P(A \text{ or } B) = P(A) + P(B) - P(A \text{ and } B)$$

where $P(A \text{ and } B)$ represents the probability of event A and B both occurring at the same time. An example of two events that are mutually exclusive are rolling a 6 on a die and rolling an odd number on a die. The probability of rolling a 6 or rolling an odd number is:

$$\frac{1}{6}+\frac{3}{6}=\frac{4}{6}=\frac{2}{3}$$

Rolling a 6 and rolling an even number are not mutually exclusive because there is some overlap. The probability of rolling a 6 or rolling an even number is:

$$\frac{1}{6}+\frac{3}{6}-\frac{1}{6}=\frac{3}{6}=\frac{1}{2}$$

Conditional Probability

The **multiplication rule** is necessary when finding the probability that event A occurs in a first trial and event B occurs in a second trial, which is written as $P(A \text{ and } B)$. This rule differs if the events are independent or dependent. Two events A and B are **independent** if the occurrence of one event does not affect the probability that the other will occur. If A and B are not independent, they are **dependent**, and the outcome of the first event somehow affects the outcome of the second. If events A and B are independent:

$$P(A \text{ and } B) = P(A)P(B)$$

and if events A and B are dependent:

$$P(A \text{ and } B) = P(A)P(B|A)$$

$P(B|A)$ represents the probability event B occurs given that event A has already occurred.

$P(B|A)$ represents **conditional probability**, or the probability of event B occurring given that event A has already occurred. $P(B|A)$ can be found by dividing the probability of events A and B both occurring by the probability of event A occurring using the formula:

$$P(B|A) = \frac{P\ (A \text{ and } B)}{P(A)}$$

and represents the total number of outcomes remaining for B to occur after A occurs. This formula is derived from the multiplication rule with dependent events by dividing both sides by $P(A)$. Note that $P(B|A)$ and $P(A|B)$ are not the same. The first quantity shows that event B has occurred after event A, and the second quantity shows that event A has occurred after event B. Incorrectly interchanging these ideas is known as **confusing the inverse**.

Consider the case of drawing two cards from a deck of fifty-two cards. The probability of pulling two queens would vary based on whether the initial card was placed back in the deck for the second pull. If the card is placed back in, the probability of pulling two queens is:

$$\frac{4}{52}\times\frac{4}{52}=0.00592$$

If the card is not placed back in, the probability of pulling two queens is:

$$\frac{4}{52} \times \frac{3}{51} = 0.00452$$

When the card is not placed back in, both the numerator and denominator of the second probability decrease by 1. This is due to the fact that, theoretically, there is one less queen in the deck, and there is one less total card in the deck as well.

Using Probability to Evaluate the Outcomes of Decisions

A **two-way frequency table** displays categorical data with two variables, and it highlights relationships that exist between those two variables. Such tables are used frequently to summarize survey results and are also known as **contingency tables**. Each cell shows a count pertaining to that individual variable pairing, known as a **joint frequency**, and the totals of each row and column are also in the table.

Consider the following two-way frequency table:

Distribution of the Residents of a Particular Village

	70 or older	69 or younger	Totals
Women	20	40	60
Men	5	35	40
Total	25	75	100

The table shows the breakdown of ages and sexes of 100 people in a particular village. The end of each row or column displays the number of people represented by the corresponding data, and the total number of people is shown in the bottom right corner. For example, there were 25 people aged 70 or older and 60 women in the data. The 20 in the first cell shows that out of 100 total villagers, 20 were women aged 70 or older. The 5 in the cell below shows that out of 100 total villagers, 5 were men aged 70 or older.

A two-way table can also show relative frequencies by indicating the percentages of people instead of the count. If each frequency is calculated over the entire total of 100, the first cell would be 20% or 0.2.

However, the relative frequencies can also be calculated over row or column totals. If row totals were used, the first cell would be:

$$\frac{20}{60} = 0.333 = 33.3\%$$

If column totals were used, the first cell would be:

$$\frac{20}{25} = 0.8 = 80\%$$

Such tables can be used to calculate **conditional probabilities**, which are probabilities that an event occurs, given another event. Consider a randomly-selected villager. The probability of selecting a male 70 years old or older is $\frac{5}{100} = 0.05$ because there are 5 males over the age of 70 and 100 total villagers.

Practice Quiz

1. Use the graph below entitled "Projected Temperatures for Tomorrow's Winter Storm" to answer the question.

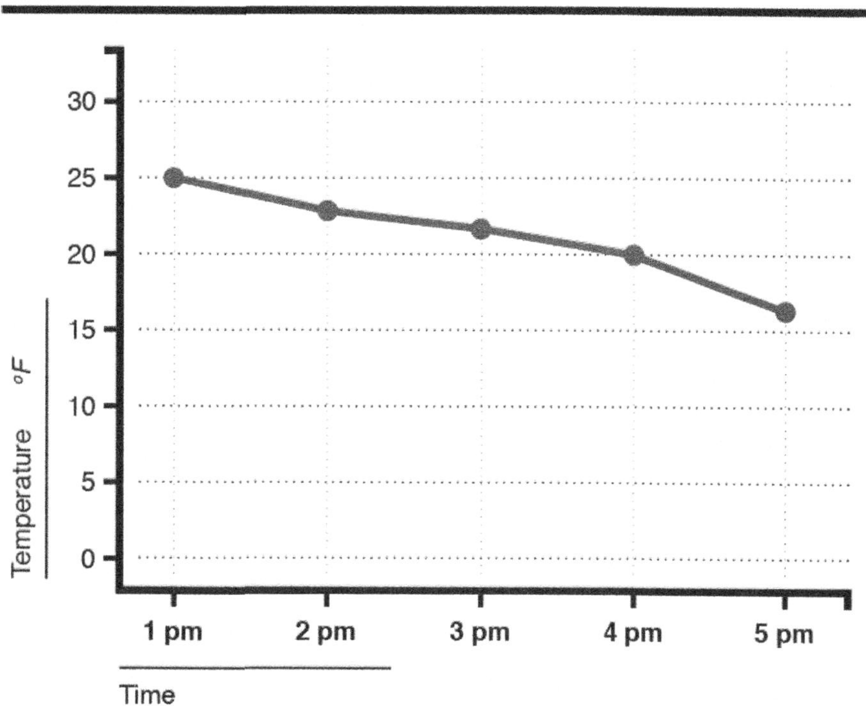

What is the expected temperature at 3:00 p.m.?

a. 25 degrees
b. 22 degrees
c. 20 degrees
d. 16 degrees

2. How many cases of cola can Lexi purchase if each case is $3.50 and she has $40?

a. 10
b. 12
c. 11.4
d. 11

3. The function $f(x) = 3.1x + 240$ models the total U.S. population, in millions, x years after the year 1980. Use this function to answer the following question: What is the total U.S. population in 2011? Round to the nearest million.

a. 336 people
b. 336 million people
c. 6,474 people
d. 647 million people

4. What are the zeros of the following quadratic function?

$$f(x) = 2x^2 - 12x + 16$$

a. $x = 2$ and $x = 4$
b. $x = 8$ and $x = 2$
c. $x = 2$ and $x = 0$
d. $x = 0$ and $x = 4$

5. Simplify: $\frac{x^3+4x^2y-5xy^2}{x^2-xy}$.

a. $x - y$
b. $x^2 + 5xy$
c. $x + 5y$
d. $x^2 - xy$

6. Solve for r: $A = P(1 + rt)$

a. $r = \frac{A}{Pt} - \frac{1}{t}$
b. $r = \frac{At}{P} - t$
c. $r = \frac{A}{P} - t$
d. $r = AP - \frac{1}{t}$

7. What is the volume of the cylinder below? Use 3.14 for π.

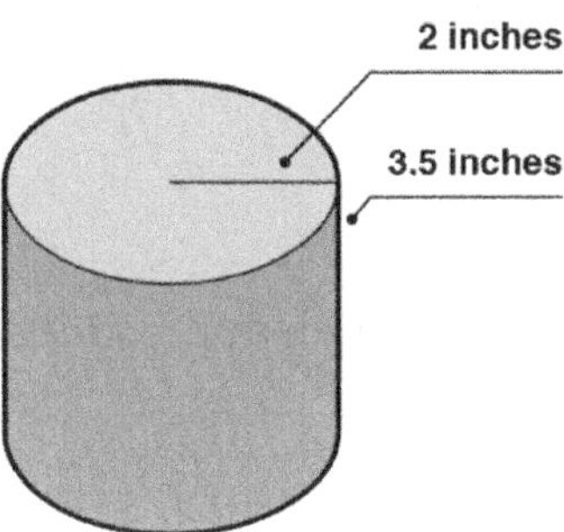

a. 18.84 in^3
b. 45.00 in^3
c. 70.43 in^3
d. 43.96 in^3

8. Which of the following pairs of angles could NOT be the smaller and larger interior angles of a parallelogram?

a. 120°, 60°
b. 125°, 55°
c. 110°, 60°
d. 20°, 160°

9. A study of adult drivers finds that it is likely that an adult driver wears their seatbelt. Which of the following could be the probability that an adult driver wears their seat belt?

a. 0.90
b. 0.05
c. 0.25
d. 0

10. A set of cards contains n numbers, one of which is an odd number. If one card is randomly selected from the set, what is the probability that the card is even?

a. $\frac{1}{n}$
b. $\frac{1}{n-1}$
c. $\frac{n-2}{n-1}$
d. $\frac{n-1}{n}$

See answers on the next page.

Answer Explanations

1. B: Look on the horizontal axis to find 3:00 p.m. Move up from 3:00 p.m. to reach the dot on the graph. Move directly left to the vertical axis between 20 and 25; the best answer choice is 22. The answer of 25 is too high above the projected time on the graph, and the answers of 20 and 16 degrees are too low.

2. D: This is a one-step, real-world application problem. The unknown quantity is the number of cases of cola to be purchased. Let x be equal to this amount. Because each case costs $3.50, the total number of cases multiplied by $3.50 must equal $40. This translates to the mathematical equation $3.5x = 40$. Divide both sides by 3.5 to obtain $x = 11.4286$, which has been rounded to four decimal places. Because cases are sold whole, and there is not enough money to purchase 12 cases, 11 cases is the correct answer.

3. B: The variable x represents the number of years after 1980. The year 2011 was 31 years after 1980, so plug 31 into the function to obtain:

$$f(31) = 3.1 \times 31 + 240 = 336.1$$

This value rounds to 336 and represents 336 million people.

4. A: The zeros of a polynomial function are the x-values where the graph crosses the x-axis, or where $y = 0$. Therefore, set y equal to 0 and solve the polynomial equation. This quadratic can be solved using factoring, as follows:

$$0 = 2x^2 - 12x + 16$$

$$2(x^2 - 6x + 8)$$

$$2(x - 4)(x - 2)$$

Setting both factors equal to 0 results in the two solutions $x = 4$ and $x = 2$, which are the zeros of the original function.

Setting each factor equal to zero and solving results in the three zeros -3, 3, and 2.

5. C: In order to simplify this expression, a common factor can be taken out of the numerator and denominator. The expression then becomes:

$$\frac{x(x^2 + 4xy - 5y^2)}{x(x - y)}$$

When those values for x cancel out, then the new polynomial on top can be factored into:

$$\frac{(x - y)(x + 5y)}{x - y}$$

The two equivalent binomials can be canceled, and the simplified expression becomes $x + 5y$.

6. A: Solving an equation for another variable involved manipulating each part. It requires performing inverse operations to move variables across the equal sign. The first step in solving for r is dividing by P. Then the equation becomes:

$$\frac{A}{P} = 1 + rt$$

Then, the 1 can be subtracted to move it to the left side: $\frac{A}{P} - 1 = rt$. The final step is dividing by t, which makes the new equation:

$$\frac{A}{Pt} - \frac{1}{t} = r$$

7. D: The volume for a cylinder is found by using the formula:

$$V = \pi r^2 h = (3.14)(2\text{ in})^2 \times 3.5\text{ in} = 43.96\text{ in}^3$$

8. C: The smaller and larger interior angles in a parallelogram must add up to 180°. This pair is the only duo that does not have a sum of 180.

9. A: The probability of 0.9 is closer to 1 than any of the other answers. The closer a probability is to 1, the greater the likelihood that the event will occur. The probability of 0.05 shows that it is very unlikely that an adult driver will wear their seatbelt because it is close to zero. A zero probability means that it will not occur. The probability of 0.25 is closer to zero than to one, so it shows that it is unlikely an adult will wear their seatbelt.

10. D: There are n total cards, which means that the denominator needs to be n (the total number of outcomes). If there is only 1 odd number, then the rest are even. There are $n - 1$ even cards. Therefore, the probability of selecting an even card is $\frac{n-1}{n}$.

English Language Arts and Reading

Reading: Literary and Informational Text Analysis

Comparing Themes

The **theme** of a text is the central idea the author communicates. Whereas the topic of a passage of text may be concrete in nature, by contrast the theme is always conceptual. For example, while the topic of Mark Twain's novel *The Adventures of Huckleberry Finn* might be described as something like the coming-of-age experiences of a poor, illiterate, functionally orphaned boy around and on the Mississippi River in 19th-century Missouri, one theme of the book might be that human beings are corrupted by society. Another might be that slavery and "civilized" society itself are hypocritical. Whereas the main idea in a text is the most important single point that the author wants to make, the theme is the concept or view around which the author centers the text.

Throughout time, humans have told stories with similar themes. Some themes are universal across time, space, and culture. These include themes of the individual as a hero, conflicts of the individual against nature, the individual against society, change vs. tradition, the circle of life, coming-of-age, and the complexities of love. Themes involving war and peace have featured prominently in diverse works, like Homer's *Iliad*, Tolstoy's *War and Peace* (1869), Stephen Crane's *The Red Badge of Courage* (1895), Hemingway's *A Farewell to Arms* (1929), and Margaret Mitchell's *Gone with the Wind* (1936). Another universal literary theme is that of the quest. These appear in folklore from countries and cultures worldwide, including the Gilgamesh Epic, Arthurian legend's Holy Grail quest, Virgil's *Aeneid*, Homer's *Odyssey*, and the *Argonautica*. Cervantes' *Don Quixote* is a parody of chivalric quests. J.R.R. Tolkien's *The Lord of the Rings* trilogy (1954) also features a quest.

Similar themes across cultures often occur in countries that share a border or are otherwise geographically close together. For example, a folklore story of a rabbit in the moon using a mortar and pestle is shared among China, Japan, Korea, and Thailand—making medicine in China, making rice cakes in Japan and Korea, and hulling rice in Thailand. Another instance is when cultures are more distant geographically, but their languages are related. For example, East Turkestan's Uighurs and people in Turkey share tales of folk hero Effendi Nasreddin Hodja. Another instance, which may either be called cultural diffusion or simply reflect commonalities in the human imagination, involves shared themes among geographically- and linguistically-different cultures: both Cameroon's and Greece's folklore tell of centaurs; Cameroon, India, Malaysia, Thailand, and Japan, of mermaids; Brazil, Peru, China, Japan, Malaysia, Indonesia, and Cameroon, of underwater civilizations; and China, Japan, Thailand, Vietnam, Malaysia, Brazil, and Peru, of shape-shifters.

Two prevalent literary themes are love and friendship, which can end happily, sadly, or both. William Shakespeare's *Romeo and Juliet*, Emily Brontë's *Wuthering Heights*, Leo Tolstoy's *Anna Karenina*, and both *Pride and Prejudice* and *Sense and Sensibility* by Jane Austen are famous examples. Another theme recurring in popular literature is of revenge, an old theme in dramatic literature, e.g. Elizabethans Thomas Kyd's *The Spanish Tragedy* and Thomas Middleton's *The Revenger's Tragedy*. Some more well-known instances include Shakespeare's tragedies *Hamlet* and *Macbeth*, Alexandre Dumas' *The Count of Monte Cristo*, John Grisham's *A Time to Kill*, and Stieg Larsson's *The Girl Who Kicked the Hornet's Nest*.

Identifying the Main Idea of a Passage

The **topic** of a text is the general subject matter. Text topics can usually be expressed in one word, or a few words at most. Additionally, readers should ask themselves what point the author is trying to make. This point is the **main idea** of the text—the one thing the author wants readers to know about the topic. Once the author has established the main idea, he or she will support the main idea with supporting details. **Supporting details** are evidence that support the main idea and include personal testimonies, examples, or statistics.

One analogy for these components and their relationships is that a text is like a well-designed house. The topic is the roof, covering all rooms. The main idea is the frame. The supporting details are the various rooms. To identify the topic of a text, readers can ask themselves what or who the author is writing about in the paragraph. To locate the main idea, readers can ask themselves what one idea the author wants readers to know about the topic. To identify supporting details, readers can put the main idea into question form and ask, "what does the author use to prove or explain their main idea?"

Let's look at an example. An author is writing an essay about the Amazon rainforest and trying to convince the audience that more funding should go into protecting the area from deforestation. The author makes the argument stronger by including evidence of the benefits of the rainforest: it provides habitats to a variety of species, it provides much of the earth's oxygen which in turn cleans the atmosphere, and it is the home to medicinal plants that are useful against some of the world's deadliest diseases. Here is an outline of the essay looking at topic, main idea, and supporting details:

> Topic: Amazon rainforest
> Main Idea: The Amazon rainforest should receive more funding to protect it from deforestation.
> Supporting Details:
> 1. It provides habitats to a variety of species
> 2. It provides much of the earth's oxygen which in turn cleans the atmosphere
> 3. It is home to medicinal plants that are useful against some of the deadliest diseases.

Notice that the topic of the essay is listed in a few key words: "Amazon rainforest." The main idea tells us what about the topic is important: that the topic should be funded to prevent deforestation. Finally, the supporting details are what author relies on to convince the audience to act or to believe in the truth of the main idea.

Determining How Ideas or Details Inform the Author's Argument

When authors want to strengthen the support for an argument, evidence-based data in the form of statistics or concrete examples can be used. Statistics and examples are often accompanied by detailed explanations to help increase the audience's understanding and shape their ideas. Expert opinions are another way to strengthen an argument. But all this effort toward supporting a given argument does not necessarily make the argument absolute. After all, the word "argument" implies that there is more than one way to think about the subject. Arguments are meant to be challenged, questioned, and analyzed.

Authors will use one of two argument models: deductive or inductive. **Deductive arguments** require two general statements to support the argument. **Inductive arguments** employ specific data, examples, or facts to support the argument.

Deductive	Inductive
All fruits contain seeds. Tomatoes contain seeds. Therefore, tomatoes are fruits.	9 out of 10 dentists prefer soft-bristled toothbrushes. Therefore, soft-bristled toothbrushes are the best type of toothbrush for optimal dental health.

No matter what evidence is presented, readers should still challenge the argument. In any text, readers are encouraged to ask specific questions to evaluate the overall validity of the argument. Some important points to consider include:

- Has the author employed logic in the argument?
- Is the argument clearly explained?
- Is the argument sufficiently supported?
- Who conducted the research, and for what purpose?
- Is the supporting data qualitative, quantitative, or a mixture of both?
- Is the presented data representative of the typical cross-section of society or of the phenomenon being discussed?
- Does the author present any bias?
- Has the author overlooked anything that should be explored to form a well-rounded argument?

Although informational writing should be written objectively, such writing still constitutes the author's particular point of view or belief about a given subject. The author's main idea will be backed up with reasons, evidence, and supporting details, but it is important for the audience to question the main idea and evaluate the presented evidence. Although the author's ideas and shared details drive the overall argument, readers should feel compelled to explore the topic further, assess the evidence, and determine whether they agree with the overall message. Authors present the argument in order to convince their readers, but readers must strive to evaluate and assess the information to arrive at an informed opinion of the subject matter.

Comprehending Explicit Textual Information in a Passage

In the Reading Test of the TSI Exam, test takers will be asked questions based on their direct knowledge of the passage. The information explicitly stated in the passage leaves the reader no room for confusion. Information explicitly stated in the passage can be identified and used as text evidence. Additionally, test takers should consider if the information is an author's opinion or an objective fact, and whether the information contains bias or stereotypes. Also important to consider is the following question: Within the information stated, which words are directly stated and what words leave room for a connotative interpretation? Being cautious of the author's presentation of information will aid the test taker in determining the correct answer choice for the question stem.

Facts and Opinions

A fact is a statement that is true empirically or an event that has actually occurred in reality and can be proven or supported by evidence; it is objective. In contrast, an opinion is subjective, representing something that someone believes rather than something that exists in the absolute. People's individual

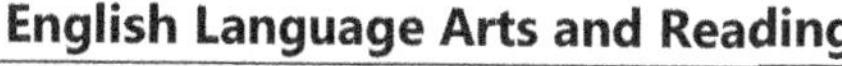

understandings, feelings, and perspectives contribute to variations in opinion. Although facts are typically objective in nature, in some instances, a statement of fact may be both factual and yet also subjective. For example, emotions are individual subjective experiences. If an individual says that they feel happy or sad, the feeling is subjective, but the statement is factual; hence, it is a subjective fact. In contrast, if one person tells another that the other is feeling happy or sad—whether this is true or not—that is an assumption or an opinion.

Biases

Biases usually occur when someone allows their personal preferences or ideologies to interfere with what should be an objective decision. In personal situations, someone is biased towards someone if they favor them in an unfair way. In academic writing, being biased in your sources means leaving out objective information that would turn the argument one way or the other. The evidence of bias in academic writing makes the text less credible, so be sure to present all viewpoints when writing, not just your own, so to avoid coming off as biased. Being objective when presenting information or dealing with people usually allows the author to gain more credibility.

Stereotypes

Stereotypes are preconceived notions that place a particular rule or characteristics on an entire group of people. Stereotypes are usually offensive to the group they refer to or to allies of that group and often have negative connotations. The reinforcement of stereotypes isn't always obvious. Sometimes stereotypes can be very subtle and are still widely used in order for people to understand categories within the world. For example, saying that women are more intuitive or nurturing than men is a stereotype, although this is still an assumption used by many in order to understand differences between one another.

Denotation and Connotation

Denotation, a word's explicit definition, is often set in comparison to connotation, the emotional, cultural, social, or personal implications associated with a word. Denotation is more of an objective definition, whereas connotation can be more subjective, although many connotative meanings of words are similar for certain cultures. The denotative meanings of words are usually based on facts, and the connotative meanings of words are usually based on emotion.

Here are some examples of words and their denotative and connotative meanings in Western culture:

Word	Denotative Meaning	Connotative Meaning
Home	A permanent place where one lives, usually as a member of a family.	A place of warmth; a place of familiarity; comforting; a place of safety and security. "Home" usually has a positive connotation.
Snake	A long reptile with no limbs and strong jaws that moves along the ground; some snakes have a poisonous bite.	An evil omen; a slithery creature (human or nonhuman) that is deceitful or unwelcome. "Snake" usually has a negative connotation.
Winter	A season of the year that is the coldest, usually from December to February in the northern hemisphere and from June to August in the southern hemisphere.	Circle of life, especially that of death and dying; cold or icy; dark and gloomy; hibernation, sleep, or rest. Winter can have a negative connotation, although many who have access to heat may enjoy the snowy season from their homes.

Literal and Figurative Language

Authors of a text use language with multiple levels of meaning for many different reasons. When the meaning of a text requires directness, the author will use literal language to provide clarity. On the other hand, an author will use figurative language to produce an emotional effect or facilitate a deeper understanding of a word or passage. For example, a set of instructions on how to use a computer would require literal language. However, a commentary on the social implications of immigration bans might contain a wide range of figurative language to elicit an empathetic response. A single text can have a mixture of both literal and figurative language.

Literal Language

Literal language uses words in accordance with their actual definition. Many informational texts employ literal language because it is straightforward and precise. Documents such as instructions, proposals, technical documents, and workplace documents use literal language for the majority of their writing, so there is no confusion or complexity of meaning for readers to decipher. The information is best communicated through clear and precise language. The following are brief examples of literal language:

- I cook with olive oil.
- There are 365 days in a year.
- My grandma's name is Barbara.
- Yesterday we had some scattered thunderstorms.
- World War II began in 1939.
- Blue whales are the largest species of whale.

Figurative Language

Not meant to be taken literal, figurative language is useful when the author of a text wants to produce an emotional effect in the reader or add a heightened complexity to the meaning of the text. Figurative language is used more heavily in texts such as literary fiction, poetry, critical theory, and speeches. It goes beyond literal language, allowing readers to form associations they wouldn't normally form. Using language in a figurative sense appeals to the imagination of the reader. It is important to remember that words signify objects and ideas and are not the objects and ideas themselves. Figurative language can highlight this detachment by creating multiple associations, but it also points to the fact that language is fluid and capable of creating a world full of linguistic possibilities. It can be argued that figurative language is the heart of communication even outside of fiction and poetry. People connect through humor, metaphors, cultural allusions, puns, and symbolism in their everyday rhetoric. The following are terms associated with figurative language:

Simile

A simile is a comparison of two things using *like, than,* or *as.* A simile usually takes objects that have no apparent connection, such as a mind and an orchid, and compares them:

> His mind was as complex and rare as a field of ghost orchids.

Similes encourage new, fresh perspectives on objects or ideas that would not otherwise occur. Unlike similes, metaphors are comparisons that do not use *like, than,* or *as.* So, a metaphor from the above example would be:

> His mind was a field of ghost orchids.

Thus, similes highlight the comparison by focusing on the figurative side of the language, elucidating the author's intent. With the metaphor, however, we get a beautiful yet equivocal comparison.

Metaphor

A popular use of figurative language, metaphors compare objects or ideas directly, asserting that something *is* a certain thing, even if it isn't. The following is an example of a metaphor used by writer Virginia Woolf:

> Books are the mirrors of the soul.

Metaphors have a vehicle and a tenor. The tenor is "books" and the vehicle is "mirrors of the soul." That is, the tenor is what is meant to be described, and the vehicle is that which carries the weight of the comparison. In this metaphor, perhaps the author means to say that written language (books) reflect a person's most inner thoughts and desires.

Dead metaphors are phrases that have been overused to the point where the figurative language has taken on a literal meaning, like "crystal clear." This phrase is in such popular use that the meaning seems literal ("perfectly clear") even when it is not.

Finally, an extended metaphor is one that goes on for several paragraphs, or even an entire text. "On First Looking into Chapman's Homer," a poem by John Keats, begins, "Much have I travell'd in the realms of gold," and goes on to explain the first time he hears Chapman's translation of Homer's writing. We see the extended metaphor begin in the first line. Keats is comparing travelling into "realms of gold" and exploration of new lands to the act of hearing a certain kind of literature for the first time. The extended metaphor goes on until the end of the poem where Keats stands "Silent, upon a peak in Darien," having heard the end of Chapman's translation. Keats has gained insight into new lands (new text) and is the richer for it.

The following are brief definitions and examples of popular figurative language:

Onomatopoeia: A word that, when spoken, imitates the sound to which it refers. Ex: "We heard a loud *boom* while driving to the beach yesterday."

Personification: When human characteristics are given to animals, inanimate objects, or abstractions. An example would be in William Wordsworth's poem "Daffodils" where he sees a "crowd ... / of golden daffodils ... / Fluttering and dancing in the breeze." Dancing is usually a characteristic attributed solely to humans, but Wordsworth personifies the daffodils here as a crowd of people dancing.

Juxtaposition: Juxtaposition places two objects side by side for comparison or contrast. For example, Milton juxtaposes God and Satan in "Paradise Lost."

Paradox: A paradox is a statement that appears self-contradictory but is actually true. One example of a paradox is when Socrates said, "I know one thing; that I know nothing." Seemingly, if Socrates knew nothing, he wouldn't know that he knew nothing. However, he is using figurative language not to say that he literally knows nothing, but that true wisdom begins with casting all presuppositions about the world aside.

Hyperbole: A hyperbole is an exaggeration. Ex: "I'm so tired I could sleep for centuries."

Allusion: An allusion is a reference to a character or event that happened in the past. T.S. Eliot's "The Waste Land" is a poem littered with allusions, including, "I will show you fear in a handful of dust," alluding to Genesis 3:19: "For you are dust, and to dust you shall return."

Pun: Puns are used in popular culture to invoke humor by exploiting the meanings of words. They can also be used in literature to give hints of meaning in unexpected places. In "Romeo and Juliet," Mercutio makes a pun after he is stabbed by Tybalt: "look for me tomorrow and you will find me a grave man."

Imagery: This is a collection of images given to the reader by the author. If a text is rich in imagery, it is easier for the reader to imagine themselves in the author's world. One example of a poem that relies on imagery is William Carlos Williams' "The Red Wheelbarrow":

> so much depends
> upon
>
> a red wheel
> barrow
>
> glazed with rain
> water
>
> beside the white
> chickens

The starkness of the imagery and the placement of the words in this poem bring to life the images of a purely simple world. Through its imagery, this poem tells a story in just sixteen words.

Symbolism: A symbol is used to represent an idea or belief system. For example, poets in Western civilization have been using the symbol of a rose for hundreds of years to represent love. In Japan, poets have used the firefly to symbolize passionate love, and sometimes even spirits of those who have died. Symbols can also express powerful political commentary and can be used in propaganda.

Irony: There are three types of irony: verbal, dramatic, and situational. Verbal irony is when a person states one thing and means the opposite. For example, a person is probably using irony when they say, "I can't wait to study for this exam next week." Dramatic irony occurs in a narrative and happens when the audience knows something that the characters do not. In the modern TV series Hannibal, the audience knows that Hannibal Lecter is a serial killer, but most of the main characters do not. This is dramatic irony. Finally, situational irony is when one expects something to happen, and the opposite occurs. For example, we can say that a police station being robbed would be an instance of situation irony.

Information that is Not Explicitly Stated

Not all information in a passage will be explicitly stated. In such cases, readers may need to make inferences. An inference is an educated guess or conclusion based on sound evidence and reasoning within the text. The test may include multiple-choice questions asking about the logical conclusion that can be drawn from reading a text, and you will have to identify the choice that unavoidably leads to that conclusion. In order to eliminate the incorrect choices, the test-taker should come up with a hypothetical situation wherein an answer choice is true, but the conclusion is not true.

Here is an example:

> Fred purchased the newest PC available on the market. Therefore, he purchased the most expensive PC in the computer store.

What can one assume for this conclusion to follow logically?

a. Fred enjoys purchasing expensive items.
b. PCs are some of the most expensive personal technology products available.
c. The newest PC is the most expensive one.

The premise of the text is the first sentence: Fred purchased the newest PC. The conclusion is the second sentence: Fred purchased the most expensive PC. Recent release and price are two different factors; the difference between them is the logical gap. To eliminate the gap, one must connect the new information from the conclusion with the pertinent information from the premise. In this example, there must be a connection between product recency and product price. Therefore, a possible bridge to the logical gap could be a sentence stating that the newest PCs always cost the most.

Synthesizing Ideas by Making a Connection or Comparison Between Two Passages

One effective way to compare and connect two different passages is to summarize both of them, which helps hone in on the important points. This makes the comparison process more manageable.

An important skill is the ability to read a complex text and then reduce its length and complexity by focusing on the key events and details. A summary is a shortened version of the original text, written by the reader in their own words. The summary should be shorter than the original text, and it must include the most critical points.

In order to effectively summarize a complex text, it's necessary to understand the original source and identify the major points covered. It may be helpful to outline the original text to get the big picture and avoid getting bogged down in the minor details. For example, a summary wouldn't include a statistic from the original source unless it was the major focus of the text. It's also important for readers to use their own words yet retain the original meaning of the passage. The key to a good summary is emphasizing the main idea without changing the focus of the original information.

Complex texts will likely be more difficult to summarize. Readers must evaluate all points from the original source, filter out the unnecessary details, and maintain only the essential ideas. The summary often mirrors the original text's organizational structure. For example, in a problem-solution text structure, the author typically presents readers with a problem and then develops solutions through the course of the text. An effective summary would likely retain this general structure, rephrasing the problem and then reporting the most useful or plausible solutions.

Paraphrasing is somewhat similar to summarizing. It calls for the reader to take a small part of the passage and list or describe its main points. Paraphrasing is more than rewording the original passage, though. As with summary, a paraphrase should be written in the reader's own words, while still retaining the meaning of the original source. The main difference between summarizing and paraphrasing is that a summary would be appropriate for a much larger text, while paraphrase might focus on just a few lines of text. Effective paraphrasing will indicate an understanding of the original source, yet still help the reader expand on their interpretation. A paraphrase should neither add new information nor remove essential facts that change the meaning of the source.

Making an Appropriate Inference about Single Passages

One technique authors often use to make their fictional stories more interesting is not giving away too much information easily; instead, they sprinkle in hints and descriptions. It is then up to the reader to draw a conclusion about the author's meaning by connecting textual clues with the reader's own pre-existing experiences and knowledge. Drawing conclusions is important as a reading strategy for understanding what is occurring in a text. Rather than directly stating who, what, where, when, or why, authors often describe story elements. Then, readers must draw conclusions to understand significant story components. As they go through a text, readers can think about the setting, characters, plot, problem, and solution; whether the author provided any clues for consideration; and combine any story clues with their existing knowledge and experiences to draw conclusions about what occurs in the text.

Making Predictions

Before and during reading, readers can apply the reading strategy of making predictions about what they think may happen next. For example, what plot and character developments will occur in fiction? What points will the author discuss in nonfiction? Making predictions about portions of text they have not yet read prepares readers mentally for reading, and also gives them a purpose for reading. To inform and make predictions about text, the reader can do the following:

- Consider the title of the text and what it implies
- Look at the cover of the book
- Look at any illustrations or diagrams for additional visual information
- Analyze the structure of the text
- Apply outside experience and knowledge to the text

Readers may adjust their predictions as they read. Reader predictions may or may not come true in the text but as readers become more experienced as consumers of different texts, their ability to make accurate predictions will improve.

Making Inferences

Authors describe settings, characters, characters' emotions, and events. Readers must infer to understand a text fully. Inferring enables readers to figure out meanings of unfamiliar words, make predictions about upcoming text, draw conclusions, and reflect on reading. Readers can infer about text before, during, and after reading. In everyday life, we use sensory information to infer. Readers can do the same with text. When authors do not answer all readers' questions, readers must infer by saying "I think ... This could be ... This is because ... Maybe ... This means ... I guess ..." etc. Looking at illustrations, considering characters' behaviors, and asking questions during reading facilitate inference. Taking clues from text and connecting text to prior knowledge help to draw conclusions. Readers can infer word meanings, settings, reasons for occurrences, character emotions, pronoun referents, author messages, and answers to questions unstated in text. To practice making inferences, students can read sentences written/selected by the instructor, discuss the setting and character, draw conclusions, and make predictions.

Making inferences and drawing conclusions involve skills that are quite similar: both require readers to fill in information the author has omitted. Authors may omit information as a technique for inducing readers to discover the outcomes themselves; or they may consider certain information unimportant; or they may assume their reading audience already knows certain information. To make an inference or draw a conclusion about text, readers should observe all facts and arguments the author has presented and consider what they already know from their own personal experiences. Reading students taking multiple-choice tests that refer to text passages can determine correct and incorrect choices based on the information in the passage. For example, from a text passage describing an individual's signs of anxiety while unloading groceries and nervously clutching their wallet at a grocery store checkout, readers can infer or conclude that the individual may not have enough money to pay for everything.

Identifying an Author's Purpose, Tone, and Organization or Rhetorical Strategies and Use of Evidence

Analyzing the Structure of a Text

Text structure is the way in which the author organizes and presents textual information so readers can follow and comprehend it. One kind of text structure is sequence. This means the author arranges the text in a logical order from beginning to middle to end. There are three types of sequences:

- Chronological: Ordering events in time from earliest to latest
- Spatial: Describing objects, people, or spaces according to their relationships to one another in space
- Order of Importance: Addressing topics, characters, or ideas according to how important they are, from either least important to most important

Chronological sequence is the most common sequential text structure. Readers can identify sequential structure by looking for words that signal it, like *first, earlier, meanwhile, next, then, later, finally;* and specific times and dates the author includes as chronological references.

In writing, some sentences naturally lead to others, whereas in other cases, a new sentence expresses a new idea. Transitional phrases connect sentences and the ideas they convey, which makes the writing coherent. Transitional language also guides the reader from one thought to the next. For example, when pointing out an objection to the previous idea, starting a sentence with "However," "But," or "On the other hand" is transitional. When adding another idea or detail, writers use "Also," "In addition," "Furthermore," "Further," "Moreover," "Not only," etc. Readers have difficulty perceiving connections between ideas without such transitional wording.

Problem-Solution Text Structure

Comparison identifies similarities between two or more things. **Contrast** identifies differences between two or more things. Authors typically employ both to illustrate relationships between things by highlighting their commonalities and deviations. For example, a writer might compare Windows and Linux as operating systems, and contrast Linux as free and open-source vs. Windows as proprietary. When writing an essay, sometimes it is useful to create an image of the two objects or events you are comparing or contrasting. Venn diagrams are useful because they show the differences as well as the similarities between two things. Once you've seen the similarities and differences on paper, it might be helpful to create an outline of the essay with both comparison and contrast. Every outline will look different because every two or more things will have a different number of comparisons and contrasts. Say you are trying to compare and contrast carrots with sweet potatoes.

Here is an example of a compare/contrast outline using those topics:

A. Introduction: Share why you are comparing and contrasting the foods. Give the thesis statement.

- Body paragraph 1: Sweet potatoes and carrots are both root vegetables (similarity)
- Body paragraph 2: Sweet potatoes and carrots are both orange (similarity)
- Body paragraph 3: Sweet potatoes and carrots have different nutritional components (difference)
- Conclusion: Restate the purpose of your comparison/contrast essay.

Of course, if there is only one similarity between your topics and two differences, you will want to rearrange your outline. Always tailor your essay to what works best with your topic.

Descriptive Text Structure

Description can be both a type of text structure and a type of text. Some texts are descriptive throughout entire books. For example, a book may describe the geography of a certain country, state, or region, or tell readers all about dolphins by describing many of their characteristics. Many other texts are not descriptive throughout but use descriptive passages within the overall text. The following are a few examples of descriptive text:

- When the author describes a character in a novel
- When the author sets the scene for an event by describing the setting
- When a biographer describes the personality and behaviors of a real-life individual
- When a historian describes the details of a particular battle within a book about a specific war
- When a travel writer describes the climate, people, foods, and/or customs of a certain place

A hallmark of description is using sensory details, painting a vivid picture so readers can imagine it almost as if they were experiencing it personally.

Cause and Effect Text Structure

When using cause and effect to extrapolate meaning from text, readers must determine the cause when the author only communicates effects. For example, if a description of a man walking down the sidewalk includes details such as his jacket billowing or his hat nearly flying off his head, the reader can infer or conclude that it must be windy outside. A useful technique for making such decisions is wording them in "If...then" form, e.g. "If the man's jacket is billowing and his hat nearly flys off his head, then it may be a windy day." Cause and effect text structures explain why certain events or actions resulted in particular outcomes. For example, an author might describe America's historical large flocks of dodo birds, the fact that gunshots did not startle/frighten dodos, and that because dodos did not flee, settlers killed whole flocks in one hunting session, explaining how the dodo was hunted into extinction.

Recognizing Events in a Sequence

Sequence structure is the order of events in which a story or information is presented to the audience. Sometimes the text will be presented in chronological order, or sometimes it will be presented by displaying the most recent information first, then moving backwards in time. The sequence structure depends on the author, the context, and the audience. The structure of a text also depends on the genre in which the text is written. Is it literary fiction? Is it a magazine article? Is it instructions for how to complete a certain task? Different genres will have different purposes for switching up the sequence.

Narrative Structure

The structure presented in literary fiction, called **narrative structure**, is the foundation on which the text moves. The narrative structure comes from the plot and setting. The **plot** is the sequence of events in the narrative that move the text forward through cause and effect. The setting is the place or time period in which the story takes place. Narrative structure has two main categories: linear and nonlinear.

A narrative is linear when it is told in chronological order. Traditional linear narratives will follow the plot diagram below depicting the narrative arc. The narrative arc consists of the exposition, conflict, rising action, climax, falling action, and resolution.

- Exposition: The exposition is in the beginning of a narrative and introduces the characters, setting, and background information of the story. The exposition provides the context for the upcoming narrative. Exposition literally means "a showing forth" in Latin.

- Conflict: In a traditional narrative, the conflict appears toward the beginning of the story after the audience becomes familiar with the characters and setting. The conflict is a single instance between characters, nature, or the self, in which the central character is forced to make a decision or move forward with some kind of action. The conflict presents something for the main character, or protagonist, to overcome.

- Rising Action: The rising action is the part of the story that leads into the climax. The rising action will develop the characters and plot while creating tension and suspense that eventually lead to the climax.

- Climax: The climax is the part of the story where the tension produced in the rising action culminates. The climax is the peak of the story. In a traditional structure, everything before the climax builds up to it, and everything after the climax falls from it. It is the height of the narrative and is usually either the most exciting part of the story or is marked by some turning point in the character's journey.
- Falling Action: The falling action happens as a result of the climax. Characters continue to develop, although there is a wrapping up of loose ends here. The falling action leads to the resolution.
- Resolution: The resolution is where the story comes to an end and usually leaves the reader with the satisfaction of knowing what happened within the story and why. However, stories do not always end in this fashion. Sometimes readers can be confused or frustrated at the end from the lack of information or the absence of a happy ending.

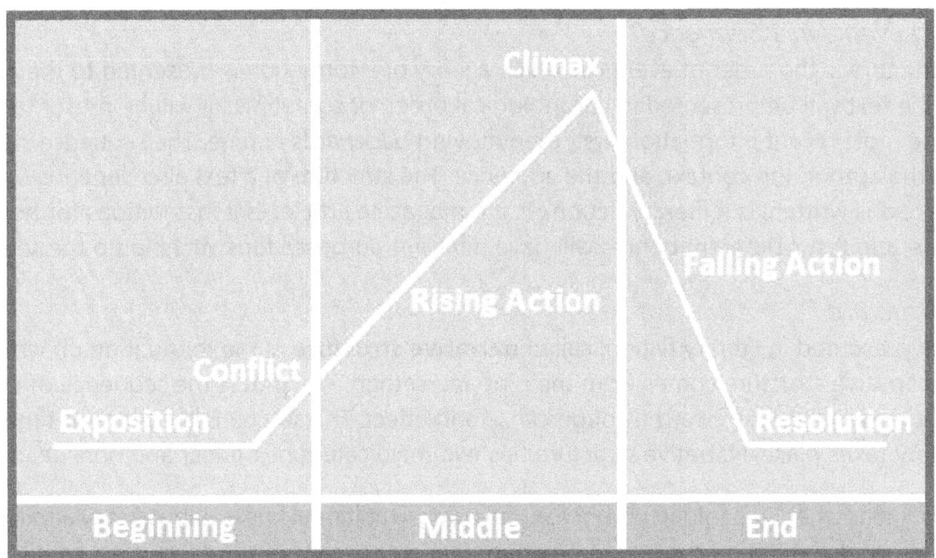

A **nonlinear narrative** deviates from the traditional narrative because it does not always follow the traditional plot structure of the narrative arc. Nonlinear narratives may include structures that are disjointed, circular, or disruptive, in the sense that they do not follow chronological order. **In medias res** is an example of a nonlinear structure. *In medias res* is Latin for "in the middle of things," which is how many ancient texts, especially epic poems, began their story, such as Homer's *Iliad*. Instead of having a clear exposition with a full development of characters, they would begin right in the middle of the action.

Many modernist texts in the late nineteenth and early twentieth centuries experimented with disjointed narratives, moving away from traditional linear narrative. Disjointed narratives are depicted in novels like *Catch 22*, where the author, Joseph Heller, structures the narrative based on free association of ideas rather than chronology. Another nonlinear narrative can be seen in the novel *Wuthering Heights*, written by Emily Brontë; after the first chapter, the narrative progresses retrospectively instead of chronologically. It seems that there are two narratives in *Wuthering Heights* working at the same time: a present narrative as well as a past narrative. Authors employ disrupting narratives for various reasons; some use it to create situational irony for the readers, while some use it to create a certain effect, such as excitement, discomfort, or fear.

Evaluating the Author's Purpose in a Given Text

Authors may have many purposes for writing a specific text. They could be imparting information, entertaining their audience, expressing their own feelings, or trying to persuade their readers of a particular position. Authors' purposes are their reasons for writing something. A single author may have one overriding purpose for writing or multiple reasons. An author may explicitly state their intention in the text, or the reader may need to infer that intention. When readers can identify the author's purpose, they are better able to analyze information in the text. By knowing why the author wrote the text, readers can glean ideas for how to approach it.

The following is a list of questions readers can ask in order to discern an author's purpose for writing a text:

- Does the title of the text give you any clues about its purpose?
- Was the purpose of the text to give information to readers?
- Did the author want to describe an event, issue, or individual?
- Was it written to express emotions and thoughts?
- Did the author want to convince readers to consider a particular issue?
- Do you think the author's primary purpose was to entertain?
- Why do you think the author wrote this text from a certain point of view?
- What is your response to the text as a reader?
- Did the author state their purpose for writing it?

Rather than simply consuming the text, readers should attempt to interpret the information being presented. Being able to identify an author's purpose efficiently improves reading comprehension, develops critical thinking, and makes students more likely to consider issues in depth before accepting writer viewpoints. Authors of fiction frequently write to entertain readers. Another purpose for writing fiction is making a political statement; for example, Jonathan Swift wrote "A Modest Proposal" (1729) as a political satire. Another purpose for writing fiction as well as nonfiction is to persuade readers to take some action or further a particular cause. Fiction authors and poets both frequently write to evoke certain moods; for example, Edgar Allan Poe wrote novels, short stories, and poems that evoke moods of gloom, guilt, terror, and dread. Another purpose of poets is evoking certain emotions: love is popular, as in Shakespeare's sonnets and numerous others. In "The Waste Land" (1922), T.S. Eliot evokes society's alienation, disaffection, sterility, and fragmentation.

Authors seldom directly state their purposes in texts. Some students may be confronted with nonfiction texts such as biographies, histories, magazine and newspaper articles, and instruction manuals, among others. To identify the purpose in nonfiction texts, students can ask the following questions:

- Is the author trying to teach something?
- Is the author trying to persuade the reader?
- Is the author imparting factual information only?
- Is this a reliable source?
- Does the author have some kind of hidden agenda?

To apply author purpose in nonfictional passages, students can also analyze sentence structure, word choice, and transitions to answer the aforementioned questions and to make inferences. For example, authors wanting to convince readers to view a topic negatively often choose words with negative connotations.

Narrative Writing

Narrative writing tells a story. The most prominent type of narrative writing is the fictional novel. Here are some examples:

- Mark Twain's *The Adventures of Tom Sawyer* and *The Adventures of Huckleberry Finn*
- Victor Hugo's *Les Misérables*
- Charles Dickens' *Great Expectations, David Copperfield,* and *A Tale of Two Cities*
- Jane Austen's *Northanger Abbey, Mansfield Park, Pride and Prejudice,* and *Sense and Sensibility*
- Toni Morrison's *Beloved, The Bluest Eye,* and *Song of Solomon*
- Gabriel García Márquez's *One Hundred Years of Solitude* and *Love in the Time of Cholera*

Nonfiction works can also appear in narrative form. For example, some authors choose a narrative style to convey factual information about a topic, such as a specific animal, country, geographic region, and scientific or natural phenomenon.

Narrative writing tells a story, and the one telling the story is called the narrator. The narrator may be a fictional character telling the story from their own viewpoint. This narrator uses the first person (*I, me, my, mine* and *we, us, our,* and *ours*). The narrator may also be the author; for example, when Louisa May Alcott writes "Dear reader" in *Little Women*, she (the author) addresses us as readers. In this case, the novel is typically told in third person, referring to the characters as he, she, they, or them. Another more common technique is the omniscient narrator; in other words, the story is told by an unidentified individual who sees and knows everything about the events and characters—not only their externalized actions, but also their internalized feelings and thoughts. Second person narration, which addresses readers as you throughout the text, is more uncommon than the first and third person options.

Expository Writing

Expository writing is also known as informational writing. Its purpose is not to tell a story as in narrative writing, to paint a picture as in descriptive writing, or to persuade readers to agree with something as in argumentative writing. Rather, its point is to communicate information to the reader. As such, the point of view of the author will be more objective. Whereas other types of writing appeal to the reader's emotions, appeal to the reader's reason by using logic, or use subjective descriptions to sway the reader's opinion or thinking, expository writing seeks simply to provide facts, evidence, observations, and objective descriptions of the subject matter instead. Some examples of expository writing include research reports, journal articles, books about history, academic textbooks, essays, how-to articles, user instruction manuals, news articles, and other factual journalistic reports.

Technical Writing

Technical writing is similar to expository writing because it provides factual and objective information. Indeed, it may even be considered a subcategory of expository writing. However, technical writing differs from expository writing in two ways: (1) it is specific to a particular field, discipline, or subject, and (2) it uses technical terminology that belongs only to that area. Writing that uses technical terms is intended only for an audience familiar with those terms. An example of technical writing would be a manual on computer programming and use.

Persuasive Writing

Persuasive writing, or ***argumentative writing***, attempts to convince the reader to agree with the author's position. Some writers may be responding to other writers' arguments, in which case they refer to those authors or text and then disagree with them. However, another common technique is for the author to anticipate opposing viewpoints, both from other authors and from readers. The author brings up these opposing viewpoints, and then refutes them before they can even be raised, strengthening the author's argument. Writers persuade readers by appealing to the readers' reason and emotion, as well as to their own character and credibility. Aristotle called these appeals ***logos***, ***pathos***, and ***ethos***, respectively.

Evaluating the Author's Point of View in a Given Text

When a writer tells a story using the first person, readers can identify this by the use of first-person pronouns, like *I, me, we, us,* etc. However, first-person narratives can be told by different people or from different points of view. For example, some authors write in the first person to tell the story from the main character's viewpoint, as Charles Dickens did in his novels *David Copperfield* and *Great Expectations.* Some authors write in the first person from the viewpoint of a fictional character in the story, but not necessarily the main character. For example, F. Scott Fitzgerald wrote *The Great Gatsby* as narrated by Nick Carraway, a character in the story, about the main characters, Jay Gatsby and Daisy Buchanan. Other authors write in the first person, but as the omniscient narrator—an often unnamed person who knows all of the characters' inner thoughts and feelings. Writing in first person as oneself is more common in nonfiction.

Third Person

The third-person narrative is probably the most prevalent voice used in fictional literature. While some authors tell stories from the point of view and in the voice of a fictional character using the first person, it is a more common practice to describe the actions, thoughts, and feelings of fictional characters in the third person using *he, him, she, her, they, them,* etc.

Although plot and character development are both necessary and possible when writing narrative texts from a first-person point of view, they are also more difficult, particularly for new writers and those who find it unnatural or uncomfortable to write from that perspective. Therefore, writing experts advise beginning writers to start out writing in the third person. A big advantage of third-person narration is that the writer can describe the thoughts, feelings, and motivations of every character in a story, which is not possible for the first-person narrator. Third-person narrative can impart information to readers that the characters do not know. On the other hand, beginning writers often regard using the third-person point of view as more difficult because they must write about the feelings and thoughts of every character, rather than only about those of the protagonist.

Second Person

Narrative texts written in the second person address someone else as "you." In novels and other fictional works, the second person is the narrative voice most seldom used. The primary reason for this is that it often reads in an awkward manner, which prevents readers from being drawn into the fictional world of the novel. The second person is more often used in informational text, especially in how-to manuals, guides, and other instructions.

First Person

First person uses pronouns such as *I, me, we, my, us,* and *our.* Some writers naturally find it easier to tell stories from their own points of view, so writing in the first person offers advantages for them. The first-person voice is better for interpreting the world from a single viewpoint, and for enabling reader immersion in one protagonist's experiences. However, others find it difficult to use the first-person narrative voice. Its disadvantages can include overlooking the emotions of characters, forgetting to include description, producing stilted writing, using too many sentence structures involving "I did...", and not devoting enough attention to the story's "here-and-now" immediacy.

How an Author's Word Choice Conveys Attitude and Shapes Meaning, Style, and Tone

Words can be very powerful. When written words are used with the intent to make an argument or support a position, the words used—and the way in which they are arranged—can have a dramatic effect on the readers. Clichés, colloquialisms, run-on sentences, and misused words are all examples of ways that word choice can negatively affect writing quality. Unless the writer carefully considers word choice, a written work stands to lose credibility.

If a writer's overall intent is to provide a clear meaning on a subject, he or she must consider not only the exact words to use, but also their placement, repetition, and suitability. Academic writing should be intentional and clear, and it should be devoid of awkward or vague descriptions that can easily lead to misunderstandings. When readers find themselves reading and rereading just to gain a clear understanding of the writer's intent, there may be an issue with word choice. Although the words used in academic writing are different from those used in a casual conversation, they shouldn't necessarily be overly academic either. It may be relevant to employ key words that are associated with the subject, but struggling to inject these words into a paper just to sound academic may defeat the purpose. If the message cannot be clearly understood the first time, word choice may be the culprit.

Word choice also conveys the author's attitude and sets a tone. Although each word in a sentence carries a specific denotation, it might also carry positive or negative connotations—and it is the connotations that set the tone and convey the author's attitude. Consider the following similar sentences:

> It was the same old routine that happens every Saturday morning—eat, exercise, chores.
>
> The Saturday morning routine went off without a hitch—eat, exercise, chores.

The first sentence carries a negative connotation with the author's "same old routine" word choice. The feelings and attitudes associated with this phrase suggest that the author is bored or annoyed at the Saturday morning routine. Although the second sentence carries the same topic—explaining the Saturday morning routine—the choice to use the expression "without a hitch" conveys a positive or cheery attitude.

An author's writing style can likewise be greatly affected by word choice. When writing for an academic audience, for example, it is necessary for the author to consider how to convey the message by carefully considering word choice. If the author interchanges between third-person formal writing and second-person informal writing, the author's writing quality and credibility are at risk. Formal writing involves complex sentences, an objective viewpoint, and the use of full words as opposed to the use of a subjective viewpoint, contractions, and first- or second-person usage commonly found in informal writing.

Content validity, the author's ability to support the argument, and the audience's ability to comprehend the written work are all affected by the author's word choice.

An Author's Tone, Message, and Effect

Tone conveys the author's attitude toward the topic and the audience. The tone also reveals their level of confidence on the subject, and whether they intend to bring humor, emotion, or seriousness to the writing. Setting the tone determines how readers will receive the overall message.

In professional writing, it is imperative that authors maintain an appropriate and professional tone that strengthens the writing quality. Framing the writing ahead of time, determining the purpose of the paper, and even considering the author's own bias on the subject will help to set the appropriate tone. Why is the paper being written? What message does the author want to convey, and to whom? Why would the intended audience find this paper interesting, and how does the author expect the audience to react? These are just some of the questions that can help to frame a piece of writing and develop an appropriate tone. To help develop the tone before writing, it sometimes helps to consider the intended audience's perspective.

When an author wishes to convey a clear message but does not want to compromise credibility by writing subjectively, using emphasis can be very effective. This is done by introducing and stressing the important points of the subject in the opening sentence or at the beginning of specific paragraphs. Consider the following:

> Music soothes the soul and captures our hearts. The following is a study on how music has affected North American society during the past five decades.
>
> The following is a study on how music has affected North American society during the past five decades. Music soothes the soul and captures our hearts.

Clearly, the author's attitude toward music is captured in the first sentence of the first example. When the sentences are rearranged in the second example, however, the emphasis is lost. With the subtle positioning of key words and phrases, an author can emphasize important points of the paper and set the tone.

Written tone can either capture readers' attention or turn them away. Considering the intended audience and how readers will perceive the message helps to develop the appropriate tone. In academic or professional writing, writers tend to employ a more serious tone, but serious does not mean dull or boring. Academic writing can engage readers by setting a tone that, although serious, also reveals a connection to readers. Authors who wish to connect with their audience on a more personal level might introduce their topic with a surprising or entertaining fact or quote a famous individual who reinforces the paper's topic.

An Author's Attitude as Revealed in the Tone of a Passage or the Language Used

Some question stems will ask about the author's attitude toward a certain person or idea. While it may seem impossible to know exactly what the author felt toward their subject, there are clues to indicate the emotion, or lack thereof, of the author. Clues like word choice or style will alert readers to the author's attitude.

Some possible words that name the author's attitude are listed below:

- Admiring
- Angry
- Critical
- Defensive
- Enthusiastic
- Humorous
- Moralizing
- Neutral
- Objective

- Patriotic
- Persuasive
- Playful
- Sentimental
- Serious
- Supportive
- Sympathetic
- Unsupportive

An author's tone is the author's attitude toward their subject and is usually indicated by word choice. If an author's attitude toward their subject is one of disdain, the author will show the subject in a negative light, using deflating words or words that are negatively-charged. If an author's attitude toward their subject is one of praise, the author will use agreeable words and show the subject in a positive light. If an author takes a neutral tone towards their subject, their words will be neutral as well, and they probably will show all sides of their subject, not just the negative or positive side.

Style is another indication of the author's attitude and includes aspects such as sentence structure, type of language, and formatting. Sentence structure is how a sentence is put together. Sometimes, short, choppy sentences will indicate a certain tone given the surrounding context, while longer sentences may serve to create a buffer to avoid being too harsh, or may be used to explain additional information. Style may also include formal or informal language. Using formal language to talk about a subject may indicate a level of respect. Using informal language may be used to create an atmosphere of friendliness or familiarity with a subject. Again, it depends on the surrounding context whether or not language is used in a negative or positive way. Style may also include formatting, such as determining the length of paragraphs or figuring out how to address the reader at the very beginning of the text.

Determining the Meaning of Words in Context

The English language is highly complex and writing in English can pose particular challenges. If an author makes repeated mistakes with spelling, grammar, or punctuation, the reader will likely experience difficulty with comprehension. Words with similar spellings can often be misused. Consider the words "affect" and "effect." The former is typically a verb and the latter is typically a noun. The words "except" and "accept" are also commonly misused. Another common error in writing is the misuse of pronouns, including "he," "she," "it," and "they." When pronouns are used to replace a singular noun, the pronouns, too, must remain singular.

Consider the two sentences below:

> A bicycle is considered an antique if *they* were made prior to 1920.
>
> A bicycle is considered an antique if *it* was made prior to 1920.

Because the passage is referring to "a bicycle," the pronoun that replaces this noun must be singular. Pronouns can also lead to ambiguity. Consider the following sentences:

> The peaceful accord between the two nations led to an established truce. **It** was the beginning of a long-lasting alliance.

Does the pronoun "it" in the second sentence refer to the peaceful accord or the established truce? The author's word choice creates ambiguity. The following word choice avoids ambiguity by focusing on the clarity of the message:

> The peaceful accord between the two nations not only led to an established truce but marked the beginning of a long-lasting alliance.

Having a command of the basics in the written structure of a language, however, is not enough to ensure a reader's comprehension. Academic writing requires a rich vocabulary and a logical order. In academic writing, the introduction should be compelling enough to draw in the audience. Within the first few sentences, the argument should be clearly stated, along with background information and subtle or overt reasons why the paper is worth reading. Once the introduction is complete, a well-organized academic paper will begin to unfold the evidence, data, and information that supports the argument. The importance of evidence cannot be overstated because the audience will immediately begin to weigh the evidence. The more objective the data, the more credible the argument. It isn't enough for the author to simply unfold the data. The data should be clearly explained and analyzed in a way that supports the argument, leaving little doubt in the reader's mind about the argument's strength. Concluding the academic paper with a concise summary, restating the evidence, and reasserting the argument without sounding redundant will add strength to the overall message and will leave the audience with a sense of closure.

When readers encounter an unfamiliar word in text, they can use the surrounding context—the overall subject matter, specific chapter/section topic, and especially the immediate sentence context. Among others, one category of context clues is grammar. For example, the position of a word in a sentence and its relationship to the other words can help the reader establish whether the unfamiliar word is a verb, a noun, an adjective, an adverb, etc. This narrows down the possible meanings of the word to one part of speech. However, this may be insufficient. In a sentence that many birds *migrate* twice yearly, the reader can determine the word is a verb, and probably does not mean eat or drink; but it could mean travel, mate, lay eggs, hatch, molt, etc.

Some words can have a number of different meanings depending on how they are used. For example, the word *fly* has a different meaning in each of the following sentences:

- "His trousers have a fly on them."
- "He swatted the fly on his trousers."
- "Those are some fly trousers."
- "They went fly fishing."
- "She hates to fly."
- "If humans were meant to fly, they would have wings."

As strategies, readers can try substituting a familiar word for an unfamiliar one and see whether it makes sense in the sentence. They can also identify other words in a sentence, offering clues to an unfamiliar word's meaning.

Writing: Essay Revision and Editing

Sustaining a Well-Focused, Coherent Discussion

Formal and Informal Language

Formal language is more impersonal than informal language. It is more "buttoned-up" and business-like, adhering to proper grammatical rules. It is used in professional or academic contexts, to convey respect or authority. For example, one would use formal language to write an informative or argumentative essay for school or to address a superior. Formal language avoids contractions, slang, colloquialisms, and first-person pronouns. Formal language uses sentences that are usually more complex and often in passive voice. Punctuation can differ as well. For example, *exclamation points (!)* are used to show strong emotion or can be used as an *interjection* but should be used sparingly in formal writing situations.

Informal language is often used when communicating with family members, friends, peers, and those known more personally. It is more casual, spontaneous, and forgiving in its conformity to grammatical rules and conventions. Informal language is used for personal emails and correspondence between coworkers or other familial relationships. The tone is more relaxed. In informal writing, slang, contractions, clichés, and the first- and second-person are often used.

Elements of the Writing Process

Skilled writers undergo a series of steps that comprise the writing process. The purpose of adhering to a structured approach to writing is to develop clear, meaningful, coherent work.

The stages are pre-writing or planning, organizing, drafting/writing, revising, and editing. Not every writer will necessarily follow all five stages for every project but will judiciously employ the crucial components of the stages for most formal or important work. For example, a brief informal response to a short reading passage may not necessitate the need for significant organization after idea generation, but larger assignments and essays will mandate use of the full process.

Pre-Writing/Planning

Brainstorming

Before beginning the essay, read the prompt thoroughly and make sure you understand its expectations. Brainstorm as many ideas as you can think of that relate to the topic and list them or put them into a graphic organizer. Refer to this list as you organize your essay outline.

Freewriting

Like brainstorming, freewriting is another prewriting activity to help the writer generate ideas. This method involves setting a timer for two or three minutes and writing down all ideas that come to mind about the topic using complete sentences. Once time is up, writers should review the sentences to see what observations have been made and how these ideas might translate into a more unified direction for the topic. Even if sentences lack sense as a whole, freewriting is an excellent way to get ideas onto the page in the very beginning stages of writing. Using complete sentences can make this a bit more challenging than brainstorming, but overall, it is a worthwhile exercise, as it may force the writer to come up with more complete thoughts about the topic.

Take the ideas you generated during pre-writing and organize them in the form of an outline.

Organizing

Although sometimes it is difficult to get going on the brainstorming or prewriting phase, once ideas start flowing, writers often find that they have amassed too many thoughts that will not make for a cohesive and unified essay. During the organization stage, writers should examine the generated ideas, hone in on the important ones central to their main idea, and arrange the points in a logical and effective manner. Writers may also determine that some of the ideas generated in the planning process need further elaboration, potentially necessitating the need for research to gather information to fill the gaps.

Once a writer has chosen their thesis and main argument, selected the most applicable details and evidence, and eliminated the "clutter," it is time to strategically organize the ideas. This is often accomplished with an outline.

Outlining

Outlines are organizational tools that arrange a piece of writing's main ideas and the evidence that supports them. After pre-writing, organize your ideas by topic, select the best ones, and put them into the outline. Be sure to include an introduction, main points, and a conclusion. Typically, it is a good idea to have three main points with at least two pieces of supporting evidence each.

The following displays the format of an outline:

- I. Introduction
    1. Background
    2. Thesis statement
- II. Body
    1. Point A
        - a. Supporting evidence
        - b. Supporting evidence
    2. Point B
        - a. Supporting evidence
        - b. Supporting evidence
    3. Point C
        - a. Supporting evidence
        - b. Supporting evidence
- III. Conclusion
    1. Restatement of main points
    2. Memorable ending

Drafting/Writing

Now it comes time to actually write the essay. In this stage, writers should follow the outline they developed in the brainstorming process and try to incorporate the useful sentences penned in the freewriting exercise. The main goal of this phase is to put all the thoughts together in cohesive sentences and paragraphs.

It is helpful for writers to remember that their work here does not have to be perfect. This process is often referred to as **drafting** because writers are just creating a rough draft of their work. Because of this, writers should avoid getting bogged down on the small details.

Referencing Sources

Anytime a writer quotes or paraphrases another text, they will need to include a citation. A citation is a short description of the work that a quote or information came from. The style manual your teacher wants you to follow will dictate exactly how to format that citation. For example, this is how one would cite a book according to the APA manual of style:

- *Format*: Last name, First initial, Middle initial. (Year Published) *Book Title*. City, State: Publisher.
- *Example*: Sampson, M. R. (1989). *Diaries from an Alien Invasion. Springfield, IL*: Campbell Press.

Revising

Revising involves going back over a piece of writing and improving it. Try to read your essay from the perspective of a potential reader to ensure that it makes sense. When revising, check that the main points are clearly stated, logically organized, and directly supported by the sub-points. Remove unnecessary details that do not contribute to the argument.

The main goal of the revision phase is to improve the essay's flow, cohesiveness, readability, and focus. For example, an essay will make a less persuasive argument if the various pieces of evidence are scattered and presented illogically or clouded with unnecessary thought. Therefore, writers should consider their essay's structure and organization, ensuring that there are smooth transitions between sentences and paragraphs. There should be a discernable introduction and conclusion as well, as these crucial components of an essay provide readers with a blueprint to follow.

Additionally, if the writer includes copious details that do little to enhance the argument, they may actually distract readers from focusing on the main ideas and detract from the strength of their work. The ultimate goal is to retain the purpose or focus of the essay and provide a reader-friendly experience. Because of this, writers often need to delete parts of their essay to improve its flow and focus. Removing sentences, entire paragraphs, or large chunks of writing can be one of the toughest parts of the writing process because it is difficult to part with work one has done. However, these types of cuts can significantly improve one's essay.

Lastly, writers should consider their voice and word choice. The voice should be consistent throughout and maintain a balance between an authoritative and warm style, to both inform and engage readers. One way to alter voice is through word choice. Writers should consider changing weak verbs to stronger ones and selecting more precise language in areas where wording is vague. In some cases, it is useful to modify sentence beginnings or to combine or split up sentences to provide a more varied sentence structure.

Editing

Rather than focusing on content (as is the aim in the revising stage), the editing phase is all about the mechanics of the essay: the syntax, word choice, and grammar. This can be considered the proofreading stage. Successful editing is what sets apart a messy essay from a polished document.

Look for the following types of errors when checking over your work:

- Spelling
- Tense usage
- Punctuation and capitalization

- Unclear, confusing, or incomplete sentences
- Subject/verb and noun/pronoun agreement

One of the most effective ways of identifying grammatical errors, awkward phrases, or unclear sentences is to read the essay out loud. Listening to one's own work can help move the writer from simply the author to the reader.

During the editing phase, it's also important to ensure the essay follows the correct formatting and citation rules as dictated by the assignment.

Recursive Writing Process

While the writing process may have specific steps, the good news is that the process is recursive, meaning the steps need not be completed in a particular order. Many writers find that they complete steps at the same time such as drafting and revising, where the writing and rearranging of ideas occur simultaneously or in very close order. Similarly, a writer may find that a particular section of a draft needs more development and will go back to the prewriting stage to generate new ideas. The steps can be repeated at any time, and the more these steps of the recursive writing process are employed, the better the final product will be.

Practice Makes Prepared Writers

Like any other useful skill, writing only improves with practice. While writing may come more easily to some than others, it is still a skill to be honed and improved. Regardless of a person's natural abilities, there is always room for growth in writing. Practicing the basic skills of writing can aid in preparations for the exam.

One way to build vocabulary and enhance exposure to the written word is through reading. This can be through reading books, but reading of any materials such as newspapers, magazines, and even social media count towards practice with the written word. This also helps to enhance critical reading and thinking skills, through analysis of the ideas and concepts read. Think of each new reading experience as a chance to sharpen these skills.

Developing a Well-Organized Paragraph

A paragraph is a series of connected and related sentences addressing one topic. Writing good paragraphs benefits writers by helping them to stay on target while drafting and revising their work. It benefits readers by helping them to follow the writing more easily. Regardless of how brilliant their ideas may be, writers who do not present them in organized ways will fail to engage readers—and fail to accomplish their writing goals. A fundamental rule for paragraphing is to confine each paragraph to a single idea. When writers find themselves transitioning to a new idea, they should start a new paragraph. However, a paragraph can include several pieces of evidence supporting its single idea; and it can include several points if they are all related to the overall paragraph topic. When writers find each point becoming lengthy, they may choose instead to devote a separate paragraph to every point and elaborate upon each more fully.

An effective paragraph should have these elements:

- Unity: One major discussion point or focus should occupy the whole paragraph from beginning to end.
- Coherence: For readers to understand a paragraph, it must be coherent. Two components of coherence are logical and verbal bridges. In logical bridges, the writer may write consecutive sentences with parallel structure or carry an idea over across sentences. In verbal bridges, writers may repeat key words across sentences.
- A topic sentence: The paragraph should have a sentence that identifies the paragraph's thesis or main idea.
- Sufficient development: To develop a paragraph, writers can use the following techniques after stating their topic sentence:
    - Define terms
    - Cite data
    - Use illustrations, anecdotes, and examples
    - Evaluate causes and effects
    - Analyze the topic
    - Explain the topic using chronological order

A topic sentence identifies the main idea of the paragraph. Some are explicit, some implicit. The topic sentence can appear anywhere in the paragraph. However, many experts advise beginning writers to place each paragraph topic sentence at or near the beginning of its paragraph to ensure that their readers understand what the topic of each paragraph is. Even without having written an explicit topic sentence, the writer should still be able to summarize readily what subject matter each paragraph addresses. The writer must then fully develop the topic that is introduced or identified in the topic sentence. Depending on what the writer's purpose is, they may use different methods for developing each paragraph.

Two main steps in the process of organizing paragraphs and essays should both be completed after determining the writing's main point, while the writer is planning or outlining the work. The initial step is to give an order to the topics addressed in each paragraph. Writers must have logical reasons for putting one paragraph first, another second, etc. The second step is to sequence the sentences in each paragraph. As with the first step, writers must have logical reasons for the order of sentences. Sometimes the work's main point obviously indicates a specific order.

Topic Sentences

To be effective, a topic sentence should be concise so that readers get its point without losing the meaning among too many words. As an example, in *Only Yesterday: An Informal History of the 1920s* (1931), author Frederick Lewis Allen's topic sentence introduces his paragraph describing the 1929 stock market crash: "The Bull Market was dead." This example illustrates the criteria of conciseness and brevity. It is also a strong sentence, expressed clearly and unambiguously. The topic sentence also introduces the paragraph, alerting the reader's attention to the main idea of the paragraph and the subject matter that follows the topic sentence.

Experts often recommend opening a paragraph with the topic sentences to enable the reader to realize the main point of the paragraph immediately. Application letters for jobs and university admissions also benefit from opening with topic sentences. However, positioning the topic sentence at the end of a paragraph is more logical when the paragraph identifies a number of specific details that accumulate evidence and then culminates with a generalization. While paragraphs with extremely obvious main ideas need no topic sentences, more often—and particularly for students learning to write—the topic sentence is the most important sentence in the paragraph. It not only communicates the main idea quickly to readers; it also helps writers produce and control information.

Use of Evidence

When authors write text for the purpose of persuading others to agree with them, they assume a position with the subject matter about which they are writing. Rather than presenting information objectively, the author treats the subject matter subjectively so that the information presented supports their position. In their argumentation, the author presents information that refutes or weakens opposing positions. Another technique authors use in persuasive writing is to anticipate arguments against the position. When students learn to read subjectively, they gain experience with the concept of persuasion in writing and learn to identify positions taken by authors. This enhances their reading comprehension and develops their skills for identifying pro and con arguments and biases.

There are five main parts of the classical argument that writers employ in a well-designed stance:

- Introduction: In the introduction to a classical argument, the author forms a bond with the readers, warms them up to the story, and gives the thesis or theme of the argument.
- Narration: In the narration portion, the author gives a summary of pertinent background information, informs the readers of anything they need to know regarding the circumstances and environment surrounding and/or stimulating the argument, and establishes what is at risk or the stakes in the issue or topic. Literature reviews are common examples of narrations in academic writing.
- Confirmation: The confirmation states all claims supporting the thesis and furnishes evidence for each claim, arranging this material in logical order—e.g. from most obvious to most subtle or strongest to weakest.
- Refutation and Concession: The refutation and concession discuss opposing views and anticipate reader objections without weakening the thesis yet permitting as many oppositions as possible.
- Summation: The summation strengthens the argument while summarizing it, supplying a strong conclusion and showing readers the superiority of the author's solution.

Introduction

A classical argument's introduction must pique reader interest, get readers to perceive the author as a writer, and establish the author's position. Shocking statistics, new ways of restating issues, or quotations or anecdotes focusing the text can pique reader interest. Personal statements, parallel instances, or analogies can also begin introductions—so can bold thesis statements if the author believes readers will agree. Word choice is also important for establishing author image with readers.

The introduction should typically narrow down to a clear, sound thesis statement. If readers cannot locate one sentence in the introduction explicitly stating the writer's position or the point they support, the writer has not refined the introduction sufficiently.

Narration and Confirmation

The narration part of a classical argument should create a context for the argument by explaining the issue to which the argument is responding, and by supplying any background information that influences the issue. Readers should understand the issues, alternatives, and stakes in the argument by the end of the narration to enable them to evaluate the author's claims equitably. The confirmation part of the classical argument enables the author to explain why they believe in the argument's thesis. The author builds a chain of reasoning by developing several individual supporting claims and explaining why that evidence supports each claim and also supports the overall thesis of the argument.

Refutation and Concession and Summation

The classical argument is the model for argumentative/persuasive writing, so authors often use it to establish, promote, and defend their positions. In the refutation aspect of the refutation and concession part of the argument, authors disarm reader opposition by anticipating and answering their possible objections, persuading them to accept the author's viewpoint. In the concession aspect, authors can concede those opposing viewpoints with which they agree. This can avoid weakening the author's thesis while establishing reader respect and goodwill for the author: all refutation and no concession can antagonize readers who disagree with the author's position. In the conclusion part of the classical argument, a less skilled writer might simply summarize or restate the thesis and related claims; however, this does not provide the argument with either momentum or closure. More skilled authors revisit the issues and the narration part of the argument, reminding readers of what is at stake.

Writing: Sentence Revision, Editing, and Completion

Subject-Verb Agreement

Lack of subject-verb agreement is a very common grammatical error. One of the most common examples is when people use a series of nouns as a compound subject with a singular instead of a plural verb. Here is an example:

> Identifying the best books, locating the sellers with the lowest prices, and paying for them *is* difficult

Instead of saying "*are* difficult." Additionally, when a sentence subject is compound, the verb is plural:

> He and his cousins *were* at the reunion.

However, if the conjunction connecting two or more singular nouns or pronouns is "or" or "nor," the verb must be singular to agree:

> That pen or another one like it is in the desk drawer.

If a compound subject includes both a singular noun and a plural one, and they are connected by "or" or "nor," the verb must agree with the subject closest to the verb: "Sally or her sisters go jogging daily"; but "Her sisters or Sally goes jogging daily."

Singular subjects need singular verbs and plural subjects need plural verbs. A common source of agreement errors is not identifying the sentence subject correctly. For example, people often write sentences incorrectly like, "The group of students *were* complaining about the test." The subject is not the plural "students" but the singular "group." Therefore, the correct sentence should read, "The group of students *was* complaining about the test." The inverse also applies, for example, in this incorrect sentence: "The facts in that complicated court case *is* open to question." The subject of the sentence is not the singular "case" but the plural "facts." Hence the sentence would correctly be written: "The facts in that complicated court case *are* open to question." New writers should not be misled by the distance between the subject and verb, especially when another noun with a different number intervenes as in these examples. The verb must agree with the subject, not the noun closest to it.

Pronoun Agreement

Pronouns within a sentence must refer specifically to one noun, known as the *antecedent*. Sometimes, if there are multiple nouns within a sentence, it may be difficult to ascertain which noun belongs to the pronoun. It's important that the pronouns always clearly reference the nouns in the sentence so as not to confuse the reader. Here's an example of an unclear pronoun reference:

> After Catherine cut Libby's hair, David bought her some lunch.

The pronoun in the examples above is *her*. The pronoun could either be referring to *Catherine* or *Libby*. Here are some ways to write the above sentence with a clear pronoun reference:

> After Catherine cut Libby's hair, David bought Libby some lunch.

> David bought Libby some lunch after Catherine cut Libby's hair.

But many times, the pronoun will clearly refer to its antecedent, like the following:

> After David cut Catherine's hair, he bought her some lunch.

Verb Tense

A verb is a word or phrase that expresses action, feeling, or state of being. Verbs explain what their subject is *doing*. Three different types of verbs used in a sentence are action verbs, linking verbs, and helping verbs.

Action verbs show a physical or mental action. Some examples of action verbs are *play, type, jump, write, examine, study, invent, develop,* and *taste*. The following example uses an action verb:

> Kat *imagines* that she is a mermaid in the ocean.

The verb *imagines* explains what Kat is doing: she is imagining being a mermaid.

Linking verbs connect the subject to the predicate without expressing an action. The following sentence shows an example of a linking verb:

> The mango *tastes* sweet.

The verb *tastes* is a linking verb. The mango doesn't *do* the tasting, but the word *taste* links the mango to its predicate, sweet. Most linking verbs can also be used as action verbs, such as *smell, taste, look, seem, grow,* and *sound*. Saying something *is* something else is also an example of a linking verb. For example, if we were to say, "Peaches is a dog," the verb *is* would be a linking verb in this sentence, since it links the subject to its predicate.

Helping verbs assist the main verb in a sentence. Examples of helping verbs are *be, am, is, was, have, has, do, did, can, could, may, might, should,* and *must,* among others. The following are examples of helping verbs:

Jessica *is* planning a trip to Hawaii.

Brenda *does* not like camping.

Xavier *should* go to the dance tonight.

Notice that after each of these helping verbs is the main verb of the sentence: *planning, like,* and *go.* Helping verbs usually show an aspect of time.

Adjectives

Adjectives are descriptive words that modify nouns or pronouns. They may occur before or after the nouns or pronouns they modify in sentences. For example, in "This is a big house," *big* is an adjective modifying or describing the noun *house.* In "This house is big," the adjective is at the end of the sentence rather than preceding the noun it modifies.

A rule of punctuation that applies to adjectives is to separate a series of adjectives with commas. For example, "Their home was a large, rambling, old, white, two-story house." A comma should never separate the last adjective from the noun, though.

Adverbs

Whereas adjectives modify and describe nouns or pronouns, adverbs modify and describe adjectives, verbs, or other adverbs. Adverbs can be thought of as answers to questions in that they describe when, where, how, how often, how much, or to what extent.

Many (but not all) adjectives can be converted to adverbs by adding *–ly.* For example, in "She is a quick learner," *quick* is an adjective modifying *learner.* In "She learns quickly," *quickly* is an adverb modifying *learns.* One exception is *fast. Fast* is an adjective in "She is a fast learner." However, *–ly* is never added to the word *fast;* it retains the same form as an adverb in "She learns fast."

Comma Splices and Run-On Sentences

Comma Splices

Commas separate words or phrases in a series of three or more. The Oxford comma is the last comma in a series. Many people omit this last comma, but many times it causes confusion. Here is an example:

I love my sisters, the Queen of England and Madonna.

This example without the comma implies that the "Queen of England and Madonna" are the speaker's sisters. However, if the speaker was trying to say that they love their sisters, the Queen of England, as well as Madonna, there should be a comma after "Queen of England" to signify this.

Commas also separate two coordinate adjectives ("big, heavy dog") but not cumulative ones, which should be arranged in a particular order for them to make sense ("beautiful ancient ruins").

A comma ends the first of two independent clauses connected by conjunctions. Here is an example:

> I ate a bowl of tomato soup, and I was hungry very shortly after.

Here are some brief rules for commas:

1. Commas follow introductory words like *however, furthermore, well, why,* and *actually,* among others.

2. Commas go between city and state: Houston, Texas.

3. If using a comma between a surname and Jr. or Sr. or a degree like M.D., also follow the whole name with a comma: "Martin Luther King, Jr., wrote that."

4. A comma follows a dependent clause beginning a sentence: "Although she was very small, ..."

5. Nonessential modifying words/phrases/clauses are enclosed by commas: "Wendy, who is Peter's sister, closed the window."

6. Commas introduce or interrupt direct quotations: "She said, 'I hate him.' 'Why,' I asked, 'do you hate him?'"

Run-On Sentences

A run-on sentence combines two or more complete sentences without punctuating them correctly or separating them. For example, a run-on sentence caused by a lack of punctuation is the following:

> There is a malfunction in the computer system however there is nobody available right now who knows how to troubleshoot it.

One correction is, "There is a malfunction in the computer system; however, there is nobody available right now who knows how to troubleshoot it." Another is, "There is a malfunction in the computer system. However, there is nobody available right now who knows how to troubleshoot it."

An example of a comma splice of two sentences is the following:

> Jim decided not to take the bus, he walked home.

Replacing the comma with a period or a semicolon corrects this. Commas that try and separate two independent clauses without a conjunction are considered comma splices.

Improper Punctuation

Rules of Capitalization

The first word of any document, and of each new sentence, is capitalized. Proper nouns, like names and adjectives derived from proper nouns, should also be capitalized. Here are some examples:

- Grand Canyon
- Pacific Palisades
- Golden Gate Bridge
- Freudian slip

- Shakespearian, Spenserian, or Petrarchan sonnet
- Irish song

Some exceptions are adjectives, originally derived from proper nouns, which through time and usage are no longer capitalized, like *quixotic*, *herculean*, or *draconian*. Capitals draw attention to specific instances of people, places, and things.

Some categories that should be capitalized include the following:

- Brand names
- Companies
- Months
- Governmental divisions or agencies
- Historical eras
- Major historical events
- Holidays
- Institutions
- Famous buildings
- Ships and other manmade constructions
- Natural and manmade landmarks
- Territories
- Nicknames
- Organizations
- Planets
- Nationalities
- Tribes
- Religions
- Names of religious deities
- Roads
- Special occasions, like the Cannes Film Festival or the Olympic Games

Exceptions

Related to American government, capitalize the noun Congress but not the related adjective congressional. Capitalize the noun U.S. Constitution, but not the related adjective constitutional. Many experts advise leaving the adjectives federal and state in lowercase, as in federal regulations or state water board, and only capitalizing these when they are parts of official titles or names, like Federal Communications Commission or State Water Resources Control Board. While the names of the other planets in the solar system are capitalized as names, Earth is more often capitalized only when being described specifically as a planet, like Earth's orbit, but lowercase otherwise since it is used not only as a proper noun but also to mean *land*, *ground*, *soil*, etc.

Names of animal species or breeds are not capitalized unless they include a proper noun. Then, only the proper noun is capitalized. Antelope, black bear, and yellow-bellied sapsucker are not capitalized. However, Bengal tiger, German shepherd, Australian shepherd, French poodle, and Russian blue cat are capitalized.

Stars, moons, and suns are not capitalized, but planets specific names and the Sun and the Moon, when referring to the Earth's specific sun and moon, are capitalized as proper nouns. Medical conditions like tuberculosis or diabetes are lowercase; again, exceptions are proper nouns, like Epstein-Barr syndrome,

Alzheimer's disease, and Down syndrome. Seasons and related terms like winter solstice or autumnal equinox are lowercase. Plants, including fruits and vegetables, like poinsettia, celery, or avocados, are not capitalized unless they include proper names, like Douglas fir, Jerusalem artichoke, Damson plums, or Golden Delicious apples.

Titles and Names

When official titles precede names, they should be capitalized, except when there is a comma between the title and name. But if a title follows or replaces a name, it should not be capitalized. For example, "the president" without a name is not capitalized, as in "The president addressed Congress." But with a name it is capitalized, like "President Obama addressed Congress." Or, "Chair of the Board Janet Yellen was appointed by President Obama." One exception is that some publishers and writers nevertheless capitalize President, Queen, Pope, etc., when these are not accompanied by names to show respect for these high offices. However, many writers in America object to this practice for violating democratic principles of equality. Occupations before full names are not capitalized, like owner Mark Cuban, director Martin Scorsese, or coach Roger McDowell.

Some universal rules for capitalization in composition titles include capitalizing the following:

- The first and last words of the title
- Forms of the verb *to be* and all other verbs
- Pronouns
- The word *not*

Universal rules for NOT capitalizing include the articles *the, a,* or *an*; the conjunctions *and, or,* or *nor*, and the preposition *to,* or *to* as part of the infinitive form of a verb. The exception to all of these is UNLESS any of them is the first or last word in the title, in which case they are capitalized. Other words are subject to differences of opinion and differences among various stylebooks or methods. These include *as, but, if,* and *or,* which some capitalize and others do not. Some authorities say no preposition should ever be capitalized; some say prepositions five or more letters long should be capitalized. The *Associated Press Stylebook* advises capitalizing prepositions longer than three letters (like *about, across,* or *with*).

Fragments and Parallelism

Fragments

Sentence fragments are caused by absent subjects, absent verbs, or dangling/uncompleted dependent clauses. Every sentence must have a subject and a verb to be complete. An example of a fragment is "Raining all night long," because there is no subject present. "It was raining all night long" is one correction. Another example of a sentence fragment is the second part in "Many scientists think in unusual ways. Einstein, for instance." The second phrase is a fragment because it has no verb. One correction is "Many scientists, like Einstein, think in unusual ways." Finally, look for "cliffhanger" words like *if, when, because,* or *although* that introduce dependent clauses, which cannot stand alone without an independent clause. For example, to correct the sentence fragment "If you get home early," add an independent clause: "If you get home early, we can go dancing."

Parallelism

Parallel structure in a sentence matches the forms of sentence components. Any sentence containing more than one description or phrase should keep them consistent in wording and form. Readers can easily follow writers' ideas when they are written in parallel structure, making it an important element of correct sentence construction. For example, this sentence lacks parallelism: "Our coach is a skilled manager, a clever strategist, and works hard." The first two phrases are parallel, but the third is not. Correction: "Our coach is a skilled manager, a clever strategist, and a hard worker." Now all three phrases match in form.

Here is another example:

> Fred intercepted the ball, escaped tacklers, and a touchdown was scored.

This is also non-parallel. Here is the sentence corrected:

> Fred intercepted the ball, escaped tacklers, and scored a touchdown.

Subordination and Coordination

One way writers can increase fluency is by varying the beginnings of sentences. Writers do this by starting most of their sentences with different words and phrases rather than monotonously repeating the same ones across multiple sentences. Another way writers can increase fluency is by varying the lengths of sentences. Since run-on sentences are incorrect, writers make sentences longer by also converting them from simple to compound, complex, and compound-complex sentences. The coordination and subordination involved in these also give the text more variation and interest, hence more fluency.

Here are a few more ways writers can increase fluency:

- Varying the transitional language and conjunctions used makes sentences more fluent.
- Writing sentences with a variety of rhythms by using prepositional phrases.
- Varying sentence structure adds fluency.

Logical Transitions

In writing, some sentences naturally lead to others, whereas in other cases, a new sentence expresses a new idea. Transitional phrases connect sentences and the ideas they convey, which makes the writing coherent. Transitional language also guides the reader from one thought to the next. For example, when pointing out an objection to the previous idea, starting a sentence with "However," "But," or "On the other hand" is transitional. When adding another idea or detail, writers use "Also," "In addition," "Furthermore," "Further," "Moreover," "Not only," etc. Readers have difficulty perceiving connections between ideas without such transitional wording.

Sentence Fluency

For fluent composition, writers must use a variety of sentence types and structures, and also ensure that they smoothly flow together when they are read. To accomplish this, they must first be able to identify fluent writing when they read it. This includes being able to distinguish among simple, compound, complex, and compound-complex sentences in text; to observe variations among sentence types, lengths, and beginnings; and to notice figurative language and understand how it augments sentence length and imparts musicality. Once students/writers recognize superior fluency, they should revise their own writing to be more readable and fluent. They must be able to apply acquired skills to revisions before being able to apply them to new drafts.

One strategy for revising writing to increase its sentence fluency is flipping sentences. This involves rearranging the word order in a sentence without deleting, changing, or adding any words. For example, the student or other writer who has written the sentence, "We went bicycling on Saturday" can revise it to, "On Saturday, we went bicycling." Another technique is using appositives. An appositive is a phrase or word that renames or identifies another adjacent word or phrase. Writers can revise for sentence fluency by inserting main phrases/words from one shorter sentence into another shorter sentence, combining them into one longer sentence, e.g. from "My cat Peanut is a gray and brown tabby. He loves hunting rats." to "My cat Peanut, a gray and brown tabby, loves hunting rats." Revisions can also connect shorter sentences by using conjunctions and commas and removing repeated words: "Scott likes eggs. Scott is allergic to eggs" becomes "Scott likes eggs, but he is allergic to them."

One technique for revising writing to increase sentence fluency is "padding" short, simple sentences by adding phrases that provide more details specifying why, how, when, and/or where something took place. For example, a writer might have these two simple sentences: "I went to the market. I purchased a cake." To revise these, the writer can add the following informative dependent and independent clauses and prepositional phrases, respectively: "Before my mother woke up, I sneaked out of the house and went to the supermarket. As a birthday surprise, I purchased a cake for her." When revising sentences to make them longer, writers must also punctuate them correctly to change them from simple sentences to compound, complex, or compound-complex sentences.

Context Clues

Readers can often figure out what unfamiliar words mean without interrupting their reading to look them up in dictionaries by examining context. Context includes the other words or sentences in a passage. One common context clue is the root word and any affixes (prefixes/suffixes). Another common context clue is a synonym or definition included in the sentence. Sometimes both exist in the same sentence. Here's an example:

> Scientists who study birds are *ornithologists*.

Many readers may not know the word *ornithologist*. However, the example contains a definition (scientists who study birds). The reader may also have the ability to analyze the suffix (*-logy*, meaning the study of) and root (*ornitho-*, meaning bird).

Another common context clue is a sentence that shows differences. Here's an example:

> Birds *incubate* their eggs outside of their bodies, unlike mammals.

Some readers may be unfamiliar with the word *incubate*. However, since we know that "unlike mammals," birds incubate their eggs outside of their bodies, we can infer that *incubate* has something to do with keeping eggs warm outside the body until they are hatched.

In addition to analyzing the etymology of a word's root and affixes and extrapolating word meaning from sentences that contrast an unknown word with an antonym, readers can also determine word meanings from sentence context clues based on logic. Here's an example:

> Birds are always looking out for predators that could attack their young.

The reader who is unfamiliar with the word *predator* could determine from the context of the sentence that predators usually prey upon baby birds and possibly other young animals. Readers might also use the context clue of etymology here, as *predator* and *prey* have the same root.

Analyzing Word Parts

By learning some of the etymologies of words and their parts, readers can break new words down into components and analyze their combined meanings. For example, the root word *soph* is Greek for wise or knowledge. Knowing this informs the meanings of English words including *sophomore, sophisticated,* and *philosophy.* Those who also know that *phil* is Greek for love will realize that *philosophy* means the love of knowledge. They can then extend this knowledge of *phil* to understand *philanthropist* (one who loves people), *bibliophile* (book lover), *philharmonic* (loving harmony), *hydrophilic* (water-loving), and so on. In addition, *phob-* derives from the Greek *phobos,* meaning fear. This informs all words ending with it as meaning fear of various things: *acrophobia* (fear of heights), *arachnophobia* (fear of spiders), *claustrophobia* (fear of enclosed spaces), *ergophobia* (fear of work), and *hydrophobia* (fear of water), among others.

Some English word origins from other languages, like ancient Greek, are found in large numbers and varieties of English words. An advantage of the shared ancestry of these words is that once readers recognize the meanings of some Greek words or word roots, they can determine or at least get an idea of what many different English words mean. As an example, the Greek word *métron* means to measure, a measure, or something used to measure; the English word *meter* derives from it. Knowing this informs many other English words, including *altimeter, barometer, diameter, hexameter, isometric,* and *metric.* While readers must know the meanings of the other parts of these words to decipher their meaning fully, they already have an idea that they are all related in some way to measures or measuring.

While all English words derive from a proto-language known as Indo-European, many of them historically came into the developing English vocabulary later, from sources like the ancient Greeks' language, the Latin used throughout Europe and much of the Middle East during the reign of the Roman Empire, and the Anglo-Saxon languages used by England's early tribes. In addition to classic revivals and native foundations, by the Renaissance era other influences included French, German, Italian, and Spanish. Today we can often discern English word meanings by knowing common roots and affixes, particularly from Greek and Latin.

The following is a list of common prefixes and their meanings:

Prefix	Definition	Examples
a-	without	atheist, agnostic
ad-	to, toward	advance
ante-	before	antecedent, antedate
anti-	opposing	antipathy, antidote
auto-	self	autonomy, autobiography
bene-	well, good	benefit, benefactor
bi-	two	bisect, biennial
bio-	life	biology, biosphere
chron-	time	chronometer, synchronize
circum-	around	circumspect, circumference
com-	with, together	commotion, complicate
contra-	against, opposing	contradict, contravene
cred-	belief, trust	credible, credit
de-	from	depart
dem-	people	demographics, democracy
dis-	away, off, down, not	dissent, disappear
equi-	equal, equally	equivalent
ex-	former, out of	extract
for-	away, off, from	forget, forswear
fore-	before, previous	foretell, forefathers
homo-	same, equal	homogenized
hyper-	excessive, over	hypercritical, hypertension
in-	in, into	intrude, invade
inter-	among, between	intercede, interrupt
mal-	bad, poorly, not	malfunction
micr-	small	microbe, microscope
mis-	bad, poorly, not	misspell, misfire
mono-	one, single	monogamy, monologue
mor-	die, death	mortality, mortuary
neo-	new	neolithic, neoconservative
non-	not	nonentity, nonsense
omni-	all, everywhere	omniscient
over-	above	overbearing
pan-	all, entire	panorama, pandemonium
para-	beside, beyond	parallel, paradox
phil-	love, affection	philosophy, philanthropic
poly-	many	polymorphous, polygamous
pre-	before, previous	prevent, preclude
prim-	first, early	primitive, primary
pro-	forward, in place of	propel, pronoun
re-	back, backward, again	revoke, recur

Prefix	Definition	Examples
sub-	under, beneath	subjugate, substitute
super-	above, extra	supersede, supernumerary
trans-	across, beyond, over	transact, transport
ultra-	beyond, excessively	ultramodern, ultrasonic, ultraviolet
un-	not, reverse of	unhappy, unlock
vis-	to see	visage, visible

The following is a list of common suffixes and their meanings:

Suffix	Definition	Examples
-able	likely, able to	capable, tolerable
-ance	act, condition	acceptance, vigilance
-ard	one that does excessively	drunkard, wizard
-ation	action, state	occupation, starvation
-cy	state, condition	accuracy, captaincy
-er	one who does	teacher
-esce	become, grow, continue	convalesce, acquiesce
-esque	in the style of, like	picturesque, grotesque
-ess	feminine	waitress, lioness
-ful	full of, marked by	thankful, zestful
-ible	able, fit	edible, possible, divisible
-ion	action, result, state	union, fusion
-ish	suggesting, like	churlish, childish
-ism	act, manner, doctrine	barbarism, socialism
-ist	doer, believer	monopolist, socialist
-ition	action, result, state,	sedition, expedition
-ity	quality, condition	acidity, civility
-ize	cause to be, treat with	sterilize, mechanize, criticize
-less	lacking, without	hopeless, countless
-like	like, similar	childlike, dreamlike
-ly	like, of the nature of	friendly, positively
-ment	means, result, action	refreshment, disappointment
-ness	quality, state	greatness, tallness
-or	doer, office, action	juror, elevator, honor
-ous	marked by, given to	religious, riotous
-some	apt to, showing	tiresome, lonesome
-th	act, state, quality	warmth, width
-ty	quality, state	enmity, activity

Practice Quiz

The next three questions are based off the following passage from Virginia Woolf's Mrs. Dalloway*:*

> What a lark! What a plunge! For so it had always seemed to her, when, with a little squeak of the hinges, which she could hear now, she had burst open the French windows and plunged at Bourton into the open air. How fresh, how calm, stiller than this of course, the air was in the early morning; like the flap of a wave; the kiss of a wave; chill and sharp and yet (for a girl of eighteen as she then was) solemn, feeling as she did, standing there at the open window, that something awful was about to happen; looking at the flowers, at the trees with the smoke winding off them and the rooks rising, falling; standing and looking until Peter Walsh said, "Musing among the vegetables?"—was that it?—"I prefer men to cauliflowers"—was that it? He must have said it at breakfast one morning when she had gone out on to the terrace—Peter Walsh. He would be back from India one of these days, June or July, she forgot which, for his letters were awfully dull; it was his sayings one remembered; his eyes, his pocket-knife, his smile, his grumpiness and, when millions of things had utterly vanished—how strange it was!—a few sayings like this about cabbages.

1. The passage is reflective of which of the following types of writing?
   a. Persuasive
   b. Expository
   c. Technical
   d. Narrative

2. What was the narrator feeling right before Peter Walsh's voice distracted her?
   a. A spark of excitement for the morning
   b. Anger at the larks
   c. A sense of foreboding
   d. Confusion at the weather

3. What is the main point of the passage?
   a. To present the events leading up to a party.
   b. To show the audience that the narrator is resentful towards Peter.
   c. To introduce Peter Walsh back into the narrator's memory.
   d. To reveal what mornings are like in the narrator's life.

The next question is based on the following passage from The Federalist No. 78 *by Alexander Hamilton.*

> According to the plan of the convention, all judges who may be appointed by the United States are to hold their offices *during good behavior*, which is conformable to the most approved of the State constitutions and among the rest, to that of this State. Its propriety having been drawn into question by the adversaries of that plan, is no light symptom of the rage for objection, which disorders their imaginations and judgments. The standard of good behavior for the continuance in office of the judicial magistracy, is certainly one of the most valuable of the modern improvements in the practice of government. In a monarchy it is an excellent barrier to the despotism of the prince; in a republic it is a no less excellent barrier to the encroachments and oppressions of the representative body. And it is the best expedient which can be devised in any government, to secure a steady, upright, and impartial administration of the laws.

4. What is Hamilton's point in this excerpt?
    a. To show the audience that despotism within a monarchy is no longer the standard practice in the states.
    b. Hamilton is trying to convince the audience that judges holding their positions based on good behavior is a practical way to avoid corruption.
    c. To persuade the audience that having good behavior should be the primary characteristic of a person in a government body and that their voting habits should reflect this.
    d. To convey the position that judges who serve for a lifetime will not be perfect and, therefore, should be forgiven for their bad behavior when it arises.

5. Felicia knew she had to be <u>prudent</u> if she was going to cross the bridge over the choppy water; one wrong move and she would be falling toward the rocky rapids.

> Which of the following is the definition of the underlined word based on the context of the sentence above?

    a. Patient
    b. Afraid
    c. Dangerous
    d. Careful

The next three questions are based on the following passage from The Life, Crime, and Capture of John Wilkes Booth *by George Alfred Townsend.*

> (1) The box in which the President sat consisted of two boxes turned into one. As on all occasions when a state party visited the theater, the middle partition was removed. (2) The box was on a level with the dress circle; about twelve feet above the stage. (3) There were two entrances—the door nearest to the wall having been closed and locked; the door nearest the balustrades of the dress circle, and at right angles with it, being open and left open, after the visitors had entered. (4) The interior was carpeted, lined with crimson paper, and furnished with a sofa covered with crimson velvet, three arm chairs similarly covered, and six cane-bottomed chairs.

> (5) President Lincoln took one of the arm-chairs and seated himself in the front of the box, in the angle nearest the audience, where, partially screened from observation, he had the best view of what was transpiring on the stage. (6) Mrs. Lincoln sat next to him, and Miss Harris in the opposite angle nearest the stage. (7) Major Rathbone sat just behind Mrs. Lincoln and Miss Harris. (8) These four were the only persons in the box.

> (9) The play proceeded, although "Our American Cousin," without Mr. Sothern, has, since that gentleman's departure from this country, been justly esteemed a very dull affair. (10) The audience at Ford's Theater including Mrs. Lincoln seemed to enjoy it very much. (11) The worthy wife of the President leaned forward, her hand upon her husband's knee, watching every scene in the drama with amused attention.

6. In context, which of the following is the best way to revise and combine sentences 1 & 2 (reproduced below)?

> The box in which the President sat consisted of two boxes turned into one. As on all occasions when a state party visited the theater, the middle partition was removed.

a. The box in which the President sat consisted of two boxes turned into one, the middle partition was removed, as on all occasions when a state party visited the theater.
b. The middle partition being removed due to the state party visiting the theater, the box in which the President sat two boxes turned into one.
c. The box in which the President sat consisted of two boxes turned into one, the middle partition being removed, as on all occasions when a state party visited the theater.
d. As on all occasions when a state party visited the theater, the middle partition as in the box in which the President sat consisted of two boxes turned into one.

7. In context, which of the following phrases is best to insert at the beginning of sentence 8 (reproduced below)?

> These four were the only persons in the box.

a. Next,
b. After the fact,
c. Immediately following,
d. All in all,

8. In context, which is the best revision to sentence 10 (reproduced below)?

> The audience at Ford's Theatre including Mrs. Lincoln seemed to enjoy it very much.

a. The audience at Ford's Theater; including Mrs. Lincoln; seemed to enjoy it very much.
b. The audience at Ford's Theater, including Mrs. Lincoln, seemed to enjoy it very much.
c. The audience at Fords Theater, including Mrs. Lincoln, seemed to enjoy it very much.
d. The audience at Fords Theater including Mrs. Lincoln seemed to enjoy it very much.

Select the choice you think best fits the underlined part of the sentence. If the original is the best answer choice, then choose Choice A.

9. After getting a cat, Billy <u>learned the meaning of</u> take care of something other than himself.
a. learned the meaning of
b. learned what it meant to
c. meant to learning the
d. made to learn of the

10. A toothache does not always denote tooth decay or a cavity; sometimes <u>it was the direct</u> result of having a sinus infection.
a. it was the direct
b. it be the direct
c. it directly was
d. it is the direct

See answers on the next page.

Answer Explanations

1. D: The passage is reflective of a narrative. A narrative is used to tell a story, as we see the narrator trying to do in this passage by using memory and dialogue. Choice *A*, persuasive writing, uses rhetorical devices to try to convince the audience of something, and there is no persuasion or argument within this passage. Choice *B*, expository, is a type of writing used to inform the reader. Choice *C*, technical writing, is usually used within business communications and uses technical language to explain procedures or concepts to someone within the same technical field.

2. C: The narrator, after feeling excitement for the morning, recalls an interaction with Peter Walsh when she was 18. She states that on that day she had felt "that something awful was about to happen," which is another way to say that she had a sense of foreboding. The narrator mentions larks and weather in the passage, but there is no proof of anger or confusion at either of them.

3. C: Walsh back into the narrator's memory. Choice *A* is incorrect because, although the novel *Mrs. Dalloway* is about events leading up to a party, the passage does not mention anything about a party. Choice *B* is incorrect; the narrator calls Peter *dull* at one point, but the rest of her memories of him are more positive. Choice *D* is incorrect; although morning is described within the first few sentences of the passage, the passage quickly switches to a description of Peter Walsh and the narrator's memories of him.

4. B: Hamilton is trying to convince the audience that judges holding their positions based on good behavior is a practical way to avoid corruption. Choice *A* is incorrect because although he mentions the condition of good behavior as a barrier to despotism, he does not discuss it as a practice in the states. Choice *C* is incorrect because the author does not argue that the audience should vote based on judges' behavior, but rather that good behavior should be the condition for holding their office. Choice *D* is not represented in the passage, so it is incorrect.

5. D: Felicia had to be prudent, or *careful*, if she was going to cross the bridge over the choppy water. Choice *A*, *patient*, is close to the word *careful*. However, *careful* makes more sense here. Choices *B* and *C* don't make sense within the context—Felicia wasn't hoping to be *afraid* or *dangerous* while crossing over the bridge but was hoping to be *careful* to avoid falling.

6. C: Choice *C* is the best answer: "The box in which the President sat consisted of two boxes turned into one, the middle partition being removed, as on all occasions when a state party visited the theater." Choice *A* is incorrect because the first comma is a comma splice. A comma splice incorrectly joins two independent clauses with a comma rather than a period or semicolon. Choice *B* is incorrect; the phrase "the box in which the President sat two boxes turned into one" is missing a verb between the words "sat" and "two." Choice *D* is incorrect because the meaning is changed; the middle partition is not said to have been removed as in the original sentence.

7. D: The phrase "All in all" is the best fit here because it means taking everything in mind, or in sum, there were 4 people gathered. The other phrases don't quite fit the context and are meant for more of a transitional phrase.

8. B: Choice *B* is the best answer. The interrupting phrase "including Mrs. Lincoln" should be separated by commas. If we take out this phrase, the sentence would stand as an independent clause by itself, so the commas are needed. Choice *A* is incorrect; semicolons should only be used to separate independent clauses, not interrupting phrases. Choice *C* is incorrect; the word "Ford's" is possessive because it's known as "Ford's theater," not Fords plural. Choice *D* is incorrect; again, the "Fords" is plural instead of possessive, and there are no commas separating the interrupting phrase.

9. B: Choice *B* is the correct answer: "Billy learned what it meant to take care of something other than himself." Choice *A* is awkwardly worded and doesn't flow with the rest of the sentence. Choice *C*, "meant to learning" is also incorrect because it is missing the word "to" after the phrase, and the word "learning" is also in an incorrect verb form. Choice *D* is also worded awkwardly and makes the latter part of the sentence unclear.

10. D: The sentence should read: "sometimes it is the direct result of having a sinus infection." Choice *A* is incorrect because "was" is in past tense, and the rest of the sentence is in present tense. Choice *B* is incorrect because "it be" is not proper subject/verb agreement. "Be" should be conjugated to "is" as a be-verb. Finally, Choice *C* is incorrect; we have a past tense "was" which is incorrect, we are missing the article "the," and the choice is poorly worded.

Practice Test #1

Mathematics

1. Given the function $f(x) = 4x - 2$, what is the correct form of the simplified difference quotient:

$$\frac{f(x+h) - f(x)}{h}$$

a. $4x - 1$
b. $4x$
c. 4
d. $4x + h$

2. How many possible positive zeros does the following polynomial function have?

$$f(x) = x^4 - 3x^3 + 2x + x - 3$$

a. 4
b. 3
c. 2
d. 1

3. The sides of a triangle have the following lengths: 4 inches, 4 inches, and 7.5 inches. If the smallest angle within the triangle has a measurement of 20°, what is the measure of the largest angle?

a. 100°
b. 140°
c. 120°
d. 160°

4. On the first four tests this semester, a student received the following scores out of 100: 74, 76, 82, and 84. The student must earn at least what score on the fifth test to receive a B in the class? Assume that the final test is also out of 100 points and that to receive a B in the class, he must have at least an 80% average.

a. 80
b. 84
c. 82
d. 78

5. Evaluate the expression: $5b^2 - 3ab + 10a$, when $a = 3$ and $b = -1$.

a. 84
b. 26
c. 44
d. 30

6. What is the volume of the given figure?

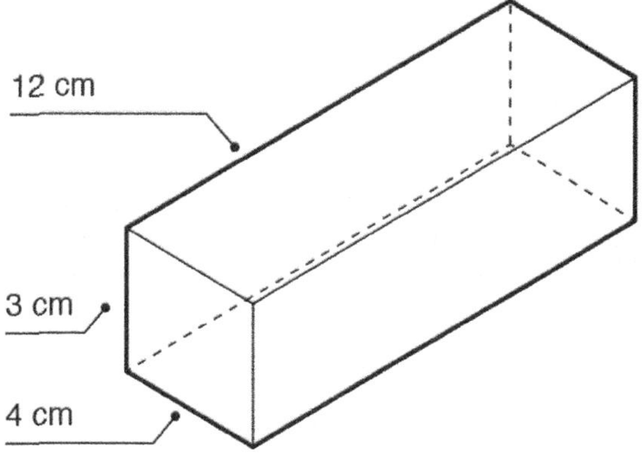

a. $36\ cm^2$
b. $144\ cm^3$
c. $72\ cm^3$
d. $36\ cm^3$

7. If Oscar's bank account totaled $4,000 in March and $4,900 in June, what was the rate of change in his bank account over those three months?
a. $900 a month
b. $300 a month
c. $4,900 a month
d. $100 a month

8. What is the perimeter of the following figure?

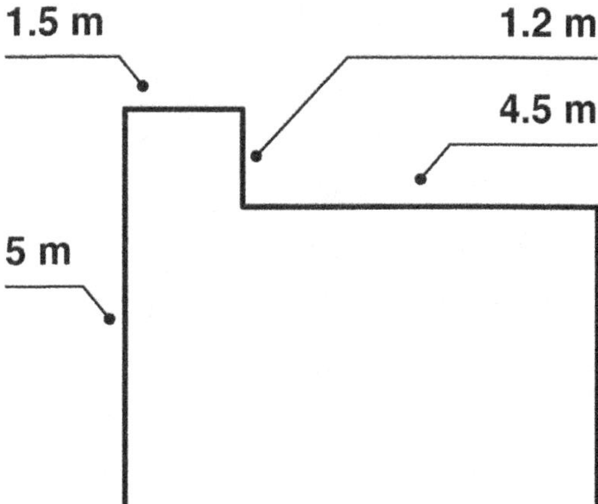

a. 13.4 m
b. 22 m
c. 12.2 m
d. 22.5 m

9. Simplify: $\frac{x^3+4x^2y-5xy^2}{x^2-xy}$.

a. $x - y$
b. $x^2 + 5xy$
c. $x + 5y$
d. $x^2 - xy$

10. A local candy store reports that, of the 100 customers that bought suckers, 35 of them bought cherry. If all 100 sucker wrappers are put in a jar, and 2 are drawn at random, what is the probability that both are cherry? Enter your answer in lowest terms.

a. $\frac{119}{990}$
b. $\frac{35}{100}$
c. $\frac{49}{400}$
d. $\frac{69}{99}$

11. The number of members of the House of Representatives varies directly with the total population in a state. If the state of New York has 19,800,000 residents and has 27 total representatives, how many should Ohio have with a population of 11,800,000?

a. 10
b. 16
c. 11
d. 5

12. The table below shows tickets purchased during the week for entry to the local zoo. What is the mean of adult tickets sold for the week?

Day of the Week	Age	Tickets Sold
Monday	Adult	22
Monday	Child	30
Tuesday	Adult	16
Tuesday	Child	15
Wednesday	Adult	24
Wednesday	Child	23
Thursday	Adult	19
Thursday	Child	26
Friday	Adult	29
Friday	Child	38

a. 24.2
b. 21
c. 22
d. 26.4

13. What is the mode for the grades shown in the chart below?

Science Grades	
Jerry	65
Bill	95
Anna	80
Beth	95
Sara	85
Ben	72
Jordan	98

a. 65
b. 33
c. 95
d. 90

14. Which of the following is the result when solving the equation $4(x+5)+6=2(2x+3)$?
a. $x=26$
b. $x=6$
c. All real numbers
d. There is no solution

15. Two consecutive integers exist such that the sum of three times the first and two less than the second is equal to 411. What are those integers?
a. 103 and 104
b. 104 and 105
c. 102 and 103
d. 100 and 101

16. Which are the values of x that satisfy the equation $2x^2-10x+3=0$?
a. $5\pm\frac{\sqrt{19}}{2}$
b. $5\pm\sqrt{19}$
c. $\frac{5}{2}\pm\frac{\sqrt{19}}{2}$
d. $-\frac{5}{2}\pm\sqrt{19}$

17. What is the simplified form of $(4y^3)^4(3y^7)^2$?
a. $12y^{26}$
b. $2{,}304y^{16}$
c. $12y^{14}$
d. $2{,}304y^{26}$

18. What type of relationship is there between age and attention span as represented in the graph below?

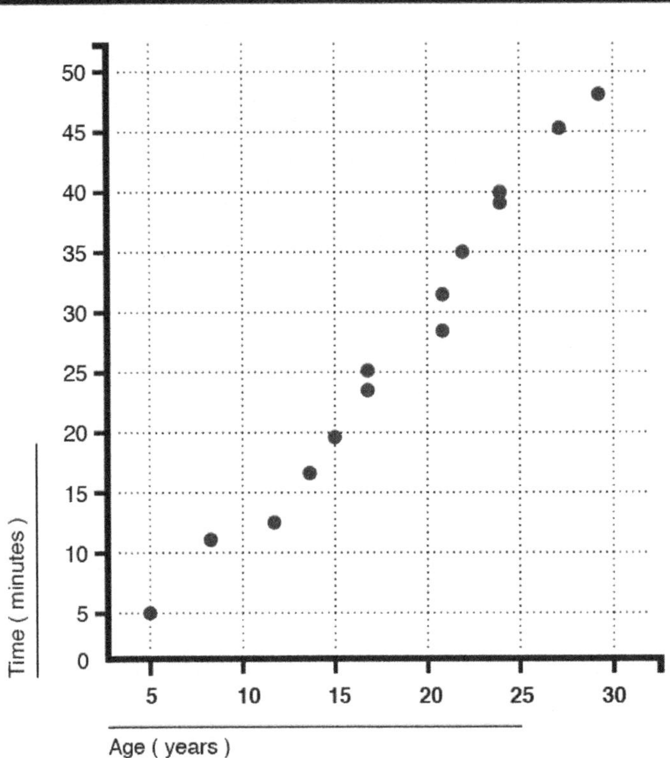

a. No correlation
b. Positive correlation
c. Negative correlation
d. Weak correlation

19. A grocery store sold 48 bags of apples in one day. If 9 of the bags contained Granny Smith apples and the rest contained Red Delicious apples, what is the ratio of bags of Granny Smith to bags of Red Delicious that were sold?

a. 48:9
b. 39:9
c. 9:48
d. 9:39

20. The mass of the Moon is about 7.348×10^{22} kilograms, and the mass of Earth is 5.972×10^{24} kilograms. How many times greater is Earth's mass than the Moon's mass?

a. 8.127×10^{1}
b. 8.127
c. 812.7
d. 8.127×10^{-1}

English Language Arts and Reading

The following is an excerpt from Architecture and Democracy *by Claude Bragdon. The next four questions are based on the following passage:*

The world war represents not the triumph, but the birth of democracy. The true ideal of democracy—the rule of a people by the *demos*, or group soul—is a thing unrealized. How then is it possible to consider or discuss an architecture of democracy—the shadow of a shade? It is not possible to do so with any degree of finality, but by an intention of consciousness upon this juxtaposition of ideas—architecture and democracy—signs of the times may yield new meanings, relations may emerge between things apparently unrelated, and the future, always existent in every present moment, may be evoked by that strange magic which resides in the human mind.

Architecture, at its worst as at its best, reflects always a true image of the thing that produced it; a building is revealing even though it is false, just as the face of a liar tells the thing his words endeavor to conceal. This being so, let us make such architecture as is ours declare to us our true estate.

The architecture of the United States, from the period of the Civil War, up to the beginning of the present crisis, everywhere reflects a struggle to be free of a vicious and depraved form of feudalism, grown strong under the very ægis of democracy. The qualities that made feudalism endeared and enduring; qualities written in beauty on the cathedral cities of mediaeval Europe—faith, worship, loyalty, magnanimity—were either vanished or banished from this pseudo-democratic, aridly scientific feudalism, leaving an inheritance of strife and tyranny—a strife grown mean, a tyranny grown prudent, but full of sinister power the weight of which we have by no means ceased to feel.

Power, strangely mingled with timidity; ingenuity, frequently misdirected; ugliness, the result of a false ideal of beauty—these in general characterize the architecture of our immediate past; an architecture "without ancestry or hope of posterity," an architecture devoid of coherence or conviction; willing to lie, willing to steal. What impression such a city as Chicago or Pittsburgh might have made upon some denizen of those cathedral-crowned feudal cities of the past we do not know. He would certainly have been amazed at its giant energy, and probably revolted at its grimy dreariness. We are wont to pity the mediaeval man for the dirt he lived in, even while smoke greys our sky and dirt permeates the very air we breathe: we think of castles as grim and cathedrals as dim, but they were beautiful and gay with color compared with the grim, dim canyons of our city streets.

1. Which of the following does the author NOT consider to be a characteristic of modern architecture?
    a. Power, strangely mingled with timidity
    b. Ugliness as a result of the false ideal of beauty
    c. Giant energy with grimy dreariness
    d. Grim castles and dim cathedrals

2. By stating that "Architecture, at its worst as at its best, reflects always a true image of the thing that produced it," the author most likely intends to suggest that:
   a. People always create buildings to look like themselves.
   b. Architecture gets more grim, drab, and depressing as the years go by.
   c. Architecture reflects—in shape, color, and form—the attitude of the society which built it.
   d. Modern architecture is a lot like democracy because it is uniform yet made up of more pieces than your traditional architecture.

3. The author refers to "mediaeval man" in the fourth paragraph in order to:
   a. Make the audience look at feudalism with a sense of nostalgia and desire.
   b. Make the audience feel gratitude for modern comforts such as architecture.
   c. Make the audience realize the irony produced from pitying him.
   d. Make the audience look back at feudalism as a time which was dark and dreary.

4. The author's attitude toward modern architecture can best be characterized as:
   a. Narcissistic
   b. Aggrieved
   c. Virtuous
   d. Sarcastic

The next question is based on the following passage:

> A surging, seething, murmuring crowd of beings that are human only in name, for to the eye and ear they seem naught but savage creatures, animated by vile passions and by the lust of vengeance and of hate. The hour, some little time before sunset, and the place, the West Barricade, at the very spot where, a decade later, a proud tyrant raised an undying monument to the nation's glory and his own vanity.
>
> During the greater part of the day the guillotine had been kept busy at its ghastly work: all that France had boasted of in the past centuries, of ancient names, and blue blood, had paid toll to her desire for liberty and for fraternity. The carnage had only ceased at this late hour of the day because there were other more interesting sights for the people to witness, a little while before the final closing of the barricades for the night.
>
> Excerpt from *The Scarlet Pimpernel* by Baroness Orczy, 1905

5. Which choice best describes why the author calls the humans "savage creatures"?
   a. They happily watch guillotine executions for entertainment.
   b. They support a tyrant who is damaging the nation.
   c. They only come out at night and do not see the daytime.
   d. They freely fight each other in the streets of France.

The next question is based on the following passage from Walden *by Henry David Thoreau:*

> When I wrote the following passages, or rather the bulk of them, I lived alone, in the woods, a mile from any neighbor, in a house which I had built myself on the shore of Walden Pond, in Concord, Massachusetts, and earned my living by the labor of my hands

only. I lived there two years and two months. At present I am a sojourner in civilized life again.

6. What does the word *sojourner* most likely mean at the end of the passage?
    a. Illegal immigrant
    b. Temporary resident
    c. Lifetime partner
    d. Farm crop

The next question is based on the following passage:

> Now the facts of life are conveyed by our senses to the consciousness within us, and stimulate the world of thought and feeling that constitutes our real life. Thought and feeling are very intimately connected, few of our mental perceptions, particularly when they first dawn upon us, being unaccompanied by some feeling. But there is this general division to be made, on one extreme of which is what we call pure intellect, and on the other pure feeling or emotion. The arts, I take it, are a means of giving expression to the emotional side of this mental activity, intimately related as it often is to the more purely intellectual side. The more sensual side of this feeling is perhaps its lowest, while the feelings associated with the intelligence, the little sensitivenesses of perception that escape pure intellect, are possibly its noblest experiences.

Excerpt from *The Practice & Science of Drawing* by Harold Speed, 1913

7. Which choice best explains the central idea of this passage?
    a. Art is based purely on our senses and not our mental perceptions.
    b. The arts are primarily an intellectual expression rather than one of feeling.
    c. The arts are primarily an emotional expression rather than one of intellect.
    d. Sensitivity inhibits the human ability to create expressive art.

The next question is based on the following passage:

> In approaching this problem of interpretation, we may first put out of consideration certain obvious limitations upon the generality of all guaranties of free speech. An occasional unthinking malcontent may urge that the only meaning not fraught with danger to liberty is the literal one that no utterance may be forbidden, no matter what its intent or result; but in fact it is nowhere seriously argued by anyone whose opinion is entitled to respect that direct and intentional incitations to crime may not be forbidden by the state. If a state may properly forbid murder or robbery or treason, it may also punish those who induce or counsel the commission of such crimes. Any other view makes a mockery of the state's power to declare and punish offences. And what the state may do to prevent the incitement of serious crimes which are universally condemned, it may also do to prevent the incitement of lesser crimes, or of those in regard to the bad tendency of which public opinion is divided. That is, if the state may punish John for burning straw in an alley, it may also constitutionally punish Frank for inciting John to do it, though Frank did so by speech or writing. And if, in 1857, the United States could punish John for helping a fugitive slave to escape, it could also punish Frank for inducing

John to do this, even though a large section of public opinion might applaud John and condemn the Fugitive Slave Law.

From "Free Speech in War Time" by James Parker Hall, written in 1921, published in Columbia Law Review, Vol. 21 No. 6

8. Which of the following, if true, would most seriously undermine the claim proposed by the author that if the state can punish a crime then it can punish the incitement of that crime?

a. The idea that human beings are able and likely to change their mind between the utterance and execution of an event that may harm others
b. The idea that human beings will always choose what they think is right based on their cultural upbringing
c. The idea that the limitation of free speech by the government during wartime will protect the country from any group that causes a threat to that country's freedom
d. The idea that those who support freedom of speech probably have intentions of subverting the government

The next question is based on the following passage:

The true boundary line of the First Amendment can be fixed only when Congress and the courts realize that the principle on which speech is classified as lawful or unlawful involves the balancing against each other of two very important social interests, in public safety and in the search for truth. Every reasonable attempt should be made to maintain both interests unimpaired, and the great interest in free speech should be sacrificed only when the interest in public safety is really imperiled, and not, as most men believe, when it is barely conceivable that it may be slightly affected. In war time, therefore, speech should be unrestricted by the censorship or by punishment, unless it is clearly liable to cause direct and dangerous interference with the conduct of the war.

Thus our problem of locating the boundary line of free speech is solved. It is fixed close to the point where words will give rise to unlawful acts. We cannot define the right of free speech with the precision of the Rule against Perpetuities or the Rule in Shelley's Case, because it involves national policies which are much more flexible than private property, but we can establish a workable principle of classification in this method of balancing and this broad test of certain danger. There is a similar balancing in the determination of what is "due process of law." And we can with certitude declare that the First Amendment forbids the punishment of words merely for their injurious tendencies. The history of the Amendment and the political function of free speech corroborate each other and make this conclusion plain.

From "Freedom of Speech in War Time" by Zechariah Chafee, Jr. written in 1919, published in Harvard Law Review, Vol. 32 No. 8

9. What is the primary purpose of the passage?
    a. To analyze the First Amendment in historical situations in order to make an analogy to the current war at hand in the nation
    b. To demonstrate that the boundaries set during wartime are different from those set when the country is at peace, and that we should change our laws accordingly
    c. To offer the idea that during wartime, the principle of freedom of speech should be limited to exclude even minor utterances in relation to a crime
    d. To claim the interpretation of freedom of speech is already evident in the First Amendment and to offer a clear perimeter of the principle during war time

The next question is based on the following passage:

> For any journey, by rail or by boat, one has a general idea of the direction to be taken, the character of the land or water to be crossed, and of what one will find at the end. So it should be in striking the trail. Learn all you can about the path you are to follow. Whether it is plain or obscure, wet or dry; where it leads; and its length, measured more by time than by actual miles. A smooth, even trail of five miles will not consume the time and strength that must be expended upon a trail of half that length which leads over uneven ground, varied by bogs and obstructed by rocks and fallen trees, or a trail that is all up-hill climbing. If you are a novice and accustomed to walking only over smooth and level ground, you must allow more time for covering the distance than an experienced person would require and must count upon the expenditure of more strength, because your feet are not trained to the wilderness paths with their pitfalls and traps for the unwary, and every nerve and muscle will be strained to secure a safe foothold amid the tangled roots, on the slippery, moss-covered logs, over precipitous rocks that lie in your path. It will take time to pick your way over boggy places where the water oozes up through the thin, loamy soil as through a sponge; and experience alone will teach you which hummock of grass or moss will make a safe stepping-place and will not sink beneath your weight and soak your feet with hidden water. Do not scorn to learn all you can about the trail you are to take ... It is not that you hesitate to encounter difficulties, but that you may prepare for them. In unknown regions take a responsible guide with you, unless the trail is short, easily followed, and a frequented one. Do not go alone through lonely places; and, being on the trail, keep it and try no explorations of your own, at least not until you are quite familiar with the country and the ways of the wild.
>
> Excerpt from *On the Trail* by Lina Beard and Adelia Belle Beard, 1915

10. ________ is NOT a detail from the passage.
    a. Learning about the trail beforehand is imperative
    b. Time will differ depending on the land
    c. Once you are familiar with the outdoors you can go places on your own
    d. Be careful for wild animals on the trail you are on

The next question is based on the following passage:

> Journalist: Our newspaper should only consider the truth in its reporting. When a party is clearly in the wrong, like if he or she is spreading a pernicious, false narrative, their position should never be presented alongside the truth without comment. The purpose of journalism is to deliver facts and context. Both sides of an issue should be called for

comment, but their responses should be framed appropriately, especially when there's a potential conflict of interest or source of bias at play. Our editorial board needs to seriously consider how our newspaper isn't currently meeting these basic standards, exposing us to charges of bias from all sides.

11. The primary purpose of the journalist's argument is to ________
    a. persuade the newspaper to adopt a more rigorous approach to journalism.
    b. defend the newspaper against charges of bias in its reporting.
    c. argue for the newspaper to hire more journalists with the appropriate skills.
    d. define the professional responsibilities of a journalist.

The next question is based on the following passage.

Rehabilitation, rather than punitive justice, is becoming much more popular in prisons around the world. Prisons in America, where the recidivism rate is 67%, would especially benefit from mimicking the prison tactics used in Norway, where the recidivism rate is only 20%. In Norway, the idea is that a rehabilitated prisoner is much less likely to offend than one who was harshly punished. Rehabilitation includes proper treatment for substance abuse, psychotherapy, healthcare and dental care, and education programs.

12. Which of the following best captures the author's purpose?
    a. To show the audience one of the effects of criminal rehabilitation by comparison
    b. To persuade the audience to donate to American prisons for education programs
    c. To convince the audience of the harsh conditions of American prisons
    d. To inform the audience of the incredibly lax system of Norwegian prisons

The next question is based on the following passage:

Dennis Hanks claims to have taught his young cousin to read, write, and cipher. "He knew his letters pretty wellish, but no more. His mother had taught him. If ever there was a good woman on earth, she was one,—a true Christian of the Baptist church. But she died soon after we arrived, and Abe was left without a teacher. His father couldn't read a word. The boy had only about one quarter of schooling, hardly that. I then set in to help him. I didn't know much, but I did the best I could. Sometimes he would write with a piece of charcoal or the p'int of a burnt stick on the fence or floor. We got a little paper at the country town, and I made some ink out of blackberry briar-root and a little copperas in it. It was black, but the copperas ate the paper after a while. I made Abe's first pen out of a turkey-buzzard feather. We had no geese them days. After he learned to write his name he was scrawlin' it everywhere. Sometimes he would write it in the white sand down by the crick bank and leave it there till the waves would blot it out. He didn't take to books in the beginnin'. We had to hire him at first, but after he got a taste on't it was the old story—we had to pull the sow's ears to get her to the trough, and then pull her tail to get her away. He read a great deal, and had a wonderful memory—wonderful. Never forgot anything."

Excerpt from *The Every-Day Life of Abraham Lincoln* by Francis Fisher Browne, 1886

13. What can reasonably be inferred from this passage?
    a. Abe hated school and learning new things.
    b. Abe had an informal yet successful education.
    c. Abe was uneducated until adulthood.
    d. Abe enjoyed learning but not from Dennis.

The next question is based on the following passage:

> The old castle soon proved to be too small for the family, and in September 1853 the foundation-stone of a new house was laid. After the ceremony the workmen were entertained at dinner, which was followed by Highland games and dancing in the ballroom.
>
> Two years later they entered the new castle, which the Queen described as "charming; the rooms delightful; the furniture, papers, everything perfection."
>
> The Prince was untiring in planning improvements, and in 1856 the Queen wrote: "Every year my heart becomes more fixed in this dear Paradise, and so much more so now, that *all* has become my dearest Albert's *own* creation, own work, own building, own laying out as at Osborne; and his great taste, and the impress of his dear hand, have been stamped everywhere. He was very busy today, settling and arranging many things for next year."
>
> From the biography *Queen Victoria* by E. Gordon Browne, M.A.

14. What does the word *impress* mean in the above passage?
    a. To affect strongly in feeling
    b. To urge something to be done
    c. A certain characteristic or quality imposed upon something else
    d. To press a thing onto something else

The next question is based on the following passage:

> Portland is a very beautiful city of 60,000 inhabitants, and situated on the Willamette river twelve miles from its junction with the Columbia. It is perhaps true of many of the growing cities of the West, that they do not offer the same social advantages as the older cities of the East. But this is principally the case as to what may be called boom cities, where the larger part of the population is of that floating class which follows in the line of temporary growth for the purposes of speculation, and in no sense applies to those centers of trade whose prosperity is based on the solid foundation of legitimate business. As the metropolis of a vast section of country, having broad agricultural valleys filled with improved farms, surrounded by mountains rich in mineral wealth, and boundless forests of as fine timber as the world produces, the cause of Portland's growth and prosperity is the trade which it has as the center of collection and distribution of this great wealth of natural resources, and it has attracted, not the boomer and speculator, who find their profits in the wild excitement of the boom, but the merchant, manufacturer, and investor, who seek the surer if slower channels of legitimate business and investment. These have come from the East, most of them within the last few years. They came as seeking a better and wider field to engage in the same occupations they had followed in their Eastern homes, and bringing with them all the love of polite life which they had acquired

there, have established here a new society, equaling in all respects that which they left behind. Here are as fine churches, as complete a system of schools, as fine residences, as great a love of music and art, as can be found at any city of the East of equal size.

From *Oregon, Washington, and Alaska. Sights and Scenes for the Tourist*, written by E.L. Lomax in 1890

15. What is a characteristic of a "boom city," as indicated by the passage?
    a. It is built on the solid business foundations of mineral wealth and farming.
    b. It is an area of land on the west coast that quickly becomes populated by residents from the east coast.
    c. Due to the hot weather and dry climate, it catches fire frequently, resulting in a devastating population drop.
    d. It is a city whose population is made up of people who seek quick fortunes rather than building a solid business foundation.

The next four questions are based on the following passage:

(1) The first and most universal change effected in milk is its souring. (2) So universal is this phenomenon that it is generally regarded as an inevitable change which cannot be avoided, and, as already pointed out, has in the past been regarded as a normal property of milk. (3) It is due to the action of certain of the milk bacteria upon the milk sugar which converts it into lactic acid, and this acid gives the sour taste and curdles the milk. (4) After this acid is produced in small quantity its presence proves deleterious to the growth of the bacteria, and further bacterial growth is checked. (5) After souring, the milk for some time does not ordinarily undergo any further changes.

(6) Milk souring has been commonly regarded as a single phenomenon, alike in all cases. (7) When it was first studied by bacteriologists it was thought to be due in all cases to a single species of micro-organism which was discovered to be commonly present and named *Bacillus acidi lactici.* (8) This bacterium has certainly the power of souring milk rapidly, and is found to be very common in dairies in Europe. (9) As soon as bacteriologists turned their attention more closely to the subject it was found that the spontaneous souring of milk was not always caused by the same species of bacterium. (10) The number of species of bacteria which have been found to sour milk has increased until something over a hundred are known to have this power. (11) These different species do not affect the milk in the same way. (12) All produce some acid, but they differ in the kind and the amount of acid, and especially in the other changes which are affected at the same time that the milk is soured, so that the resulting soured milk is quite variable.

From *The Story of Germ Life* by Herbert William Conn.

16. In context, which of the following phrases is best to insert at the beginning of sentence 5 (reproduced below)?

After souring, the milk for some time does not ordinarily undergo any further changes.

a. Furthermore,
b. Additionally,
c. However,
d. Therefore,

17. In context, which of the following is the best way to revise and combine sentences 10 & 11 (reproduced below)?

The number of species of bacteria which have been found to sour milk has increased until something over a hundred are known to have this power. These different species do not affect the milk in the same way.

a. The number of species of bacteria which have been found to sour milk has increased until something over a hundred are known to have this power, and these different species do not affect the milk in the same way.
b. The number of species of bacteria which have been found to sour milk has increased until something over a hundred are known to have this power, or these different species do not affect the milk in the same way.
c. The number of species of bacteria which have been found to sour milk has increased until something over a hundred are known to have this power, but these different species do not affect the milk in the same way.
d. The number of species of bacteria which have been found to sour milk has increased until something over a hundred are known to have this power, so these different species do not affect the milk in the same way.

18. In context, which is the best revision to sentence 8 (reproduced below)?

This bacterium has certainly the power of souring milk rapidly, and is found to be very common in dairies in Europe.

a. This bacterium has certainly the power of souring milk rapidly; and is found to be very common in dairies in Europe.
b. This bacterium has certainly the power of souring milk rapidly finding to be very common in dairies in Europe.
c. This bacterium has certainly the power of souring milk rapidly and is found to be very common in dairies in Europe.
d. This bacterium has certainly the power of souring milk rapidly, and is found to be very common in dairies in Europe.

19. In context, which of the following sentences would best be inserted after sentence 2 (reproduced below)?

So universal is this phenomenon that it is generally regarded as an inevitable change which cannot be avoided, and, as already pointed out, has in the past been regarded as a normal property of milk.

a. Today, however, the phenomenon is well understood.
b. However, today the phenomenon is not well understood.
c. Flowers also have unusual properties which undergo transformation.
d. The properties in milk are the same as any other product that undergoes souring.

For the following questions, select the choice you think best fits the underlined part of the sentence. If the original is the best answer choice, then choose Choice A.

20. <u>Play baseball, swimming, and dancing</u> are three of Hannah's favorite ways to be active.
a. Play baseball, swimming, and dancing
b. Playing baseball; swimming; dancing;
c. Playing baseball, to swim and to dance,
d. Playing baseball, swimming, and dancing

21. <u>I was shocked by the sound of the blast muting</u> the television and went outside to see what happened.
a. I was shocked by the sound of the blast muting
b. I was shocked by the sound of the blast, muted
c. Shocked at the sound of the blast, I muted
d. The sound of the blast shocked me, muting

22. <u>The dog turned in a circle five times before its tail</u> went between its legs and it went to sleep.
a. The dog turned in a circle five times before its tail
b. For the dog, it turned around five times before its tail
c. A dog's turning in a circle five times before its tail
d. The dog turned in a circle five times before their tail

23. <u>The food at the fashion show being the best part</u>, which was shipped in from twenty different countries and prepared by world-renowned chefs.
a. The food at the fashion show being the best part
b. The best part about being at the fashion show was the food
c. At the fashion show the food was the best part of the party
d. The best part of the fashion show been the food

24. Every time the mosquito truck came driving down the road with the poison, <u>the kids riding their bikes behind it</u>.
a. the kids riding their bikes behind it.
b. the kids' rode their bikes' behind it.
c. the kids would ride their bikes behind it.
d. the kids rides their bikes behind it.

25. <u>Gertrude is fearful and worried about her sister coming into</u> town because she knows there will be a lot of work to do.
   a. Gertrude is fearful and worried about her sister coming into
   b. Gertrude is worried about and fearful her sister coming into
   c. Gertrude is fearful, worried about her sister coming into
   d. Gertrude is fearful of and worried about her sister coming into

26. <u>Before they decided on Costa Rica for their honeymoon</u>, the couple researched at least eight other vacation spots in different countries.
   a. Before they decided on Costa Rica for their honeymoon
   b. They decided on Costa Rica for their honeymoon
   c. Before their honeymoon, deciding on Costa Rica,
   d. Costa Rica as their honeymoon,

27. On the first day of school, <u>Kayla, late to three of her classes,</u> and never found the fourth!
   a. Kayla, late to three of her classes,
   b. Kayla being late to three of her classes
   c. Kayla to three of her classes late
   d. Kayla was late to three of her classes

28. Lulu continued to play <u>in order that</u> she wouldn't scare the kitten away.
   a. in order that
   b. so,
   c. so that
   d. so that,

29. My husband works evenings about a half-hour away, and our <u>13-year-old</u> daughter, Niamh, attends a homeschooling program.
   a. 13-year-old
   b. 13 year old
   c. 13-year old
   d. 13 year-old

30. Feeling optimistic, <u>the day suddenly makes you smile</u>.
   a. the day suddenly makes you smile.
   b. the day no longer seems so sad.
   c. the day brightens your mood.
   d. you smile for the rest of the day.

Writing Prompt

In response to the following prompt, write a 300- to 600-word essay.

> Substance abuse recovery centers in Florida have doubled in the past two years. Additionally, the centers that already existed are filled to the maximum occupancy. In order to accommodate the patients, some recovery centers are expanding their residencies and adding more staff. The reason for this rise in recovery centers speaks to the state of our nation with the abuse of drugs and alcohol. The substance abuse problem is worse than ever before and will only continue to grow if we allow the trafficking and consumption of drugs to go unpunished.

Write a response in which you identify your stance on the argument above. Once you've identified your stance, use concrete evidence to support your argument.

Answer Explanations #1

Mathematics

1. C: Plugging the function into the formula results in:

$$\frac{4(x+h)-2-(4x-2)}{h}$$

This is simplified to:

$$\frac{4x+4h-2-4x+2}{h}=\frac{4h}{h}=4$$

This value is also equal to the derivative of the given function. The derivative of a linear function is its slope.

2. B: One way to determine the number of zeros is to count the number of sign changes in coefficients in the polynomial. This results in the number of possible positive zeros. The coefficients are 1, −3, 2, 1, and −3. The sign changes between 1 and −3, −3 and 2, and 1 and −3, which is a total of 3 changes. Therefore, there are at most 3 positive zeros.

3. B: Because two sides are equal, this is an isosceles triangle. The smallest sides correspond to the 20° angles. The third angle has a measure of:

$$180-20-20=140°$$

4. B: Let x be equal to the fifth test score. Therefore, in order to receive, at minimum, a B in the class, the student must have:

$$\frac{74+76+82+84+x}{5}=80$$

Therefore,

$$\frac{316+x}{5}=80$$

Solving for x gives:

$$316+x=400$$

$$x=84$$

Therefore, he must receive at least an 84 out of 100 on the fifth test to receive a B in the course.

5. C: Choice *C* is the correct simplification for the expression given. For the expression:

$$5b^2 - 3ab + 10a$$

When $a = 3$ and $b = -1$, the values for a and b can be substituted into the given expression. The new expression becomes:

$$5(-1)^2 - 3(3)(-1) + 10(3)$$

Simplifying this expression using the order of operations yields a final answer of 44.

6. B: The volume of a rectangular prism is found by multiplying the length by the width by the height. Multiplying these three values yields an answer of 144 cubic centimeters. The answer must be in cubic units because volume involves all three dimensions. Each of the other answers have only two dimensions that are multiplied and one dimension is forgotten, as in *D*, where 12 and 3 are multiplied.

7. B: The average rate of change is found by calculating the difference in dollars over the elapsed time. Therefore, the rate of change is equal to $(\$4{,}900 - \$4{,}000) \div 3 \text{ months}$, which is equal to $\$900 \div 3$ or $300 per month.

8. B: The perimeter is found by adding the length of all the exterior sides. When the given dimensions are added, the perimeter is 22 meters.

$$P = 5 + 1.5 + 1.2 + 4.5 + 3.8 + 6 = 22$$

The last two dimensions can be found by subtracting 1.2 from 5, and adding 1.5 and 4.5, respectively.

9. C: In order to simplify this expression, a common factor can be taken out of the numerator and denominator. The expression then becomes:

$$\frac{x(x^2 + 4xy - 5y^2)}{x(x - y)}$$

When those values for x cancel out, then the new polynomial on top can be factored into:

$$\frac{(x - y)(x + 5y)}{x - y}$$

The two equivalent binomials can be canceled, and the simplified expression becomes $x + 5y$.

10. A: The probability of choosing a cherry wrapper with the first selection is $\frac{35}{100}$. If the first selection is cherry, then the probability of getting cherry the second time is $\frac{34}{99}$. So, the chance that both are cherry would be:

$$\frac{35}{100} \times \frac{34}{99}$$

$$\frac{1{,}190}{9{,}900}$$

$$\frac{119}{990}$$

11. B: The number of representatives varies directly with the population, so the equation necessary is $N = k \times P$, where N is the number of representatives, k is the variation constant, and P is total population in millions. Plugging in the information for New York allows k to be solved for. This process gives $27 = k \times 19.8$, so $k \approx 1.36$. Therefore, the formula for number of representatives given total population in millions is:

$$N = 1.36 \times P$$

Plugging in $P = 11.8$ for Ohio results in $N \approx 16.05$, which rounds to 16 total representatives.

12. C: To find the mean, or average, of a data set, add all data values and divide by the number of data points in the set. Each day of the week has an adult ticket amount sold that must be added together. The equation is as follows:

$$\frac{22 + 16 + 24 + 19 + 29}{5} = 22$$

13. C: The mode for a set of data is the value that occurs the most. The grade that appears the most is 95. It's the only value that repeats in the set. The mean is around 84.3.

14. D: The distributive property is used on both sides to obtain:

$$4x + 20 + 6 = 4x + 6$$

Then, like terms are collected on the left, resulting in:

$$4x + 26 = 4x + 6$$

Next, the addition principle is used to subtract $4x$ from both sides, and this results in the false statement $26 = 6$. Therefore, there is no solution.

15. A: First, the variables have to be defined. Let x be the first integer; therefore, $x + 1$ is the second integer. This is a two-step problem. The sum of three times the first and two less than the second is translated into the following expression:

$$3x + (x + 1 - 2)$$

Set this expression equal to 411 to obtain:

$$3x + (x + 1 - 2) = 411$$

The left-hand side is simplified to obtain:

$$4x - 1 = 411$$

To solve for x, first add 1 to both sides and then divide both sides by 4 to obtain $x = 103$. The next consecutive integer is 104.

16. C: To solve this quadratic equation, the quadratic formula with $a = 2$, $b = -10$, and $c = 3$ should be used. Therefore,

$$x = \frac{-(-10) \pm \sqrt{(-10)^2 - 4(2)(3)}}{2(2)} = \frac{10 \pm \sqrt{76}}{4}$$

$$x = \frac{10 \pm 2\sqrt{19}}{4} = \frac{5}{2} \pm \frac{\sqrt{19}}{2}$$

17. D: The exponential rules $(ab)^m = a^m b^m$ and $(a^m)^n = a^{mn}$ can be used to rewrite the expression as:

$$4^4 y^{12} \times 3^2 y^{14}$$

The coefficients are multiplied together and the exponential rule $a^m a^n = a^{m+n}$ is then used to obtain the simplified form $2{,}304y^{26}$:

$$4^4 y^{12} \times 3^2 y^{14}$$

$$256y^{12} \times 9y^{14}$$

$$2{,}304y^{12} \times y^{14}$$

$$2{,}304y^{26}$$

18. B: The relationship between age and time for attention span is a positive correlation because the general trend for the data is up and to the right. As the age increases, so does attention span.

19. D: There were 48 total bags of apples sold. If 9 bags were Granny Smith and the rest were Red Delicious, then $48 - 9 = 39$ bags were Red Delicious. Therefore, the ratio of Granny Smith to Red Delicious is $9 : 39$.

20. A: Division can be used to solve this problem. The division necessary is:

$$\frac{5.972 \times 10^{24}}{7.348 \times 10^{22}}$$

To compute this division, divide the constants first then use algebraic laws of exponents to divide the exponential expression.

This results in about 0.8127×10^2, which, written in scientific notation, is 8.127×10^1.

English Language Arts and Reading

1. D: The author does not consider modern architecture to be grim and dim. The author uses this phrase to refer to feudal architecture. Choices *A*, *B*, and *C* are all mentioned in the text as characteristics of modern architecture, especially in the cities of Chicago and Pittsburgh.

2. C: Choice *A* is too specific and is taken too literally. It is not that the architecture represents the builders; it represents the builder's culture. Choice *B* is incorrect because the term "at its worst as at its best" highlights both the positive and negative aspects of architecture. Therefore, the statement that it only becomes more depressing over time is illogical. Choice *D* is incorrect; the statement does not suggest this analysis.

3. C: The author refers to the "mediaeval man" in order to make the audience realize the irony produced from pitying him. The author says that we pity him for the dirt he lived in; however, we inhale smoke and dirt from our own skies. Choices *A*, *B*, and *D* are incorrect, as they just miss the mark of the statement.

4. B: Considering the strong, negative language used throughout the passage, such as "power, strangely mingled with timidity," "ingenuity, frequently misdirected," and "grim, dim canyons of our city streets," one can assume that the author is annoyed, offended, and disgruntled by modern architecture. Therefore, Choice *B*, aggrieved, is the most likely choice. None of the other answer choices accurately match the author's attitude.

5. A: Choice *A* is the correct answer because the author is describing a crowd of people watching guillotine executions for "the greater part of the day." In the second paragraph, the author states that the carnage of the guillotine only stopped because people had more interesting things to see late in the day. She describes these people as energized by hate and violence, like savages. Choice *B* is incorrect because the passage does not state that the people support the tyrant. Choice *C* is incorrect because there is nothing to suggest that the people only come out at night. Choice *D* is incorrect because, although the people love violence and carnage, the author does not say that they enact it on one another.

6. B: Although we don't have much context to go off of, this person is probably not a "lifetime partner" or "farm crop" of civilized life. These two do not make sense, so Choices *C* and *D* are incorrect. Choice *A* is also a bit strange. To be an "illegal immigrant" of civilized life is not a used phrase, making Choice *A* incorrect.

7. C: Choice *C* is the correct answer because the author claims that the arts give expression to the emotional side of the mind. He says that human consciousness operates on a spectrum of intellect and emotion, and while art can be linked to intellect, it is primarily an expression of feelings. Choice *A* is incorrect because the passage focuses on mental perceptions rather than the senses and argues that the sensual side of feeling "is perhaps the lowest." Choice *B* is incorrect because the author says that the arts are primarily emotional expression. Choice *D* is incorrect because the passage does not focus on sensitivity, and the brief mention of it suggests that it aids in the creation of art.

8. A: The idea in Choice *A* most seriously undermines the claim because it brings into question the tendency to commit a crime and points out the difference between utterance and action in moral situations. Choice *B* is incorrect; this idea does not undermine the claim at hand but introduces an observation irrelevant to the claim. Choices *C* and *D* are incorrect because they would actually strengthen the author's claim rather than undermine it.

9. D: Choice *A* is incorrect; the passage calls upon no historical situations as precedent. Choice *B* is incorrect; we can infer that the author would not agree with this, because they state that "In war time, therefore, speech should be unrestricted ... by punishment." Choice *C* is incorrect; this is more consistent with the main idea of the first passage.

10. D: Choice *D* is correct; it may be real advice an experienced hiker would give to an inexperienced hiker. However, the question asks about details in the passage, and this is not in the passage. Choice *A* is incorrect; we do see the author encouraging the reader to learn about the trail beforehand ... "wet or dry; where it leads; and its length." Choice *B* is also incorrect, because we do see the author telling us the time will lengthen with boggy or rugged places opposed to smooth places. Choice *C* is incorrect; at the end of the passage, the author tells us "do not go alone through lonely places ... unless you are quite familiar with the country and the ways of the wild."

11. A: Choice *A* correctly identifies the argument's primary purpose. The purpose is clearly persuasive, and the focus is on the newspaper's approach to journalism. According to the conclusion, the newspaper isn't currently meeting basic editorial standards, and the journalist wants the newspaper to adopt the best practices described in the argument.

Choice *B* is incorrect. The journalist mentions that the newspaper is currently exposed to charges of bias from all sides, but the argument isn't defending the newspaper. It's calling for a change in editorial policy.

Choice *C* is incorrect. Although the journalist might agree that the newspaper needs to shake up its staff, the primary focus is on the newspaper's approach to journalism.

Choice *D* is incorrect. The journalist touches on the professional responsibilities of a journalist, but it's in the context of the newspaper's failings, which Choice *D* doesn't reference.

12. A: Although it is obvious the author favors rehabilitation, Choice *B* is incorrect because the author never asks for donations from the audience. Choices *C* and *D* are also incorrect. We can infer from the passage that American prisons are probably harsher than Norwegian prisons as a result of the author's comparisons; it is not their purpose to inform or convince us, because the author compares Norwegian and American prison recidivism rates.

13. B: Choice *B* is a reasonable inference to make from the text. The passage suggests that Abe was taught how to read and write by his cousin. The text says that he did not attend school for long, so it's reasonable to infer that most of his education was informal. Considering that Abe loved to read, had a strong mind, and eventually became president of the United States, it is also reasonable to infer that his education was successful. Choice *A* is incorrect because the text does not mention Abe's feelings about school and suggests that Abe loved to read and to write his name after learning to do so. Choice *C* is incorrect because Abe learned to read and write as a child. Choice *D* is incorrect because there is nothing to suggest that Abe took issue with Dennis being his teacher.

14. C: The sentence states that "the impress of his dear hand [has] been stamped everywhere." Choice *A* is one definition of *impress*, but this definition is used more as a verb than a noun: "She impressed us as a songwriter." Choice *B* is incorrect because it is also used as a verb: "He impressed the need for something to be done." Choice *D* is incorrect because it is part of a physical act: "The businessman impressed his mark upon the envelope." The phrase in the passage is meant as figurative, since the workmen did most of the physical labor, not the prince.

15. D: Choice *A* is a characteristic of Portland, but not of a booming city. Choice *B* is close—a boom city is one that becomes quickly populated, but it is not necessarily always populated by residents from the east coast. Choice *C* is incorrect because a boom city is not one that catches fire frequently, but one made up of people who are looking to make quick fortunes from the resources provided on the land.

16. D: Choice *D, therefore*, is the correct answer. The word *therefore* indicates a result of something. We see that in the sentence before, the acid is deleterious to growth. As a result of this, "the milk does not undergo any further changes." The other transition words indicate an addition of information, and this is more of a result of the previous information.

17. C: The correct answer is the following sentence: "The number of species of bacteria which have been found to sour milk has increased until something over a hundred are known to have this power, but these different species do not affect the milk in the same way." The conjunction "but" is the best choice for this sentence because it indicates a contrast; although one might think all bacteria would affect milk the same way, they do not.

18. C: Choice *C* is the best answer. Simple sentences with a conjunction don't require a comma. Choice *A* is incorrect because semicolons require independent clauses (complete sentences) on either side of them. Choice *B* is incorrect; the gerund "finding" coupled with "to be" is not proper verb usage. Choice *D* is incorrect because, like the original, simple sentences with a conjunction don't require a comma.

19. A: Choice *A* is the best answer. One must look at the surrounding context to choose the right answer choice. A "phenomenon" is seen as a wonder or miracle, not something that logically follows something else. Assuring the reader that this "phenomenon" is well understood today would appropriately follow sentence 2. Sentence 3 then goes on to explain how this property is "well understood," so we have two surrounding sentences that work well with Choice *A*. Choice *B* is incorrect because the following sentence goes on to explain how we understand this happening, and Choice *B* says that it is *not* well understood. Choices *C* and *D* should be ruled out because they do not fall between sentences 2 & 3 in a logical way; they deviate from the topic.

20. D: Choice *D* is the best answer choice because the gerunds are all in parallel structure: "Playing baseball, swimming, and dancing." Choice *A* is incorrect because "Play baseball" does not match the parallel structure of the other two gerunds. Choice *B* is incorrect because the answer uses semicolons instead of commas, which is incorrect. Semicolons are used to separate independent clauses. Choice *C* is incorrect because "to swim" and "to dance" do not follow parallel structure with "Playing baseball."

21. C: Choice *C* is the correct answer: "Shocked at the sound of the blast, I muted the television and went outside to see what happened." Choice *A* is incorrect because we're not sure if it is the "I" that's doing the muting or the blast. Choice *B* has incorrect sentence structure. We have "I was shocked" and that carries over to "I was muted," which is incorrect. We need someone doing the muting without the helping verb. Choice *D* is incorrect; we don't have a proper subject to go with the verb "muting." "Me muting" is not correct. In the original sentence, it's the "sound" that's doing the muting, which is incorrect.

22. A: Choice *A* is the best answer because it is the most straightforward. Choice *B* adds "For the dog, it turned around," which makes the sentence more confusing than the simple, "The dog turned in a circle." Choice *C* is incorrect because "A dog turned" is clearer subject/verb agreement than "A dog's turning," which does not match the other verb tense. Choice *D* is incorrect pronoun agreement; "their" should be "its" because there is only one dog.

23. B: Choice *B* is the correct answer choice. Choice *A* is incorrect because the verb "being" is incorrect usage; it should say "the food was the best part," not "the food being the best part." Choice *C* is incorrect because the way the sentence is worded, it seems as if the "party" was shipped from twenty different countries, not the "food"; it has a misplaced modifier. Choice *D* is incorrect; it is missing the helping verb "has."

24. C: Choice *C* is the best answer choice because we have an independent clause with correct subject/verb agreement. Choice *A* does not have an independent clause, due to the verb form "riding," which should be "would ride." Choice *B* is incorrect; "kids" and "bikes" are plural and show no possession of anything, so there should be no apostrophes behind those words. Choice *D* is incorrect; "kids rides" is incorrect subject/verb agreement. The correct phrase should be "kids ride."

25. D: Choice *D* is the best answer choice because it uses parallelism in its prepositions: "fearful of" and "worried about." Choice *A* is incorrect because one wouldn't be "fearful about" something, but "fearful of" something. Choice *B* is incorrect; the preposition after fearful is missing altogether. Choice *C* is incorrect because a comma doesn't belong in between "fearful" and "worried." This does not correct the problem of still needing a preposition after "fearful."

26. A: The answer choice is correct as-is because it is a dependent clause connected to an independent clause and contains the correct subject-verb agreement and clarity. Choice *B* is incorrect because if we were to place this sentence before the last sentence, we would have two independent clauses separated by a comma, and this would create a comma splice. Choice *C* is incorrect; this is not the best answer because it isn't the clearest, since the subject "they" or "the couple" comes later in the sentence. Choice *D* is incorrect because the phrasing is awkward and not as clear as Choice *A*.

27. D: Choice *D* is the best answer because it has the proper subject/verb agreement: "Kayla was late." Choice *A* is incorrect because there is no helping verb before "late," and the comma separates the next phrase which should be the verbal phrase. Choice *B* is incorrect because the verb is not the right form; it should be "was late" not "being late." Choice *C* is incorrect because the word order is inverted.

28. C: Choice *C* is the best answer here: "Lulu continued to play so that she wouldn't scare the kitten away." Usually the words "in order" are used with the word "to." Choice *A* is incorrect because the words "in order" are usually followed by the word "to" not "that." For Choice *D*, there is no need for a comma after "so that", and for Choice *B*, there is no need for a comma after "so."

29. A: Choice *A* is the best answer, no change, because "13-year-old" is correct. When an age is describing a noun and precedes the noun, hyphenation is required.

30. D: Choice *D* is the best answer: "you smile for the rest of the day." As the sentence is currently written, there is a dangling modifier. The sentence implies that the day, and not the person, is feeling optimistic.

Writing Prompt

When writing a persuasive-explanatory essay, it's important to use the author's words to support your claims. You can do so by quoting phrases and sentences that reinforce your point. However, it's easy to accidentally take the author's message out of context. A great tip to preserve the original message is by paraphrasing. Compare your summary to the author's initial statements. If the general idea is unchanged, you're going to do well.

For the persuasive side of an essay, you're going to try to convince the reader that your opinion is valid. You'll want to write in a convincing and deliberate manner. Avoid using words like *maybe*, *potentially*, *could be*, etc. Those words have a tendency to diminish a strong message. Remember to include the opposing argument in your paper. A balanced persuasive essay shows both sides of the argument. Acknowledge the opposing view, but don't get too worried about the minute details.

Don't forget the general structure of an essay!

- An introductory paragraph contains your initial opinion and idea. You can't have an introductory paragraph without a thesis statement. You'll also allude to your main points briefly.
- Body paragraphs are your main points. For a 300–600-word essay, two to three body paragraphs will be fine. Make sure you address your first point, add your supporting evidence, and elaborate. Repeat those steps as needed.
- The concluding paragraph summarizes your main points.

Writing can be hard, but have no fear. Try to imagine you're having a conversation. Essays are essentially structured conversations. However, it's not quite like talking with friends. Slang, inside jokes, and abbreviations don't work well for strangers. Imagine you're talking to someone you deeply admire and respect; you'd want to be thoughtful and understanding. This means you should simplify complex ideas without being reductive and condescending.

In general, it's good practice to read what you write out loud. Your ears will notice if something doesn't sound right. Our ears pick up on details that our eyes miss. It's especially true when you're completely focused on writing.

If you get stuck at any point, take a break, and come back to it. You'll have ample time to finish if you pace yourself and take it easy.

Practice Test #2

Mathematics

1. Which of the following is perpendicular to the line $4x + 7y = 23$?
   a. $y = -\frac{4}{7}x + 23$
   b. $4x + 7y = 14$
   c. $y = \frac{7}{4}x - 12$
   d. $y = -\frac{7}{4}x + 11$

2. From the chart below, which two are preferred by more men than women?

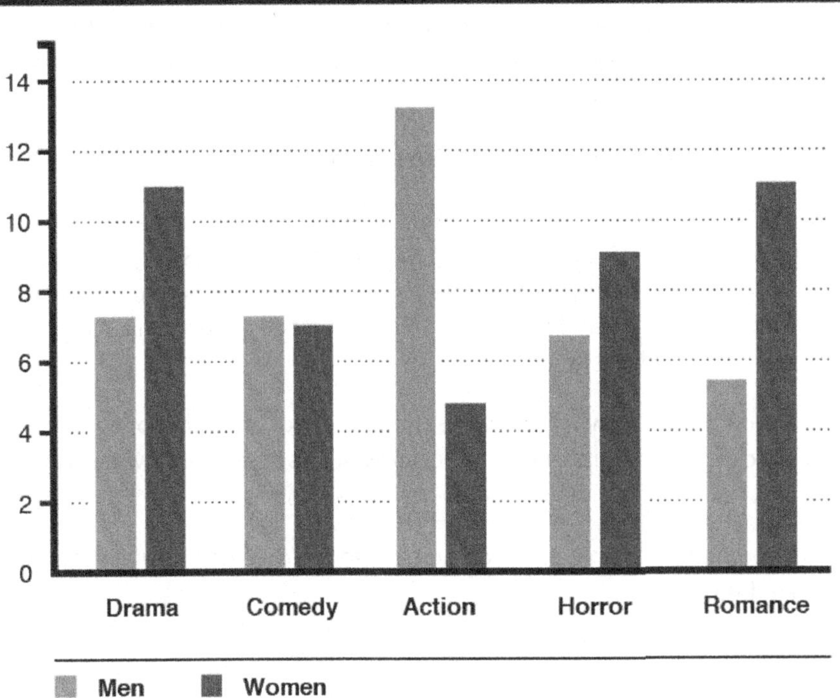

   a. Comedy and Action
   b. Drama and Comedy
   c. Action and Horror
   d. Action and Romance

3. Which type of graph best represents a continuous change over a period of time?
   a. Bar graph
   b. Line graph
   c. Pie graph
   d. Histogram

4. If the line of the following equation is graphed in the xy-plane, what is the y-intercept of the line?

$$\frac{4}{3}x - \frac{11}{9}y = -55$$

   a. 67.2
   b. 45
   c. -67.2
   d. -45

5. In a neighborhood, 15 out of 80 households have children under the age of 18. What percentage of the households have children under 18?
   a. 0.1875%
   b. 18.75%
   c. 1.875%
   d. 15%

6. Olive oil is being transferred from a rectangular storage container that has dimensions 5 inches by 9 inches by 12 inches into a cylindrical storage container that has a diameter of 5 inches. What is the minimum possible length for such a cylindrical storage container that will hold all of the olive oil?
   a. $\frac{432}{5\pi}$ inches
   b. $\frac{108}{5\pi}$ inches
   c. 6.25π inches
   d. 5π inches

7. What is an equivalent logarithmic form of the following exponential function?

$$f(x) = 10^{x+3}$$

   a. $x = 3 + \log y$
   b. $-3 + \log y = x$
   c. $\log(x - 3) = y$
   d. $\log_3 x = y$

8. Which of the following relations is a function?
   a. $\{(1,4), (1,3), (2,4), (5,6)\}$
   b. $\{(-1,-1), (-2,-2), (-3,-3), (-4,-4)\}$
   c. $\{(0,0), (1,0), (2,0), (1,1)\}$
   d. $\{(1,0), (1,2), (1,3), (1,4)\}$

9. Given the linear function $g(x) = \frac{1}{4}x - 2$, which domain value corresponds to a range value of $\frac{1}{8}$?
   a. $\frac{17}{2}$
   b. $-\frac{63}{32}$
   c. 0
   d. $\frac{2}{17}$

10. Paul took a written driving test, and he answered 12 questions correctly.. If he answered 75% of the total questions correctly, how many questions were on the test?
    a. 15
    b. 20
    c. 18
    d. 16

11. What is the mode for the grades shown in the chart below?

Science Grades	
Jerry	65
Bill	95
Anna	80
Beth	95
Sara	85
Ben	72
Jordan	98

    a. 65
    b. 90
    c. 95
    d. 84.3

12. The following two points are plotted on a number line: −18.2 and 6.3. What is the distance between these two points?
    a. -24.5
    b. 11.9
    c. 24.5
    d. -11.9

13. What is the value of the constant b in the following equation?

$$-4x(x-9) + 8(x-3) = ax^2 + bx + c$$

    a. -4
    b. -44
    c. -24
    d. 44

14. What is the missing length x?

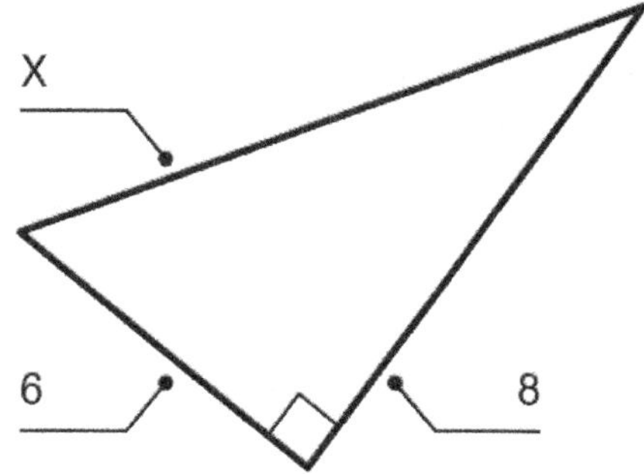

a. 6
b. -10
c. 10
d. 100

15. A circle has a radius of 8 and the y-coordinate of the center in the xy-plane is -6. Two points on the circumference of the circle are $(4, 2)$ and $(-4, -6)$. Which of the following is the x-coordinate of the center? The equation for a circle with radius r and center (h, k) is $(x - h)^2 + (y - k)^2 = r^2$.

a. 4
b. -4
c. 6
d. 11

16. At a local pet store, 70% of the animals available to adopt are dogs and 30% are cats. The average cost of adopting a dog is $100, and the average cost of adopting a cat is $80. What is the average cost of all the animals? Answer in dollars.

a. $94
b. $80
c. $72
d. $65

17. Each time a toy is manufactured, there is a 6% chance that it will be defective. What is the probability that 3 toys in a row will be defective?

a. 0.000216
b. 0.0216
c. 0.06
d. 0.0036

18. What is the correct factorization of the following binomial?

$$2y^3 - 128$$

a. $2(y + 8)(y - 8)$
b. $2(y + 4)(y^2 - 4y)$
c. $2(y + 4)(y - 4)^2$
d. $2(y - 4)(y^2 + 4y + 16)$

19. Keisha is planning a company picnic for the end of quarter celebration. She has a budget of $1,275 for renting a pavilion and purchasing catered food. There are 45 people in the office that will attend the picnic, and the cost of renting a pavilion is $310. Which of the following inequalities shows how to find the amount of money, x, that Annie can spend on a catered lunch for each employee?

a. $45x + 310 \geq 1{,}275$
b. $45x - 310 \leq 1{,}275$
c. $45x - 310 \geq 1{,}275$
d. $45x + 310 \leq 1{,}275$

20. The function $f(t) = \frac{20{,}000}{1+10e^{-2t}}$ represents the number of people who catch a disease t weeks after its initial outbreak in a population of 20,000 people. How many people initially had the disease at the time of the initial outbreak? Round to the nearest whole number.

a. 20,000
b. 1,818
c. 2,000
d. 0

English Language Arts and Reading

Question 1 is based on the following passage:

> The Industrial Revolution touched and altered almost every aspect of the economic and political life of pre-1760 Europe, which, in turn, changed the existing social order. With roots digging as deeply into the past as the thirteenth century, when capitalism and commerce began to develop, industrialization slowly became inevitable. It was aided by a gradual expansion of the market, a demand for more goods by an increasing number of consumers, and the step-by-step liberation of private enterprise from government control. (1) Industrialization began in earnest in the textile industry of Great Britain, and, due to progress in the field of technological innovations, caused a huge upswing in the amount of money necessary to establish a factory. (2) Industry became the new source of wealth, which had formerly been land, but the power remained concentrated within a small group of rich men—the capitalists. The existence of this wealthy class directly contrasted with that of the impoverished working class (people who had once worked the land until they were forced by industrialization to undertake factory labor in order to survive). The juxtaposition of a small number of people, who held great wealth, with a population for whom extreme and widespread poverty was inescapable was one of the greatest problems the Industrial Revolution created.

1. Which transition sentence would best go after the underlined sentence (1)?

a. The demand for large amounts of capital was met by a small group of wealthy investors.
b. Therefore, the need for large capitalists was predominant.
c. Capitalists, with their deep pockets, came to the rescue.
d. The economic theory of supply and demand was born.

Question 2 is based on the following passage:

> There was a man named Webster who lived in a town of twenty-five thousand people in the state of Wisconsin. He had a wife named Mary and a daughter named Jane and he

was himself a fairly prosperous manufacturer of washing machines. When the thing happened of which I am about to write, he was thirty-seven or thirty-eight years old and his one child, the daughter, was seventeen. Of the details of his life up to the time a certain revolution happened within him it will be unnecessary to speak. He was however a rather quiet man inclined to have dreams which he tried to crush out of himself in order that he function as a washing machine manufacturer; and no doubt, at odd moments, when he was on a train going some place or perhaps on Sunday afternoons in the summer when he went alone to the deserted office of the factory and sat several hours looking out at a window and along a railroad track, he gave way to dreams.

From *Many Marriages* by Sherwood Anderson

2. What does the author mean by the following sentence?

"Of the details of his life up to the time a certain revolution happened within him it will be unnecessary to speak."

a. The details of his external life don't matter; only the details of his internal life matter.
b. Whatever happened in his life before he had a certain internal change is irrelevant.
c. He had a traumatic experience earlier in his life which rendered it impossible for him to speak.
d. Before the revolution, he was a lighthearted man who always wished to speak to others no matter who they were.

The next three questions are based on the excerpt from A Christmas Carol *by Charles Dickens:*

Meanwhile the fog and darkness thickened so, that people ran about with flaring links, proffering their services to go before horses in carriages, and conduct them on their way. The ancient tower of a church, whose gruff old bell was always peeping slyly down at Scrooge out of a Gothic window in the wall, became invisible, and struck the hours and quarters in the clouds, with tremulous vibrations afterwards as if its teeth were chattering in its frozen head up there. The cold became intense. In the main street, at the corner of the court, some labourers were repairing the gas-pipes, and had lighted a great fire in a brazier, round which a party of ragged men and boys were gathered: warming their hands and winking their eyes before the blaze in rapture. The water-plug being left in solitude, its overflowings sullenly congealed, and turned to misanthropic ice.

The brightness of the shops where holly sprigs and berries crackled in the lamp heat of the windows, made pale faces ruddy as they passed. Poulterers' and grocers' trades became a splendid joke; a glorious pageant, with which it was next to impossible to believe that such dull principles as bargain and sale had anything to do. The Lord Mayor, in the stronghold of the mighty Mansion House, gave orders to his fifty cooks and butlers to keep Christmas as a Lord Mayor's household should; and even the little tailor, whom he had fined five shillings on the previous Monday for being drunk and bloodthirsty in the streets, stirred up to-morrow's pudding in his garret, while his lean wife and the baby sallied out to buy the beef.

Foggier yet, and colder. Piercing, searching, biting cold. If the good Saint Dunstan had but nipped the Evil Spirit's nose with a touch of such weather as that, instead of using his familiar weapons, then indeed he would have roared to lusty purpose. The owner of one scant young nose, gnawed and mumbled by the hungry cold as bones are gnawed by dogs, stopped down at Scrooge's keyhole to regale him with a Christmas carol: but at the first sound of

"God bless you, merry gentleman! May nothing you dismay!"

Scrooge seized the ruler with such energy of action, that the singer fled in terror, leaving the keyhole to the fog and even more congenial frost.

3. Which of the following can NOT be inferred from the passage?
   a. The narrative takes place during winter.
   b. The majority of the narrative is located in a bustling city street.
   c. This passage takes place during the nighttime.
   d. The Lord Mayor is a wealthy person within the narrative.

4. According to the passage, which of the following regarding the poulterers and grocers is true?
   a. They were so poor in the quality of their products that customers saw them as a joke.
   b. They put on a pageant in the streets every year for Christmas to entice their customers.
   c. They did not believe in Christmas, so they refused to participate in the town parade.
   d. They set their shops up to be entertaining public spectacles rather than a dull trade exchange.

5. The author's depiction of the scene in the last few paragraphs does all EXCEPT which of the following?
   a. Offer an allusion to religious affiliation in England.
   b. Attempt to evoke empathy for the character of Scrooge.
   c. Provide a palpable experience through the use of imagery and diction.
   d. Depict Scrooge as an uncaring, terrifying character to his fellows.

6. A student has been assigned the task of writing a paper about the spice trade. They have written the following paragraph:

> Christopher Columbus originally set sail on a mission to find new lands where spices were abundant. This would provide him and his country of Spain with great wealth and trade power. He was unsuccessful in his mission, yet he was still able to find other valuable culinary goods.

Which of the following details would be the most supportive addition to the text?
   a. "While Columbus is often credited with being the first to discover America, there were likely multiple explorers who made landfall on the continent earlier."
   b. "Portugal was successful in bringing spices from India to Europe."
   c. "Once Columbus arrived in North America, he was able to find potatoes, corn, tomatoes, and peppers to bring back to Spain."
   d. "John Cabot sailed from England with the same goal as Columbus."

The next question is based on the following passage:

He was, in fact, an odd mixture of small shrewdness and simple credulity. His appetite for the marvellous, and his powers of digesting it, were equally extraordinary; and both had been increased by his residence in this spell-bound region. No tale was too gross or monstrous for his capacious swallow. It was often his delight, after his school was dismissed in the afternoon, to stretch himself on the rich bed of clover bordering the little brook that whimpered by his schoolhouse, and there con over old Mather's direful tales,

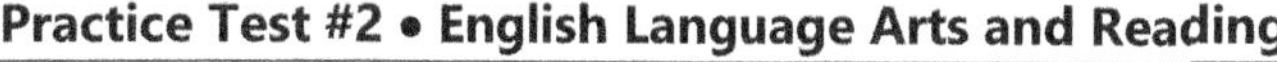

until the gathering dusk of evening made the printed page a mere mist before his eyes. Then, as he wended his way by swamp and stream and awful woodland, to the farmhouse where he happened to be quartered, every sound of nature, at that witching hour, fluttered his excited imagination,—the moan of the whip-poor-will from the hillside, the boding cry of the tree toad, that harbinger of storm, the dreary hooting of the screech owl, or the sudden rustling in the thicket of birds frightened from their roost. The fireflies, too, which sparkled most vividly in the darkest places, now and then startled him, as one of uncommon brightness would stream across his path; and if, by chance, a huge blockhead of a beetle came winging his blundering flight against him, the poor varlet was ready to give up the ghost, with the idea that he was struck with a witch's token. His only resource on such occasions, either to drown thought or drive away evil spirits, was to sing psalm tunes and the good people of Sleepy Hollow, as they sat by their doors of an evening, were often filled with awe at hearing his nasal melody, "in linked sweetness long drawn out," floating from the distant hill, or along the dusky road.

Excerpt from The Legend of Sleepy Hollow by Washington Irving, 1820

7. What can reasonably be inferred from this passage?
   a. The character described is witty.
   b. The character described is gullible.
   c. The character described is not a fan of reading.
   d. The character described is adventurous.

Questions 8–11 are based on the following passage from The Life, Crime, and Capture of John Wilkes Booth *by George Alfred Townsend.*

The box in which the President sat consisted of two boxes turned into one, the middle partition being removed, as on all occasions when a state party visited the theater. The box was on a level with the dress circle; about twelve feet above the stage. There were two entrances—the door nearest to the wall having been closed and locked; the door nearest the balustrades of the dress circle, and at right angles with it, being open and left open, after the visitors had entered. The interior was carpeted, lined with crimson paper, and furnished with a sofa covered with crimson velvet, three arm chairs similarly covered, and six cane-bottomed chairs. Festoons of flags hung before the front of the box against a background of lace.

President Lincoln took one of the arm-chairs and seated himself in the front of the box, in the angle nearest the audience, where, partially screened from observation, he had the best view of what was transpiring on the stage. Mrs. Lincoln sat next to him, and Miss Harris in the opposite angle nearest the stage. Major Rathbone sat just behind Mrs. Lincoln and Miss Harris. These four were the only persons in the box.

The play proceeded, although "Our American Cousin," without Mr. Sothern, has, since that gentleman's departure from this country, been justly esteemed a very dull affair. The audience at Ford's, including Mrs. Lincoln, seemed to enjoy it very much. The worthy wife of the President leaned forward, her hand upon her husband's knee, watching every scene in the drama with amused attention. Even across the President's face at intervals swept a smile, robbing it of its habitual sadness.

About the beginning of the second act, the mare, standing in the stable in the rear of the theater, was disturbed in the midst of her meal by the entrance of the young man who had quitted her in the afternoon. It is presumed that she was saddled and bridled with exquisite care.

Having completed these preparations, Mr. Booth entered the theater by the stage door; summoned one of the scene shifters, Mr. John Spangler, emerged through the same door with that individual, leaving the door open, and left the mare in his hands to be held until he (Booth) should return. Booth, who was even more fashionably and richly dressed than usual, walked thence around to the front of the theater, and went in. Ascending to the dress circle, he stood for a little time gazing around upon the audience and occasionally upon the stage in his usual graceful manner. He was subsequently observed by Mr. Ford, the proprietor of the theater, to be slowly elbowing his way through the crowd that packed the rear of the dress circle toward the right side, at the extremity of which was the box where Mr. and Mrs. Lincoln and their companions were seated. Mr. Ford casually noticed this as a slightly extraordinary symptom of interest on the part of an actor so familiar with the routine of the theater and the play.

8. Which of the following best describes the author's attitude toward the events leading up to the assassination of President Lincoln?
   a. Excitement due to the setting and its people
   b. Sadness due to the death of a beloved president
   c. Anger because of the impending violence
   d. Neutrality due to the style of the report

9. What does the author mean by the last sentence in the passage?
   a. Mr. Ford was suspicious of Booth and assumed he was making his way to Mr. Lincoln's box.
   b. Mr. Ford thought that Booth was elbowing his way to the dressing room to get ready for the play.
   c. Mr. Ford thought that Booth was making his way to the theater lounge to find his companions.
   d. Mr. Ford assumed Booth's movement throughout the theater was due to being familiar with the theater.

10. Given the author's description of the play *Our American Cousin*, which one of the following is most analogous to Mr. Sothern's departure from the theater?
   a. A ballet dancer leaves the New York City Ballet just before they go on to their final performance.
   b. A basketball player leaves an NBA team, and the next year they make it to the championship but lose.
   c. A lead singer leaves their band to begin a solo career, and the band drops in sales by 50 percent on their next album.
   d. A movie actor dies in the middle of making a movie, and the movie is made anyway by actors who resemble the deceased.

11. Based on the organizational structure of the passage, which of the following texts would be most similar?
    a. A chronological account in a novel of a woman and a man meeting for the first time
    b. A cause-and-effect text ruminating on the causes of global warming
    c. An autobiography that begins with the subject's death and culminates in his birth
    d. A text focusing on finding a solution to the problem of the Higgs boson particle

12. Read the following statement, written by an ethicist, and then answer the question.

    Artificial intelligence is rapidly approaching consciousness. What began as simple algorithms that locate and regurgitate information is now capable of independently drawing conclusions. Unfortunately, the free market is responsible for the advances in artificial intelligence, and private companies aren't incentivized to align artificial intelligence with humanity's goals. Without any guidance, artificial intelligence will adopt humanity's worst impulses and mirror the Internet's most violent worldviews.

The ethicist would most likely agree with which one of the following?
    a. The Internet is negatively impacting society.
    b. Artificial intelligence should be limited to simple algorithms.
    c. Humanity's goals should always be prioritized over technological advancements.
    d. Unregulated artificial intelligence is a threat to humanity.

13. Read the following statement, written by a businessman, and then answer the question.

    My cardinal rule is to only invest in privately held small businesses that exclusively sell tangible goods and have no debt.

Which one of the following is the best investment opportunity according to the businessman's cardinal rule?
    a. Jose owns his own grocery store. He's looking for a partner, because he fell behind on his mortgage and owes the bank three months' worth of payments.
    b. A multinational corporation is selling high-yield bonds for the first time.
    c. A family-owned accounting firm with no outstanding debts is looking for its first outside investor. The firm has turned a profit every year since it opened.
    d. Elizabeth is seeking a partner with business expertise to help expand her standalone store that sells niche board games. The store isn't currently profitable, but it's never been in debt.

14. The next question is based on the following passage:

    The two main types of strokes are ischemic and hemorrhagic. Ischemic stroke occurs when a blood clot blocks an artery in the central nervous system (CNS). The blockage disrupts the flow of oxygen-rich blood to CNS tissue and to the brain to the extent that the supply of oxygen and glucose is insufficient to support ongoing metabolism. Thrombotic stroke and embolic stroke are two subtypes of ischemic stroke. During a thrombotic stroke, a blood clot or atherosclerotic plaque develops locally to create blockage. <u>During an embolic stroke, a blood clot or atherosclerotic plaque develops elsewhere, such as in the heart, breaks apart, and travels in the bloodstream without blocking blood</u>

flow until it reaches a central nervous system artery, then it travels through the artery up to the brain, lodging there.

There is a semicolon missing from this run-on sentence. What is the correct position for it?

a. During an embolic stroke, a blood clot or atherosclerotic plaque develops elsewhere, such as in the heart; breaks apart, and travels in the bloodstream without blocking blood flow until it reaches a central nervous system artery, then it travels through the artery up to the brain, lodging there.
b. During an embolic stroke, a blood clot or atherosclerotic plaque develops elsewhere, such as in the heart, breaks apart, and travels in the bloodstream without blocking blood flow until it reaches a central nervous system artery; then it travels through the artery up to the brain, lodging there.
c. During an embolic stroke, a blood clot or atherosclerotic plaque develops elsewhere; such as in the heart, breaks apart, and travels in the bloodstream without blocking blood flow until it reaches a central nervous system artery, then it travels through the artery up to the brain, lodging there.
d. During an embolic stroke, a blood clot or atherosclerotic plaque develops elsewhere, such as in the heart, breaks apart; and travels in the bloodstream without blocking blood flow until it reaches a central nervous system artery, then it travels through the artery up to the brain, lodging there.

Directions for questions 15–18: The following sentence has a blank where something has been left out. Beneath the sentence are four words or phrases. Choose the word or phrase that, when inserted in the sentence, best fits the meaning of the sentence as a whole.

15. The publishers purposely kept a(n) ________ mood surrounding the novel; they knew that its secrecy would enchant its potential readers.

a. demonstrative
b. reticent
c. apathetic
d. buoyant

16. She seemed to ________ in him a new sensation, probably what others would consider a taste of first love.

a. galvanize
b. placate
c. quell
d. relinquish

17. The job description requires candidates to be ________ in English and Spanish so that they can easily communicate with native speakers of both languages.

a. notorious
b. inept
c. proficient
d. unassuming

18. The organization revised their policies and procedures since the former ones were ________ and many no longer applied.
    a. resuscitated
    b. obsolete
    c. ostentatious
    d. contemporary

19. Which word or phrase should be eliminated to make the sentence less wordy?

    The significance of the notion of three-ness is manifested in the literature of these cultures, which abounds with numerous events, occurring in patterns of three, that radically affect the lives of the main characters and those of there families, friends, and foes.

    a. The significance of
    b. the notion of
    c. of these cultures
    d. numerous

20. If there is an error in the underlined part of the sentence, what is the error?

    The significance of the notion of three-ness is manifested in the literature of these cultures, which abounds with numerous events, occurring in patterns of three, that radically affect the lives of the main characters and <u>those of there families, friends, and foes.</u>

    a. No error
    b. "Those" should be "that."
    c. "There" should be "their."
    d. There should not be a comma before "and foes."

Select the choice you think best fits the underlined part of the sentence. If the original is the best answer choice, then choose Choice A.

21. "Where could my cat have gone?" Everyone just looked at <u>each other</u> in utter silence.
    a. each other
    b. one another
    c. themselves
    d. each one

22. Lulu was only five years old and brought this kitten home only six weeks ago and she was so fond of her.
    a. Lulu was only five years old and brought this kitten home only six weeks ago and she was so fond of her.
    b. Lulu brought this kitten home only six weeks ago and she was so fond of her
    c. Lulu brought this kitten home only six weeks ago, and she was so fond of her
    d. Lulu was only five years old, and brought this kitten home only six weeks ago, and she was so fond of her

23. At night, Eva would curl up on the pillow next to Lulu and stay with her <u>across the night</u>.
    a. across the night
    b. below the night
    c. through the night
    d. amidst the night

24. When Nathaniel Hawthorne wrote *The Scarlet Letter* in 1850, he became the first American author to contribute a mature, tragic view of life <u>in</u> the literature of the young United States.
    a. in
    b. to
    c. from
    d. with

The next two questions are based on the following excerpt from Variation of Animals and Plants under Domestication *by Charles Darwin.*

> Peach (*Amygdalus persica*).—In the last chapter I gave two cases of a peach-almond and a double-flowered almond which suddenly produced fruit closely resembling true peaches. I have also recorded many cases of peach-trees producing buds, which, when developed into branches, have yielded nectarines. We have seen that no less than six named and several unnamed varieties of the peach have thus produced several varieties of nectarine. I have shown that it is highly improbable that all these peach-trees, some of which are old varieties, and have been propagated by the million, are hybrids from the peach and nectarine, and that it is opposed to all analogy to attribute the occasional production of nectarines on peach-trees to the direct action of pollen from some neighbouring nectarine-tree.
>
> Several of the cases are highly remarkable, because, firstly, the fruit thus produced has sometimes been in part a nectarine and in part a peach; secondly, because nectarines thus suddenly produced have reproduced themselves by seed; and thirdly, because nectarines are produced from peach-trees from seed as well as from buds.
>
> The seed of the nectarine, on the other hand, occasionally produces peaches; and we have seen in one instance that a nectarine-tree yielded peaches by bud-variation. As the peach is certainly the oldest or primary variety, the production of peaches from nectarines, either by seeds or buds, may perhaps be considered as a case of reversion. Certain trees have also been described as indifferently bearing peaches or nectarines, and this may be considered as bud-variation carried to an extreme degree.

25. Which of the following statements is NOT a detail from the passage?
    a. At least six named varieties of the peach have produced several varieties of nectarine.
    b. It is not probable that all of the peach-trees mentioned are hybrids from the peach and nectarine.
    c. An unremarkable case is the fact that nectarines are produced from peach-trees from seed as well as from buds.
    d. The production of peaches from nectarines might be considered a case of reversion.

26. Which of the following is an accurate paraphrasing of the following sentence?

    Certain trees have also been described as indifferently bearing peaches or nectarines, and this may be considered as bud-variation carried to an extreme degree.

    a. Some trees are described as bearing peaches and some trees have been described as bearing nectarines, but individually the buds are extreme examples of variation.
    b. One way in which bud-variation is said to be carried to an extreme degree is when specific trees have been shown to casually produce peaches or nectarines.
    c. Certain trees are indifferent to bud-variation, as recently shown in the trees that produce both peaches and nectarines in the same season.
    d. Nectarines and peaches are known to have cross-variation in their buds, which indifferently bears other sorts of fruit to an extreme degree.

After reading the passage, choose the best answer to the question based on what is expressed or suggested in the passage.

Director: Movies require the audience to suspend their disbelief. As such, directors need to create a universe with consistent internal logic. When the subject matter is based on real events and communities, the director must closely mirror reality. For example, characters should talk like people from that specific region and historical period.

Critic: Movies hold immense power in our culture in defining what is and isn't socially acceptable. Consequently, directors have a responsibility not to use language that offends various groups, especially people in vulnerable positions. Censoring hate speech and racial slurs won't break the audience's disbelief.

27. Which one of the following best describes the main point in dispute between the director and critic?
    a. Movie audiences suspend their disbelief.
    b. Hate speech and racial slurs offend people.
    c. Movies should avoid offending people.
    d. Directors enjoy full creative control over their work.

The next three questions are based on the following passage:

There is always so much going on in our family and so many scheduled events every week that without a set list of <u>chores and</u> (1) without ensuring the chores are completed, our household would be utterly chaotic.

I work days, from home. My husband works evenings about a half-hour away, and our <u>13-year-old</u> (2) daughter, Niamh, attends a homeschooling program. She is an avid hockey player and the third-highest scorer on the team. She simply lives for hockey. Three times a week, she has hockey practice, and <u>once, approximately, a week</u> (3), she has a hockey game. Niamh is responsible for washing her jerseys and her hockey pants and making sure all her gear is properly stored after every practice and game in the garage. Occasionally she forgets and leaves it all in the middle of the dining room floor. Niamh must also clean the kitchen every evening after dinner, empty the dishwasher, and feed her two guinea pigs and her cat. Every Saturday, we also give Niamh an allowance for

doing extra chores. She sweeps and washes our floors, cleans windows, vacuums, and tidies up the bathrooms.

28. Choose the best replacement (1).
    a. No change
    b. chores, and,
    c. chores and,
    d. chores, and

29. Choose the best replacement (2).
    a. No change
    b. 13 year old
    c. 13-year old
    d. 13 year-old

30. Choose the best replacement (3).
    a. No change
    b. approximately once a week
    c. approximately bi-weekly
    d. once a week

Writing Prompt

In response to the following prompt, write a 300- to 600-word essay.

> According to the plan of the convention, all judges who may be appointed by the United States are to hold their offices *during good behavior*, which is conformable to the most approved of the State constitutions and among the rest, to that of this State. Its propriety having been drawn into question by the adversaries of that plan, is no light symptom of the rage for objection, which disorders their imaginations and judgments. The standard of good behavior for the continuance in office of the judicial magistracy is certainly one of the most valuable of the modern improvements in the practice of government. In a monarchy, it is an excellent barrier to the despotism of the prince; in a republic, it is a no less excellent barrier to the encroachments and oppressions of the representative body. And it is the best expedient which can be devised in any government, to secure a steady, upright, and impartial administration of the laws.

Write an essay and explain what the author means by the passage above. Then, choose a side on the issue and argue why you agree or disagree. Give specific examples to support the argument.

Answer Explanations #2

Mathematics

1. C: The slopes of perpendicular lines are negative reciprocals, meaning their product is equal to -1. The slope of the line given needs to be found. Its equivalent form in slope-intercept form is $y = -\frac{4}{7}x + \frac{23}{7}$, so its slope is $-\frac{4}{7}$. The negative reciprocal of this number is $\frac{7}{4}$. The only line in the options given with this same slope is $y = \frac{7}{4}x - 12$.

2. A: The chart is a bar chart showing how many men and women prefer each genre of movies. The dark gray bars represent the number of women, while the light gray bars represent the number of men. The light gray bars are higher and represent more men than women for the genres of Comedy and Action.

3. B: A line graph represents continuous change over time. The line on the graph is continuous and not broken, as on a scatter plot. A bar graph may show change but isn't necessarily continuous over time. A pie graph is better for representing percentages of a whole. Histograms are best used in grouping sets of data in bins to show the frequency of a certain variable.

4. B: To find the y-intercept, plug 0 in for x and solve for y. Therefore,

$$\frac{4}{3}(0) - \frac{11}{9}y = -55$$

$$-\frac{11}{9}y = -55$$

Multiplying both sides by $-\frac{9}{11}$ gives:

$$y = \frac{495}{11} = 45$$

5. B: First, the information is translated into the ratio $\frac{15}{80}$. To find the percentage, translate this fraction into a decimal by dividing 15 by 80. The corresponding decimal is 0.1875. Move the decimal point two places to the right to obtain the percentage 18.75%.

6. A: We can assume the volume of each container is equal. The volume of the rectangular container is:

$$V = 5 \times 9 \times 12 = 540 \text{ in}^3$$

The volume of the cylindrical container is:

$$V = \pi r^2 h = \pi 0(2.5)^2 h = 6.25\pi h \text{ in}^3$$

Note that the radius is equal to the half of the given diameter, which is 5 inches. Setting these volumes equal results in:

$$540 = 6.25\pi h$$

7. B: The equivalent equation form of the function is $y = 10^{x+3}$. The expression can be written in logarithmic form as:

$$\log_{10} y = x + 3$$

A logarithm with base 10 is known as the common logarithm and is written without the base. Adding -3 to both sides results in:

$$-3 + \log y = x$$

8. B: The only relation in which every x-value corresponds to exactly one y-value is the relation given in Choice *B*, making it a function. The other relations have the same x-value paired up to different y-values, which goes against the definition of functions.

9. A: The range value is given, and this is the output of the function. Therefore, the function must be set equal to $\frac{1}{8}$ and solved for x. Thus, this needs to be solved:

$$\frac{1}{8} = \frac{1}{4}x - 2$$

The fractions can be cleared by multiplying times the LCD 8. This results in:

$$1 = 2x - 16$$

Add 16 to both sides and divide by 2 to obtain:

$$x = \frac{17}{2}$$

10. D: The unknown quantity is the number of total questions on the test. Let x be equal to this unknown quantity. Therefore, $0.75x = 12$. Divide both sides by 0.75 to obtain $x = 16$.

11. C: The mode for a set of data is the value that occurs the most. The grade that appears the most is 95. It's the only value that repeats in the set. The mean is around 84.3.

12. C: The distance between two points on a number line is equal to the absolute value of the difference between the two points. Therefore, the distance is:

$$|-18.2 - 6.3| = |-24.5| = 24.5$$

13. D: Distribute the expressions in front of the parentheses to obtain:

$$-4x^2 + 36x + 8x - 24$$

Collecting like terms results in:

$$-4x^2 + 44x - 24$$

The coefficient on the x-term is 44, so $b = 44$.

14. C: The Pythagorean theorem can be used to find the missing length x because it is a right triangle. The theorem states that $6^2 + 8^2 = x^2$, which simplifies into $100 = x^2$. Taking the positive square root of both sides results in the missing value $x = 10$.

15. A: The equation for a circle with radius r and center (h, k) is $(x-h)^2+(y-k)^2=r^2$. From the information given, the equation is:

$$(x-h)^2+(y+6)^2=64$$

Plugging in the point $(4, 2)$ results in:

$$(4-h)^2+64=64$$

Therefore:

$$(4-h)^2=0$$

$$h=4$$

The x-coordinate of the center of this circle is 4.

16. A: 94.

This is a weighted average problem. The average cost of a dog carries a weight of 70%, and the average cost of a cat carries a weight of 30%. The overall average cost is equal to the sum of each weight times the cost of each animal. The dog's contribution to the overall average is:

$$70\% \times 100=0.7 \times 100=\$70$$

The cat's contribution to the overall average is:

$$30\% \times 80=0.3 \times 80=\$24$$

Add these two amounts to obtain the overall average:

$$\$70+\$24=\$94$$

17. A: The probability of the occurrence of consecutive independent events is equal to the product of their probabilities. The probability of each toy being defective is $6\%=0.06$. Therefore, the probability of 3 toys in a row being defective is:

$$(0.06)(0.06)(0.06)=0.06^3=0.000216$$

18. D: First, the common factor 2 can be factored out of both terms, resulting in:

$$2(y^3-64)$$

The resulting binomial is a difference of cubes that can be factored using the rule:

$$a^3-b^3=(a-b)(a^2+ab+b^2)$$

$$a=y \text{ and } b=4$$

Therefore, the result is:

$$2(y-4)(y^2+4y+16)$$

19. B: The time of the initial outbreak corresponds to $t = 0$. Therefore, 0 must be plugged into the function. This results in $\frac{20,000}{1+10e^0} = \frac{20,000}{1+10} = \frac{20,000}{11} = 1,818.182$, which rounds to 1,818. Therefore, there were 1,818 people in the population that initially had the disease.

20. D: If the cost of the lunch is x, then, because there will be 45 employees attending the lunch, the cost of catering will be $45x$. The sum of this amount and $310, which is the cost of the pavilion, has to be less than or equal to the budgeted amount of $1,275. Therefore, the correct inequality is:

$$45x + 310 \leq 1,275$$

English Language Arts and Reading

1. A: Choice *A* is the best selection, because it provides the link from the expense of building factories to the capitalists, which led to industry becoming the new source of wealth. Choice *B* is awkwardly worded, and although it correctly states the need for capitalists, it does not put them into action. Choice *C* is factually correct, but it is not the best choice because the tone is more casual than that of the rest of the essay. Choice *D* is factually incorrect and does not logically link the two sentences.

2. B: Choice *B*, whatever happened in his life before he had a certain internal change is irrelevant, is the correct answer. Choices *A*, *C*, and *D* use some of the same language as the original passage, like "revolution," "speak," and "details," but they do not capture the meaning of the statement. The narrator was not concerned with the character's life before his epiphany and had no intention of talking about it.

3. C: Some of the evidence that this narrative takes place during winter is that "the cold became intense," and people were decorating their shops with "holly sprigs,"—a Christmas tradition. It also mentions that it's Christmastime at the end of the passage. We can infer that the narrative is located in a bustling city street by the actions in the story. People are running around trying to sell things, the atmosphere is busy, there is a church tolling the hours, etc. We can infer that the Lord Mayor is wealthy—he lives in the "Mansion House" and has 50 cooks. We cannot infer that the passage takes place during the nighttime. While we do have a statement that says that the darkness thickened, the darkness could be thickening because it is foggy outside.

4. D: The passage tells us that the poulterers' and grocers' trades were "a glorious pageant, with which it was next to impossible to believe that such dull principles as bargain and sale had anything to do," which means they set up their shops to be entertaining public spectacles in order to increase sales. Choice *A* is incorrect; although the word *joke* is used, it is meant to be used as a source of amusement rather than something made in poor quality. Choice *B* is incorrect; that they put on a "pageant" is figurative for the public spectacle they made with their shops, not a literal play. Choice *C* is incorrect, as this is not mentioned anywhere in the passage.

5. B: The author, at least in the last few paragraphs, does not attempt to evoke empathy for the character of Scrooge. We see Scrooge lashing out at an innocent, cold boy, with no sign of affection or feeling for his harsh conditions. We see Choice *A* when the author talks about Saint Dunstan. We see Choice *C*, providing a palpable experience and imaginable setting and character, especially with the "piercing, searching, biting cold," among other statements. Finally, we see Choice *D* when Scrooge chases the young boy away.

6. C: Choice *C* is the correct answer because it expands on the last sentence of the passage, explaining what culinary goods Columbus brought back to Spain and where he was able to find them. Choice *A* is incorrect because the text is not talking about the merit of Columbus' discovery of America—it is about what he contributed to the spice trade. Choices *B* and *D* are relevant to the overall topic, but the focus of this specific paragraph is on Columbus' contributions.

7. B: Choice *B* is a reasonable inference to make from the text. The character believes in fantastical tales. He is also superstitious and believes that singing will drive away evil spirits. Additionally, the character is described as having "simple credulity" in the first line. All of this shows that the character is quick to believe stories that are not based in reality and is most likely gullible in nature. Choice *A* is incorrect because there is nothing to suggest that the character has quick wit. Choice *C* is incorrect because the character is said to read Mather's tales in his spare time. Choice *D* is incorrect because there is nothing indicating that the character is adventurous (outside of his imagination), and he is described as easily startled, which suggests he might be too afraid to go on grand adventures.

8. D: The report is mostly objective; we see very little language that entails any strong emotion whatsoever. The story is told almost as an objective documentation of a sequence of actions—we see the president sitting in his box with his wife, their enjoyment of the show, Booth's walk through the crowd to the box, and Ford's consideration of Booth's movements. There is perhaps a small amount of bias when the author mentions the president's "worthy wife." However, the word choice and style show no signs of excitement, sadness, anger, or apprehension from the author's perspective, so the best answer is Choice *D*.

9. D: Mr. Ford assumed Booth's movement throughout the theater was due to being familiar with the theater. Choice *A* is incorrect; although Booth does eventually make his way to Lincoln's box, Mr. Ford does not make this distinction in this part of the passage. Choice *C* is incorrect; although the passage mentions "companions," it mentions Lincoln's companions rather than Booth's companions. Choice *B* is incorrect; the passage mentions "dress circle," which is the first level of the theater, not a "dressing room."

10. C: The original source of the analogy displays someone significant to an event who leaves, and then the event becomes worse for it. We see Mr. Sothern leaving the theater company, and then the play becoming a "very dull affair." Choice *A* doesn't indicate that the final performance suffered from the dancer's departure, so this is incorrect. Choice *B* shows a basketball player leaving a team, and then the team makes it to the championship but then loses. This choice could be a contestant for the right answer; however, we don't know if the team has become worse for his departure or better for it. Choice *D* is incorrect. The actor departs an event, but there is no assessment of the quality of the movie. It simply states that the actor who filled in resembles the deceased.

11. A: It's tempting to mark Choice *A* wrong because the genres are different. Choice *A* is a fiction text, and the original passage is not a fictional account. However, the question stem asks specifically about organizational structure. Choice *A* has a chronological structure just like the passage, so this is the correct answer. The passage does not have a cause-and-effect or problem/solution structure, making Choices *B* and *D* incorrect. Choice *C* is tempting because it mentions an autobiography; however, the structure of this text starts at the end and works its way toward the beginning, which is the opposite structure of the original passage.

12. D: The ethicist is troubled by the lack of incentives for private companies to regulate artificial intelligence. According to the ethicist's conclusion, artificial intelligence is adopting humanity's worst impulses and violent worldviews, and thereby threatening humanity. Choice *A* is incorrect. The ethicist might agree that artificial intelligence is negatively impacting society, but the Internet is barely mentioned in this argument. Choice *C* is incorrect. Although the ethicist would likely agree with this general sentiment, Choice *C* is too broad. Choice *B* is incorrect. The ethicist doesn't argue for limiting artificial intelligence to simple algorithms.

13. D: The cardinal rule has three requirements—privately held small business, sells tangible goods, and no debt. Elizabeth's store is a privately held small business (standalone and owned by her), it sells tangible goods (board games), and it has no debt. The lack of profitability is irrelevant, acting as a red herring. The cardinal rule doesn't mention it, presumably since the businessman thinks he can increase profitability as long as the business meets those three requirements. Choice *A* is incorrect. Jose's grocery store owes the bank three months' worth of mortgage payments, so it has debt, violating the cardinal rule. Choice *C* is incorrect. The accounting firm violates the cardinal rule because it does not sell a tangible good. Choice *B* is incorrect. A multinational corporation is not a small business, so it violates the cardinal rule.

14. B: A semicolon separates main clauses that are not joined by a coordinating conjunction, such as "and." Choice *B* breaks this long sentence into two main clauses, each of which can stand on its own as a complete sentence.

15. B: *Reticent* is the best choices for this sentence because it means reserved, secretive, or quiet. *Demonstrative* means expressive, so this is the opposite of what we are looking for. *Apathetic* is incorrect because it means uninterested or uncaring. *Buoyant* means resilient or light in weight and does not fit within the context of the sentence.

16. A: *Galvanize* is the best answer here because it means to awaken or arouse something. *Placate* is incorrect because it means to soothe or pacify. *Quell* means to suppress, so this is the opposite of the correct answer. Finally, *relinquish* is incorrect because it denotes giving up or letting go.

17. C: *Proficient* is the best choice for this sentence because it means highly skilled. *Notorious* means well known. *Inept* means unskilled. *Unassuming* means modest.

18. B: *Obsolete* is the best choice for this sentence because it means outdated or old-fashioned. *Resuscitated* means revived. *Ostentatious* means showy or pretentious. *Contemporary* means modern or current.

19. B: "The notion of" should be deleted, because "The significance of three-ness..." is much more direct. "Of these cultures", Choice *C*, is a necessary reference to the Indo-European societies. "Numerous", Choice *D*, attests to the quantity of these events, and it is stronger than simply "abounds with events."

20. C: *Their* is the correct spelling of the possessive form of *they*.

21. B: The reciprocal pronoun "one another" generally refers to more than two people.

22. C: The best answer is Choice *C*: "Lulu brought this kitten home only six weeks ago, and she was so fond of her." There are two independent clauses in one sentence, so separating the two clauses with a comma is the best option. The original line and Choice *B* do not separate the clauses with a comma. Additionally, the information that Lulu was only five years old is not necessary in this particular sentence; it is out of context, making Choice *D* incorrect.

23. C: We would use the preposition *through*, when talking about staying with someone during the night.

24. B: The underlined portion of this sentence is a preposition. Prepositions connect objects to nouns, pronouns, or phrases representing nouns. Here, incorrect because it signals that Hawthorne and the literature are co-contributors.

25. C: This question requires close attention to the passage. Choice *A* can be found where the passage says "no less than six named and several unnamed varieties of the peach have thus produced several varieties of nectarine," so this choice is incorrect. Choice *B* can be found where the passage says "it is highly improbable that all these peach-trees... are hybrids from the peach and nectarine." Choice *D* is incorrect because we see in the passage that "the production of peaches from nectarines, either by seeds or buds, may perhaps be considered as a case of reversion." Choice *C* is the correct answer because the word *unremarkable* should be changed to *remarkable* in order for it to be consistent with the details of the passage.

26. B: Choice *B* is the correct answer because the meaning holds true even if the words have been switched out or rearranged some. Choice *A* is incorrect because it has trees bearing either peaches or nectarines, and the trees in the original phrase bear both. Choice *C* is incorrect because the statement does not say these trees are "indifferent to bud-variation" but that they have "indifferently [bore] peaches or nectarines." Choice *D* is incorrect; the statement may use some of the same words, but the meaning is skewed in this sentence.

27. C: The director and critic are arguing about the director's role. The director argues that directors should be allowed to offend people, if that would accurately reflect reality, so the audience can maintain its suspension of disbelief. The critic would argue that this violates the director's social responsibility to avoid offending people. Choice *A* is incorrect. Both the director and critic would agree that movie audiences suspend their disbelief. This is the director's main point, and the critic acknowledges its existence by claiming that censoring hate speech and racial slurs won't break the audience's disbelief. Choice *B* is incorrect. This is the critic's main point, and the director would likely also agree. The director isn't claiming that movies aren't offensive, but that offending people is justified to protect the suspension of disbelief. Choice *D* is incorrect. This isn't the main point in dispute. In addition, both the director and critic imply that they believe this to be true. For the director, creative control is required to structure a universe where an audience can suspend its disbelief. For the critic, the director would need creative control to censor what the critic deems inappropriate.

28. D: In this sentence, there is an interrupting phrase that must be set apart by two commas on either side of it.

29. A: When an age is describing a noun and precedes the noun, hyphenation is required.

30. B. Choice *A* is not the best answer because the adverb *approximately* interrupts the phrase *once a week*, producing the awkward if grammatically correct phrase *once, approximately, a week*. Choice *C* is not correct because *bi-weekly* means twice a week or every two weeks. Choice *D* is not the best answer because it changes the meaning.

Writing Prompt

When writing a persuasive-explanatory essay, it's important to use the author's words to support your claims. You can do so by quoting phrases and sentences that reinforce your point. However, it's easy to accidentally take the author's message out of context. A great tip to preserve the original message is by paraphrasing. Compare your summary to the author's initial statements. If the general idea is unchanged, you're going to do well.

For the persuasive side of an essay, you're going to try to convince the reader that your opinion is valid. You'll want to write in a convincing and deliberate manner. Avoid using words like *maybe*, *potentially*, *could be*, etc. Those words have a tendency to diminish a strong message. Remember to include the opposing argument in your paper. A balanced persuasive essay shows both sides of the argument. Acknowledge the opposing view, but don't get too worried about the minute details.

Don't forget the general structure of an essay!

- An introductory paragraph contains your initial opinion and idea. You can't have an introductory paragraph without a thesis statement. You'll also allude to your main points briefly.
- Body paragraphs are your main points. For a 300–600-word essay, two to three body paragraphs will be fine. Make sure you address your first point, add your supporting evidence, and elaborate. Repeat those steps as needed.
- The concluding paragraph summarizes your main points.

Writing can be hard, but have no fear. Try to imagine you're having a conversation. Essays are essentially structured conversations. However, it's not quite like talking with friends. Slang, inside jokes, and abbreviations don't work well for strangers. Imagine you're talking to someone you deeply admire and respect; you'd want to be thoughtful and understanding. This means you should simplify complex ideas without being reductive and condescending.

In general, it's good practice to read what you write out loud. Your ears will notice if something doesn't sound right. Our ears pick up on details that our eyes miss. It's especially true when you're completely focused on writing.

If you get stuck at any point, take a break, and come back to it. You'll have ample time to finish if you pace yourself and take it easy.

Practice Test #3

Mathematics

1. What is the result of dividing 24 by $\frac{8}{5}$, in lowest possible terms?

   a. $\frac{5}{3}$

   b. $\frac{3}{5}$

   c. $\frac{120}{8}$

   d. 15

2. Debbie is taking an exam. The multiple-choice questions are worth 2.5 points and the short answer questions are worth 4 points. If she answers 15 multiple-choice questions correctly and x short answer questions correctly, which of the following expressions represents her total score on the exam?

   a. $15x + 2.5$
   b. $2.5x + 60$
   c. $4x + 37.5$
   d. 41.5

3. The following set represents the test scores from a university class: {35, 79, 80, 87, 87, 90, 92, 95, 95, 98, 99}. If the outlier is removed from this set, which of the following is TRUE?

   a. The mean and the median will decrease.
   b. The mean and the median will increase.
   c. The mean and the mode will increase.
   d. The mean and the mode will decrease.

4. What are the zeros of the following cubic function?

$$g(x) = x^3 - 2x^2 - 9x + 18$$

   a. 2, 3
   b. 2, 3, -2
   c. 2, 3, -3
   d. 2, -2

5. If $h(x) = -6x + 11$, what is $h(-2)$?

   a. 1
   b. −1
   c. 23
   d. −23

6. For which values of x is the following function undefined?

$$f(x) = \frac{x^2 + 3x + 1}{-3x + x^2}$$

a. 2, 3
b. 0, 3
c. 1, 2
d. 0, 1

7. What is the equation of the line that passes through the two points $(-3, 7)$ and $(-1, -5)$?

a. $y = 6x + 11$
b. $y = 6x$
c. $y = -6x - 11$
d. $y = -6x$

8. If the volume of a sphere is the same as a cylinder that has a radius of 6 inches and a height of 10 inches, what is the radius, in inches, of the sphere? The volume of a sphere with radius r is $V = \frac{4}{3}\pi r^3$.

a. 10
b. $3\sqrt[3]{10}$
c. $\sqrt[3]{30}$
d. 13

9. What is the area of the shaded region?

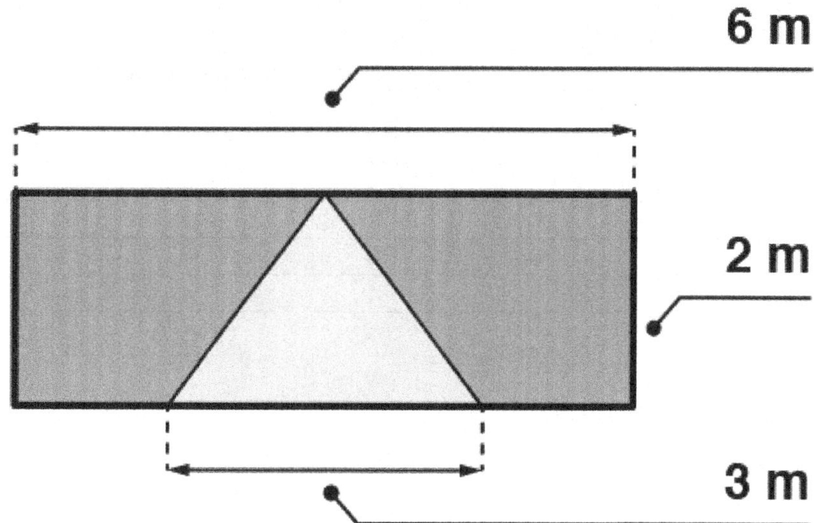

a. 9 m^2
b. 12 m^2
c. 6 m^2
d. 8 m^2

10. Which of the following is the equation of a vertical line that runs through the point $(1, 4)$?
    a. $x = 1$
    b. $y = 1$
    c. $x = 4$
    d. $y = 4$

11. In order to estimate deer population in a forest, biologists obtained a sample of deer in that forest and tagged each one of them. The sample had 300 deer in total. They returned a week later, harmlessly captured 400 deer, and found that 5 were tagged. Using this information, which of the following is the best estimate of the total number of deer in the forest?
    a. 24,000 deer
    b. 30,000 deer
    c. 40,000 deer
    d. 100,000 deer

12. What is the solution to the following system of equations?

$$2x - y = 6$$

$$y = 8x$$

    a. $(1, 8)$
    b. $(-1, -8)$
    c. All real numbers
    d. There is no solution.

13. The table below shows student names and how many classes they took during their first semester of college. If these students represent a random sample, what is the probability that a student will take at least 4 classes in their first semester?

Name	Number of classes taken
Bryan	3
Keisha	4
Mary	5
Kent	2
David	6
Courtney	4

    a. 67%
    b. 50%
    c. 75%
    d. 100%

14. The following table presents data for 100 students and whether or not they play an instrument. What is the probability that a female does not play an instrument? Enter your answer as a decimal rounded to three decimal places.

	Plays instrument	Does not play instrument	Total
Male	16	36	52
Female	13	35	48
Total	29	71	100

a. 0.493
b. 0.350
c. 0.371
d. 0.729

15. Which is equivalent to the following expression?

$$\frac{4x-2}{x+5}-\frac{2x-1}{x-5}$$

a. $\frac{6x^2-12x+5}{x^2-25}$
b. $\frac{2x-1}{x^2-25}$
c. $\frac{2x-1}{x+5}$
d. $\frac{2x^2-31x+15}{x^2-25}$

16. In order to get a B in a class, Mark needs to have an 80 average on his 5 tests. He received the following grades on his first 4 tests: 85, 76, 56, and 88. What is the lowest score he would need to receive on the fifth test to get a B in the class?

a. 90
b. 95
c. 85
d. 80
e. 100

17. A pen costs $0.50 less than three times the cost of a pencil. If the pen and pencil together cost $5.10, how much more does the pen cost than the pencil?

a. $3.70
b. $4.25
c. $2.30
d. $1.40

18. Out of 16,800 students at the state university, 1400 were history majors, 1200 were education majors, 1560 were engineering majors, and 1000 were pre-med. Using these percentages, if in a single dorm 150 were engineering majors, approximately how many students lived in the dorm?

a. 1613
b. 156
c. 1560
d. 1213

19. The following table shows values of two functions $f(x)$ and $g(x)$.

x	$f(x)$	$g(x)$
4	6	3
5	-8	5
6	2	-8

If $h(x) = -4 \times g(x) - f(x)$, what is the value of $h(6)$?

a. -30
b. 30
c. 24
d. 34

20. What is the length of side x in the following right triangle?

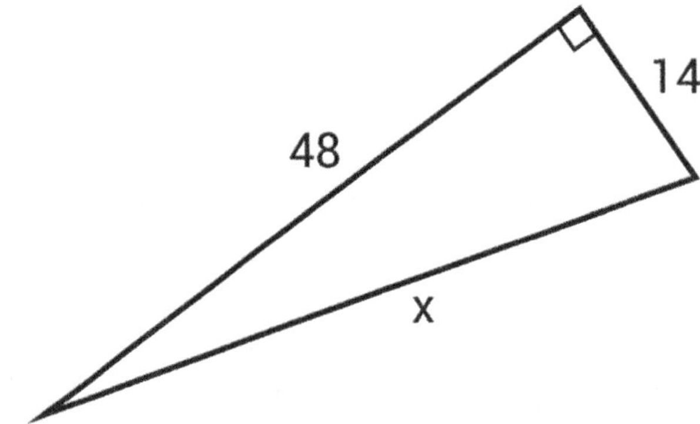

a. 42
b. 52
c. 50
d. 2,500

English Language Arts and Reading

Questions 1–4 are based on the following passage:

Alice was beginning to get very tired of sitting by her sister on the bank, and of having nothing to do: once or twice she had peeped into the book her sister was reading, but it had no pictures or conversations in it, "and what is the use of a book," thought Alice "without pictures or conversation?"

So she was considering in her own mind (as well as she could, for the hot day made her feel very sleepy and stupid), whether the pleasure of making a daisy-chain would be worth the trouble of getting up and picking the daisies, when suddenly a White Rabbit with pink eyes ran close by her.

There was nothing so VERY remarkable in that; nor did Alice think it so VERY much out of the way to hear the Rabbit say to itself, "Oh dear! Oh dear! I shall be late!" (when she thought it over afterwards, it occurred to her that she ought to have wondered at this, but at the time it all seemed quite natural); but when the Rabbit actually TOOK A WATCH OUT OF ITS WAISTCOAT-POCKET, and looked at it, and then hurried on, Alice started to her feet, for it flashed across her mind that she had never before seen a rabbit with either a waistcoat-pocket, or a watch to take out of it, and burning with curiosity, she ran across the field after it, and fortunately was just in time to see it pop down a large rabbit-hole under the hedge.

In another moment down went Alice after it, never once considering how in the world she was to get out again.

The rabbit-hole went straight on like a tunnel for some way, and then dipped suddenly down, so suddenly that Alice had not a moment to think about stopping herself before she found herself falling down a very deep well.

Either the well was very deep, or she fell very slowly, for she had plenty of time as she went down to look about her and to wonder what was going to happen next. First, she tried to look down and make out what she was coming to, but it was too dark to see anything; then she looked at the sides of the well, and noticed that they were filled with cupboards and book-shelves; here and there she saw maps and pictures hung upon pegs. She took down a jar from one of the shelves as she passed; it was labelled "ORANGE MARMALADE," but to her great disappointment it was empty: she did not like to drop the jar for fear of killing somebody, so managed to put it into one of the cupboards as she fell past it.

"Well!" thought Alice to herself, "after such a fall as this, I shall think nothing of tumbling down stairs! How brave they'll all think me at home! Why, I wouldn't say anything about it, even if I fell off the top of the house!" (Which was very likely true.)

Excerpt from *Alice's Adventures in Wonderland* by Lewis Carroll, 1865

1. Based on this passage, which three words best describe Alice?
    a. Patient, sleepy, observant
    b. Whimsical, conformist, doting
    c. Impulsive, restless, curious
    d. Thoughtful, inventive, boisterous

2. Why does Alice follow the white rabbit?
    a. She hopes to catch him and keep him for a pet.
    b. He looks like one of the pictures in her sister's book.
    c. Her sister suggested she find something to do.
    d. She was bored, and she had never seen a rabbit with a waist-coat pocket or a watch.

3. What does this passage reveal about the setting?
    a. It establishes the transition between Alice's world and the rabbit's world.
    b. It shows us the world as the rabbit sees it.
    c. It shows us that the white rabbit is equally at home in Alice's world and its own world.
    d. It establishes the characters and where they live.

4. In this passage, Alice:
    a. Reads her sister's book, picks daisies, follows the rabbit, falls down a well
    b. Falls asleep, chases a rabbit, climbs under a hedge, falls down a well
    c. Is bored, chases a rabbit across a field, follows it down a rabbit hole, falls down a very deep well
    d. Talks to her sister about a book, follows the white rabbit down the rabbit hole, eats marmalade and drops the jar, falls for a very long time

The next question is based on the following passage:

> Bet and Nan were fifteen years old—twins. They were good-hearted girls, unclean, clothed in rags, and profoundly ignorant. Their mother was like them. But the father and the grandmother were a couple of fiends. They got drunk whenever they could; then they fought each other or anybody else who came in the way; they cursed and swore always, drunk or sober; John Canty was a thief, and his mother a beggar. <u>They made beggars of the children, but failed to make thieves of them</u>. Among, but not of, the dreadful rabble that inhabited the house, was a good old priest whom the King had turned out of house and home with a pension of a few farthings, and he used to get the children aside and teach them right ways secretly.
>
> Excerpt from *The Prince and the Pauper* by Mark Twain, 1882

5. The writer is considering deleting the underlined section of text. Should this sentence be kept or deleted?
    a. Kept, because the line confirms that the children grow up to be thieves
    b. Deleted, because the focus is on the children being beggars
    c. Kept, because it explains that the children were not corrupted by the adults
    d. Deleted, because it undermines the priest's hard work in instilling morals

The next question is based on the following passage:

> Sherlock Holmes took his bottle from the corner of the mantelpiece and his hypodermic syringe from its neat Morocco case. For some little time his eyes rested thoughtfully upon the sinewy forearm and wrist all dotted and scarred with innumerable puncture-marks. Finally he thrust the sharp point home, pressed down the tiny piston, and sank back into the velvet-lined arm-chair with a long sigh of satisfaction.
>
> Excerpt from *The Sign of the Four* by Arthur Conan Doyle, 1890

6. The author wishes to insert the following sentence:

"With his long, white, nervous fingers he adjusted the delicate needle, and rolled back his left shirt-cuff."

The best placement for this sentence is:
    a. Before sentence 1
    b. After sentence 1
    c. After sentence 2
    d. After the last sentence

Questions 7–12 are based on the following passage from Rhetoric and Poetry in the Renaissance: A Study of Rhetorical Terms in English Renaissance Literary Criticism *by D. L. Clark:*

> To the Greeks and Romans, rhetoric meant the theory of oratory. As a pedagogical mechanism, it endeavored to teach students to persuade an audience. The content of rhetoric included all that the ancients had learned to be of value in persuasive public speech. It taught how to work up a case by drawing valid inferences from sound evidence, how to organize this material in the most persuasive order, and how to compose in clear and harmonious sentences. Thus, to the Greeks and Romans, rhetoric was defined by its function of discovering means to persuasion and was taught in the schools as something that every free-born man could and should learn.
>
> In both these respects, the ancients felt that poetics, the theory of poetry, was different from rhetoric. As the critical theorists believed that the poets were inspired, they endeavored less to teach men to be poets than to point out the excellences which the poets had attained. Although these critics generally, with the exceptions of Aristotle and Eratosthenes, believed the greatest value of poetry to be in the teaching of morality, no one of them endeavored to define poetry, as they did rhetoric, by its purpose. To Aristotle, and centuries later to Plutarch, the distinguishing mark of poetry was imitation. Not until the Renaissance did critics define poetry as an art of imitation endeavoring to inculcate morality...
>
> The same essential difference between classical rhetoric and poetics appears in the content of classical poetics. Whereas classical rhetoric deals with speeches which might be delivered to convict or acquit a defendant in the law court, or to secure a certain action by the deliberative assembly, or to adorn an occasion, classical poetics deals with lyric, epic, and drama. It is a commonplace that classical literary critics paid little attention to the lyric. It is less frequently realized that they devoted almost as little space to discussion of metrics. By far the greater bulk of classical treatises on poetics is devoted to characterization and to the technique of plot construction, involving as it does narrative and dramatic unity and movement as distinct from logical unity and movement.

7. What does the author say about how the purpose of poetry changed for later philosophers?
    a. The author says that at first, poetry was not defined by its purpose but was valued for its ability to be used to teach morality. Later, some philosophers would define poetry by its ability to instill morality. Finally, during the Renaissance, poetry was believed to be an imitative art, but was not necessarily believed to instill morality in its readers.
    b. The author says that the classical understanding of poetry dealt with its ability to be used to teach morality. Later, philosophers would define poetry by its ability to imitate life. Finally, during the Renaissance, poetry was believed to be an imitative art that instilled morality in its readers.
    c. The author says that at first, poetry was thought to be an imitation of reality. Later on, philosophers valued poetry more for its ability to instill morality.
    d. The author says that the classical understanding of poetry was that it dealt with the search for truth through its content; later, the purpose of poetry would be through its entertainment value.

8. What does the author of the passage say about classical literary critics in relation to poetics?
   a. That rhetoric was valued more than poetry because rhetoric had a definitive purpose to persuade an audience, and poetry's wavering purpose made it harder for critics to teach
   b. That although most poetry was written as lyric, epic, or drama, the critics were most focused on the techniques of lyric and epic and their performance of musicality and structure
   c. That although most poetry was written as lyric, epic, or drama, the critics were most focused on the techniques of the epic and drama and their performance of structure and character
   d. That the study of poetics was more pleasurable than the study of rhetoric due to its ability to assuage its audience, and the critics, therefore, focused on what poets did to create that effect

9. What is the primary purpose of this passage?
   a. To alert the readers to Greek and Roman culture regarding poetic texts and the focus on characterization and plot construction rather than lyric and meter
   b. To inform the readers of the changes in poetic critical theory throughout the years and to contrast those changes to the solidity of rhetoric
   c. To educate the audience on rhetoric by explaining the historical implications of using rhetoric in the education system
   d. To contemplate the differences between classical rhetoric and poetry and to consider their purposes in a particular culture

10. The word *inculcate* in the final sentence can be best interpreted as meaning which one of the following?
   a. Imbibe
   b. Instill
   c. Implode
   d. Inquire

11. Which of the following most closely resembles the way in which the passage is structured?
   a. The first paragraph presents an issue. The second paragraph offers a solution to the problem. The third paragraph summarizes the first two paragraphs.
   b. The first paragraph presents definitions and examples of a particular subject. The second paragraph presents a second subject in the same way. The third paragraph offers a contrast of the two subjects.
   c. The first paragraph presents an inquiry. The second paragraph explains the details of that inquiry. The last paragraph offers a solution.
   d. The first paragraph presents two subjects alongside definitions and examples. The second paragraph presents us a comparison of the two subjects. The third paragraph presents a contrast of the two subjects.

12. Given the author's description of the content of rhetoric in the first paragraph, which one of the following is most analogous to what it taught? (The sentence is shown below.)

It taught how to work up a case by drawing valid inferences from sound evidence, how to organize this material in the most persuasive order, and how to compose in clear and harmonious sentences.

a. As a musician, they taught me that the end product of the music is everything—what I did to get there was irrelevant, whether it was my ability to read music or the reliance on my intuition to compose.
b. As a detective, they taught me that time meant everything when dealing with a new case, that the simplest explanation is usually the right one, and that documentation is extremely important to credibility.
c. As a writer, they taught me the most important thing about writing was consistently showing up to the page every single day, no matter where my muse was.
d. As a football player, they taught me how to understand the logistics of the game, how my placement on the field affected the rest of the team, and how to run and throw with a mixture of finesse and strength.

The next question is based on the following sentence:

> Despite facing numerous challenges involving coworkers and bosses, her unwavering determination allowed her to succeed in a male-dominated field.

13. What can reasonably be inferred from this statement?
a. The woman was given special help due to her gender.
b. The woman faced issues in her field due to her gender.
c. The woman performed better than her male counterparts.
d. The woman had struggles balancing her work and personal life.

The next question is based on the following statements:

> Claim 1: There has been a steep decline in people shopping in malls.
>
> Claim 2: Online sales for stores have skyrocketed in the last few years.

14. What can reasonably be inferred from these statements?
a. People prefer shopping online to shopping in person.
b. People do not want to shop online more than they do in person.
c. Malls need to have more services to attract consumers.
d. Online goods are higher-quality than those found in physical stores.

The next question is based on the following sentences:

> The woman read the yellowed letter, smiling to herself with each tender word. As she came to the end, she began to weep.

15. What can reasonably be inferred from this text?
a. The author of the letter has passed away.
b. The letter's contents are hurtful to the woman.
c. The author of the letter is dear to the woman.
d. The woman is excited to reply to the letter.

16. Choose the best replacement word or phrase.

"Where could my cat have gone?" Everyone just looked at each other in utter silence.

a. No change
b. one another
c. themselves
d. each one

The next question is based on the following passage:

Sarah Boone obtained a patent for a new version of the ironing board in 1892. Boone was an African American dressmaker who sought to improve upon existing ironing board concepts. Her design made it far easier to iron women's clothing, such as dresses. She also made her ironing board collapsible so that it could be stored more easily. Although the ironing board has existed for centuries and has continued to improve over time, Boone played a crucial role in the development of the form and function of the ironing board we still use today.

17. Which choice best describes the function of the underlined sentence in this text?
a. To clarify that Boone did not invent the ironing board, but she still played an integral part in its history
b. To question why Boone is recognized as a crucial part of the ironing board's history despite not being the actual inventor
c. To convince readers that Boone was the only credited inventor for the ironing board and should be respected as such
d. To persuade readers to always try to improve upon the items that they use every day, as this is how the world continues to progress

18. Choose the best replacement.

Forced to migrate to areas rich in coal, where filthy, violence-ridden cities have sprung up, the people of agrarian communities encountered suffering, despondency, and poverty.

a. No change
b. where filthy, violence-ridden, cities have sprung up
c. where filthy, violence-ridden cities had sprung up
d. where filthy, violence ridden cities have sprung up

19. Choose the best replacement.

Both my husband and myself drive our daughter to friends' houses, school, the arena, the grocery store, medical appointments, and more.

a. No change
b. I
c. me
d. myself,

20. Choose the best replacement for the underlined portion.

    He developed a tragic vision that is fundamentally dark: man's inevitable moral downfall is determined by the workings of its own heart.

    a. No change
    b. her own heart
    c. his own heart
    d. people's own heart

21. Choose the best replacement for the underlined portion.

    To a visitor, the mouth of the cavern is bright with sunlight and flowers, but a few feet in, the light dims and warmth turns to chill; the visitor stumbles, first in confusion, then in terror.

    a. No change
    b. but a few feet in the light, dims and warmth turns to chill, the visitor stumbles, first in confusion, then in terror
    c. but a few feet in the light dims and warmth turns to chill, the visitor stumbles first in confusion then in terror
    d. but a few feet in the light dims and warmth turns to chill: the visitor stumbles first in confusion, then in terror

22. Choose the best replacement for the underlined portion.

    With roots digging deeply into the past as the thirteenth century, when capitalism and commerce began to develop, industrialization slowly became inevitable.

    a. No change
    b. With roots, digging deeply into the past as the thirteenth century
    c. With roots digging as deeply into the past as the thirteenth century
    d. With roots that were digging deeply into the past as the thirteenth century

23. Choose the best replacement for the underlined portion.

    The juxtaposition of a small number of people, who held great wealth, with a population for whom extreme and widespread poverty was inescapable was one of the greatest problems the Industrial Revolution created.

    a. No change
    b. amount
    c. quota
    d. mass

The next question is based on the following passage:

> A comparison of brown rice and white rice reveals distinct nutritional differences. Brown rice, with its unrefined whole-grain nature, is a nutrient powerhouse. It is rich in fiber, essential vitamins, and minerals. This makes it an excellent choice for those seeking a healthier grain option. White rice, although less nutritious due to refining, is a quick source of energy and a versatile ingredient in various cuisines. This makes it a viable

choice when eaten in moderation and for specific dietary needs. <u>There is also a cost difference between the two types of rice, which can factor into why one rice is chosen over another</u>.

24. Which revision improves the level of information provided in the text?
    a. NO CHANGE
    b. "Brown rice and white rice are also priced differently, which is important for those hoping to save money when buying groceries."
    c. "The two types of rice can also vary in cost, which may affect which one consumers eat on a regular basis."
    d. "White rice is also generally more affordable than brown rice, which is an important factor when choosing between the two variations."

The next question is based on the following passage:

> On the bridge, as they had been riding out of Bridgewater, they had met a vanguard of fugitives from the field of battle, weary, broken men, many of them wounded, all of them terror-stricken, staggering in speedless haste with the last remnants of their strength into the shelter which it was their vain illusion the town would afford them. Eyes glazed with lassitude and fear looked up piteously out of haggard faces at Mr. Blood and his companion as they rode forth; <u>rough</u> voices cried a warning that merciless pursuit was not far behind.

Excerpt from *Captain Blood* by Rafael Sabatini, 1922

25. Which revision improves the descriptiveness of the text's language?
    a. Scratchy
    b. Hoarse
    c. Boisterous
    d. Fearful

26. Choose the best replacement for the underlined portion.

    Yet Hawthorne's bleak vision also embraces the drama of the human heart, through which he depicts the heart as a redemptive agent, subtly affirming <u>humanities</u> inherent goodness.

    a. No change
    b. humanities'
    c. humanitys
    d. humanity's

27. To a visitor, the mouth of the cavern is bright with sunlight and flowers, but a few feet in, the light dims and warmth turns to chill; the visitor stumbles, first in confusion, then in terror.

a. but a few feet in, the light dims and warmth turns to chill; the visitor stumbles, first in confusion, then in terror.
b. but a few feet in the light, dims and warmth turns to chill, the visitor stumbles, first in confusion, then in terror
c. but a few feet in the light dims and warmth turns to chill, the visitor stumbles first in confusion then in terror
d. but a few feet in the light dims and warmth turns to chill: the visitor stumbles first in confusion, then in terror

28. Choose the best replacement for the underlined portion.

Further back, a small gleam of light appears and the visitor hurries toward it, to find a scene much like that at the entrance of the cavern, only perfect.

a. No change
b. In the back
c. To the back
d. Farther in

29. Choose the best replacement for the underlined portion.

This, to Hawthorne, is the depth of human nature; the beauty that lies beyond fear and hopelessness.

a. No change
b. human nature. The beauty that lies beyond fear and hopelessness.
c. human nature: the beauty that lies beyond fear and hopelessness.
d. human nature (the beauty that lies beyond fear and hopelessness).

The next question is based on the following passage:

There has been debate within the literary world regarding the authorship of Shakespeare's works. Some believe that many of the works accredited to Shakespeare were actually co-authored with someone else or that Shakespeare wasn't involved at all. This is because there is little documentation proving that Shakespeare was a skilled writer. Christopher Marlowe and Francis Bacon have often been offered up as potential authors of Shakespeare's work due to their writing prowess.

30. What is the main purpose of this text?

a. To encourage readers to look up Shakespeare's biography
b. To disagree with claims that Shakespeare did not write his own plays
c. To educate readers on a theory regarding Shakespeare's authorship
d. To support the argument that Shakespeare wrote all of his plays by himself

Writing Prompt

In response to the following prompt, write a 300- to 600-word essay.

> The true boundary line of the First Amendment can be fixed only when Congress and the courts realize that the principle on which speech is classified as lawful or unlawful involves the balancing against each other of two very important social interests, in public safety and in the search for truth. Every reasonable attempt should be made to maintain both interests unimpaired, and the great interest in free speech should be sacrificed only when the interest in public safety is really imperiled, and not, as most men believe, when it is barely conceivable that it may be slightly affected. In war time, therefore, speech should be unrestricted by the censorship or by punishment, unless it is clearly liable to cause direct and dangerous interference with the conduct of the war.

Write a response in which you identify your stance on the argument above. Once you've identified your stance, use concrete evidence to support your argument.

Answer Explanations #3

Mathematics

1. D: To divide fractions, multiply by the reciprocal:

$$24 \div \frac{8}{5} = \frac{24}{1} \times \frac{5}{8} = \frac{3 \times 8}{1} \times \frac{5}{8} = \frac{15}{1} = 15$$

2. C: Because each multiple-choice question is worth 2.5 points, and she answers 15 of them correctly, her total score from multiple-choice questions is $2.5(15) = 37.5$. Because each short answer question is worth 4 points, and she answers x of them correctly, her total score from short answer questions is $4x$. Adding these together results in $4x + 37.5$, her total score.

3. B: The outlier is 35. When a small outlier is removed from a data set, the mean and the median increase. The first step in this process is to identify the outlier, which is the number that lies away from the given set. Once the outlier is identified, the mean and median can be recalculated. The mean will be affected because it is the average of all of the numbers. The median will be affected because it finds the middle number, which is subject to change because a number is lost. The mode will most likely not change because it is the number that occurs the most, which will not be the outlier if there is only one outlier.

4. C: To find the zeros, set the function equal to 0 and factor the polynomial. Because there are four terms, it should be factored by grouping. Factor a common factor out of the first set of two terms, and then find a shared binomial factor in the second set of two terms. This results in:

$$x^2(x-2) - 9(x-2) = 0$$

The binomial can then be factored out of each set to get:

$$(x^2 - 9)(x - 2) = 0$$

This can be factored further as:

$$(x+3)(x-3)(x-2) = 0$$

Setting each factor equal to zero and solving results in the three zeros -3, 3, and 2.

5. C: If $h(x) = -6x + 11$, then $h(-2)$ can be found by substituting –2 in for x in the function. Therefore:

$$h(-2) = -6(-2) + 11 = 12 + 11 = 23$$

6. B: For rational functions, the denominator can never be equal to 0. Finding the undefined values for a function is the same as finding the zeros of the expression in the denominator. To find the undefined values, set the denominator equal to 0 and solve for x. This results in $-3x + x^2 = 0$, and its solutions are $x = 0$ and $x = 3$. Therefore, the undefined values of x are 0 and 3; Choice B is correct.

7. C: First, the slope of the line must be found. First, the slope of the line must be found. This is equal to the change in y over the change in x, given the two points:

$$\frac{-5-7}{-1--3}$$

$$\frac{-12}{2}=-6$$

Therefore, the slope is -6.

The slope and one of the points are then plugged into the point-slope form of a line:

$$y-y_1=m(x-x_1)$$

This results in:

$$y-7=-6(x+3)$$

The -6 is distributed and the equation is solved for y to obtain $y=-6x-11$.

8. B: The volume of a cylinder with radius r and height h is $V=\pi r^2 h$. The volume of a sphere with radius r is $V=\frac{4}{3}\pi r^3$. Therefore, the cylinder mentioned in the problem has a volume of:

$$V=\pi(6)^2(10)=360\pi \text{ in}^3$$

The sphere has the same volume, so the equations can be set equal:

$$360\pi=\frac{4}{3}\pi r^3$$

$$\frac{360\cancel{\pi}}{\cancel{\pi}}=360=\frac{4}{3}r^3$$

$$r^3=360\times\frac{3}{4}=270$$

Taking the cube root of r^3 finds the radius of the sphere:

$$r=\sqrt[3]{270}=3\sqrt[3]{10}\text{ in}$$

9. A: The area of the shaded region is calculated in a few steps. First, the area of the rectangle is found using the formula:

$$A=length\times width=6\text{ m}\times 2\text{ m}=12\text{ m}^2$$

Second, the area of the triangle is found using the formula:

$$A=\frac{1}{2}\times base\times height=\frac{1}{2}\times 3\text{ m}\times 2\text{ m}=3\text{ m}^2$$

The last step is to take the rectangle area and subtract the triangle area. The area of the shaded region is:

$$A=12\text{ m}^2-3\text{ m}^2=9\text{ m}^2$$

10. A: A vertical line has the same x-value for any point on the line. Other points on the line would be $(1,3)$, $(1,5)$, $(1,9)$, etc. Mathematically, this is written as $x = 1$. A vertical line is always of the form $x = a$ for some constant a.

11. A: A proportion should be used to solve this problem. The ratio of tagged to total deer in each instance is set equal to one another, and the unknown quantity is a variable x. The proportion is:

$$\frac{300}{x} = \frac{5}{400}$$

Cross-multiplying gives $120{,}000 = 5x$, and dividing through by 5 results in 24,000.

12. B: This system can be solved using substitution. Plug the second equation in for y in the first equation to obtain $2x - 8x = 6$, which simplifies to $-6x = 6$. Divide both sides by 6 to get $x = -1$, which is then substituted back into either original equation to obtain $y = -8$.

13. A: Four out of the six students took at least 4 classes. Probability is defined as the number of desired outcomes over the number of possible outcomes. Therefore, the correct probability is $\frac{4}{6} \approx 0.67 = 67\%$.

14. D: There are 48 total females and 35 do not play an instrument. This is a conditional probability problem. The probability that a female does not play an instrument is $\frac{35}{48} \approx 0.729$ rounded to three decimal places.

15. D: In order to add the two rational expressions, a common denominator must be used. The common denominator is $(x+5)(x-5)$. Multiply by fractions equal to 1 to build the common denominator. Multiply the first expression times $\frac{x-5}{x-5}$ and the second times $\frac{x+5}{x+5}$, and then subtract to obtain:

$$\frac{(4x-2)(x-5)}{(x+5)(x-5)} - \frac{(2x-1)(x+5)}{(x-5)(x+5)}$$

$$\frac{4x^2 - 20x - 2x + 10}{(x+5)(x-5)} - \frac{2x^2 + 10x - x - 5}{(x+5)(x-5)}$$

$$\frac{2x^2 - 31x + 15}{x^2 - 25}$$

16. B: Let x be the score on the fifth test. Therefore, to get a B in the class, $\frac{85+75+55+90+x}{5} > 80$. Therefore, $\frac{305+x}{5} > 80$. Multiplying times 5 on both sides results in $305 + x > 400$. Subtracting 305 from each side results in $x > 95$. Therefore, Mark must obtain at least a 95 on the last test to receive a B in the class.

17. C: Let x be the cost of the pencil. Therefore, $3x - 0.50$ is the cost of the pen. Together, they sum up to \$5.10, which is:

$$x + (3x - 0.50) = 5.10$$

Solve for x to find the cost of the pencil:

$$x + 3x = 5.10 + 0.50$$

$$4x = 5.60$$

$$x = 1.40$$

Therefore, the pencil costs \$1.40 and the pen costs $3(1.40) - 0.50 = 3.70$, or \$3.70. Thus, the pen costs $\$3.70 - \$1.40 = \$2.30$ more than the pen.

18. A: The percentage of engineering majors at the entire university is $\frac{1560}{16800} \approx 9.3\%$. If this data was used to estimate the number of engineering majors in the dorm, then 9.3% of those students were also engineering majors. 9.3% of the total number of students in the dorm is equal to 150. Divide 150 by 0.93 to obtain 1612.9, which is closest to 1613.

19. B: From the table, we can see that $f(6) = 2$ and $g(6) = -8$. Therefore,

$$h(6) = -4(-8) - 2$$

$$h(6) = 32 - 2$$

$$h(6) = 30$$

20. C: Because it is a right triangle, the Pythagorean theorem can be used. The missing side length is the hypotenuse. Therefore, $14^2 + 48^2 = x^2$, or $2500 = x^2$. Take the square root of 2,500 to obtain $x = 50$.

English Language Arts and Reading

1. C: Alice's behaviors in the passage suggest that she is all three of the characteristics named in Choice *C*, whereas the other answers include only one or two characteristics of Alice's character. Choice *A* suggests she is patient, Choice *B* suggests she is conformist or doting, and Choice *D* suggests she is inventive, none of which fit based on the text.

2. D: Choices *A*, *B*, and *C* are incorrect because they all include motivations that are not mentioned in the passage. Choice *D* is more complete, as we learn later in the passage that in addition to being bored, Alice has never seen anything like the rabbit.

3. A: The passage establishes the world Alice is in and the transition, via the well, into the new world as she passes the shelves and other items. The story is told from Alice's perspective, not the rabbit's, Choice *B*. We do not learn much about the white rabbit, Choice *C*, other than his being late. Though we do get introduced to two main characters, we do not know yet where they live, Choice *D*.

4. C: Choices *A*, *B*, and *D* all include actions Alice does not complete or participate in. Therefore, Choice *C* is the correct choice.

5. C: Choice *C* is the correct answer because the sentence is integral to the information being provided in the story. It should be kept for this reason. The line is clarifying that although the children had poor parental figures around them, they did not become criminals like them. This is later supported by saying that a priest helped them learn morals. Choice *A* is incorrect because the text does not focus on the children being beggars. It focuses on the children's upbringing and how they are not thieves. Choices *B* and *D* are incorrect because the sentence should not be deleted for the reason mentioned above.

6. A: Choice *B* is correct because it follows a logical chain of events. In the sentence, Sherlock Holmes already has the syringe out of its case and is in the process of rolling his sleeve up. In the first sentence of the paragraph, Holmes takes his syringe out, so the sentence must be placed sometime after this event. In the second sentence, Holmes can see his forearm, which means that he must have already rolled his sleeve back, making Choice *B* correct.

7. B: The rest of the answer choices improperly interpret this explanation in the passage. Poetry was never mentioned for its use in entertainment, which makes Choice *D* incorrect. Choices *A* and *C* are incorrect because they mix up the chronological order.

8. C: The author says that although most poetry was written as lyric, epic, or drama, the critics were most focused on the techniques of the epic and drama and their performance of structure and character. This is the best answer choice as portrayed by paragraph three. Choice *A* is incorrect because nowhere in the passage does it say rhetoric was more valued than poetry, although it did seem to have a more definitive purpose than poetry. Choice *B* is incorrect; this almost mirrors Choice *A*, but the critics were not focused on the lyric, as the passage indicates. Choice *D* is incorrect because the passage does not mention that the study of poetics was more pleasurable than the study of rhetoric.

9. D: The purpose is to contemplate the differences between classical rhetoric and poetry and to consider their purposes in a particular culture. Choice *A* is incorrect; this thought is discussed in the third paragraph, but it is not the main idea of the passage. Choice *B* is incorrect; although changes in poetics throughout the years is mentioned, this is not the main idea of the passage. Choice *C* is incorrect; although this is partly true—that rhetoric within the education system is mentioned—the subject of poetics is left out of this answer choice.

10. B: The correct answer choice is Choice *B*, *instill*. Choice *A*, *imbibe*, means to drink heavily, so this choice is incorrect. Choice *C*, *implode*, means to collapse inward, which does not make sense in this context. Choice *D*, *inquire*, means to investigate.

11. B: In the passage, we see the first paragraph defining rhetoric and offering examples of how the Greeks and Romans taught this subject. In the second paragraph, poetics is defined and examples of its dynamic definition are provided. In the third paragraph, the contrast between rhetoric and poetry is characterized through how each of these were studied in a classical context.

12. D: The passage covers three general principles—logic, organization, and style—which are paralleled in Choice *D*. Drawing inferences parallels to understanding the logistics of the game. Organization of material parallels to organization on the field. How to compose in harmonious sentences parallels to how to run with finesse and strength.

13. B: Choice *B* is the correct answer because the sentence indicates that the female worker faced issues with her coworkers and bosses in a male-dominated field. It is reasonable to infer that she faced issues in this field due to her gender. Choice *A* is incorrect because there is nothing to indicate that she received special help. Choice *C* is incorrect because, although the woman was successful, the sentence does not indicate whether she was more or less successful than her male counterparts. Choice *D* is incorrect because the worker's personal life is not mentioned.

14. A: Choice *A* is the correct answer because these sentences state two related facts: People have been shopping in malls much less, and online shopping has majorly increased. Therefore, it is reasonable to infer that people prefer shopping online to shopping in person nowadays. Choice *B* is incorrect because it is the opposite of what the statements imply. Choice *C* is incorrect because there is no indication of how services affect where people prefer to shop. Choice *D* is incorrect because there is no indication of a difference in quality.

15. C: Choice *C* is the correct answer because it is reasonable to infer that the author of the letter means something to the woman. The letter's contents are tenderly worded, and the emotions they evoke are powerful enough to make the woman cry. These are strong indicators that the woman cares for the author. Choice *A* is incorrect because even though the woman is weeping, it could be for a variety of reasons. Choice *B* is incorrect because the letter is tenderly worded and makes the woman smile, which implies that it is kind rather than hurtful. Choice *D* is incorrect because there is no indication that the woman is excited or planning to reply to the letter.

16. B: The best answer is Choice *B*. The reciprocal pronoun "one another" generally refers to more than two people. Choice *C* implies each person would look at themselves, while Choice *D* refers to individual objects.

17. A: Choice *A* is the correct answer because the sentence summarizes Boone's role in the development of the ironing board—not as a sole inventor but as someone who helped innovate the design in a major way. Choice *B* is incorrect because the text is not questioning Boone's contributions but rather affirming them. Choice *C* is incorrect because the text is not claiming that Boone is the sole inventor; she is a contributor to the design. Choice *D* is incorrect because the text is not trying to persuade the reader of anything; it is only describing Boone's contributions.

18. C: Choice *C* is the correct answer because it uses past tense (*had*), which is consistent with the rest of the paragraph. Choice *A* is incorrect because *have* is the present tense, while the passage uses past tense. Choice *B* is incorrect because it inserts an additional comma after *violence-ridden*. Choice *D* is incorrect because it leaves out the hyphen on the compound adjective *violence-ridden*.

19. B: "I" is a subject pronoun, and in this sentence, "I" is part of a compound subject, "my husband and I." A helpful way to answer this question is to take out the phrase "my husband" and read the sentence with each choice. Choice *A*, "myself drive our daughter" is incorrect, and so is Choice *D*, "myself, drive our daughter." Choice *C*, "me drive our daughter" is also incorrect. "I drive our daughter" is the best answer.

20. C: Collective nouns denote a group as a single unit, and they typically take a singular pronoun ("Mankind had its finest hour.") In this passage, *man* is taken as the universal, collective subject. *His* agrees with *man* and in this context is grammatically correct. Choice *B* (*her*) would make the valid point that traditional constructs unfairly exclude women, but that argument is irrelevant to the discussion of Hawthorne's allegory of the human heart. Choice *D*, *people's*, would require the plural *hearts* instead of the singular *heart*.

21. A: Choice *B* is incorrect because the comma separates the noun *light* from its verb dims and the introductory phrase *but a few feet in* must be followed by a comma. Choice *C* is incorrect because the commas are needed to separate the phrases within the clauses. Choice *D* is incorrect because it lacks the appropriate commas and because the clause following the colon does not introduce a summary or an explanation.

22. C: The correct answer is Choice *C* because it includes the missing word *as* ("digging as deeply").

23. A: Choice *B*, *amount* refers to items that cannot be counted, whereas *number* refers to something, such as people, that can be counted. Choice *C*, *quota*, refers to a controlled quantity of something one must acquire or receive. Choice *D* is incorrect because *mass* can be used to refer to a large quantity of people, not the relatively small number from the passage.

24. D: Choice *D* is the correct answer because it adds the most relevant information. It tells readers which rice is less expensive and says that it may affect which choice someone makes. Choice *A* is incorrect because the sentence can be improved to be more informative. Choices *B* and *C* are incorrect because they do not say which rice is less expensive.

25. B: Choice *B* is the correct answer because the word *hoarse* aligns with the original text while providing more description to the sentence. The text is detailing soldiers in the midst of action. They are crying out with rough voices. In this case, *rough* means unsmooth. *Hoarse* is a more descriptive word that describes voices as being harsh, usually due to shouting. This makes it a better choice for this sentence. Although *scratchy* has a similar meaning to *rough*, it lowers the descriptiveness of the text's language, making Choice *B* incorrect. Choice *C* is incorrect because *boisterous* is a positive word that implies a level of cheerful energy. That is not appropriate for the scenario in this text. Choice *D* is incorrect because *fearful* does not align with the original text, which is describing the quality of the voice. *Fearful* describes the emotion behind the voice rather than the auditory description of it.

26. D: Choice *D* is a singular possessive noun. Choice *A* makes no sense; *humanities* is the study of human culture, which does not possess inherent goodness. Choice *B* is the plural possessive of *humanities*. Choice *C*, *humanitys*, is not a word.

27. A: The highlighted portion is an example of two independent clauses held together by a semicolon. The first clause is "but a few feet in, the light dims and warmth turns to chill," and the second one is "the visitor stumbles, first in confusion, then in terror." The introductory phrase "but a few feet in" is an absolute phrase and must end with a comma. Inserting a comma after "dims" is inappropriate because the conjunction "and" connects only two actions. In the second clause, the comma after "confusion" substitutes for the conjunction "and." Choice *B* is incorrect because the comma separates the noun "light" from its verb "dims." Choice *C* is incorrect because the commas are needed to separate the phrases within the clauses. Choice *D* is incorrect because it lacks the appropriate commas and because the clause following the colon does not introduce a summary or an explanation.

28. D: *Farther* indicates additional distance, whereas *further* indicates an additional amount of something abstract, such as time. Choice *B* interrupts the sense of journey the writer is describing and therefore is not the best answer. Choice *C* is awkward; *toward* rather than *to* is correct.

29. C: Choice *C* is correct because a colon is used to introduce a summary or an explanation. The phrase "the beauty that lies beyond fear and hopelessness" further describes Hawthorne's vision of human nature. Choice *A* is incorrect because the semicolon is not separating two independent clauses. Choice *B* is incorrect because it creates a sentence fragment. Choice *D* is incorrect because parentheses are used to enclose nonessential elements such as minor digressions.

30. C: Choice *C* is the correct answer because the text is educating the reader about the theory that Shakespeare was not responsible for writing all of the works he's credited with by himself. Choice *A* is incorrect because the text does not encourage the reader to do anything. Choices *B* and *D* are incorrect because the author does not express agreement or disagreement with the theory.

Writing Prompt

When writing a persuasive-explanatory essay, it's important to use the author's words to support your claims. You can do so by quoting phrases and sentences that reinforce your point. However, it's easy to accidentally take the author's message out of context. A great tip to preserve the original message is by paraphrasing. Compare your summary to the author's initial statements. If the general idea is unchanged, you're going to do well.

For the persuasive side of an essay, you're going to try to convince the reader that your opinion is valid. You'll want to write in a convincing and deliberate manner. Avoid using words like *maybe*, *potentially*, *could be*, etc. Those words have a tendency to diminish a strong message. Remember to include the opposing argument in your paper. A balanced persuasive essay shows both sides of the argument. Acknowledge the opposing view, but don't get too worried about the minute details.

Don't forget the general structure of an essay!

- An introductory paragraph contains your initial opinion and idea. You can't have an introductory paragraph without a thesis statement. You'll also allude to your main points briefly.
- Body paragraphs are your main points. For a 300–600-word essay, two to three body paragraphs will be fine. Make sure you address your first point, add your supporting evidence, and elaborate. Repeat those steps as needed.
- The concluding paragraph summarizes your main points.

Writing can be hard, but have no fear. Try to imagine you're having a conversation. Essays are essentially structured conversations. However, it's not quite like talking with friends. Slang, inside jokes, and abbreviations don't work well for strangers. Imagine you're talking to someone you deeply admire and respect; you'd want to be thoughtful and understanding. This means you should simplify complex ideas without being reductive and condescending.

In general, it's good practice to read what you write out loud. Your ears will notice if something doesn't sound right. Our ears pick up on details that our eyes miss. It's especially true when you're completely focused on writing.

If you get stuck at any point, take a break, and come back to it. You'll have ample time to finish if you pace yourself and take it easy.

Index

Greetings!

First, we would like to give a huge "thank you" for choosing us and this study guide for your TSI exam. We hope that it will lead you to success on this exam and for your years to come.

Our team has tried to make your preparations as thorough as possible by covering all of the topics you should be expected to know. In addition, our writers attempted to create practice questions identical to what you will see on the day of your actual test. We have also included many test-taking strategies to help you learn the material, maintain the knowledge, and take the test with confidence.

We strive for excellence in our products, and if you have any comments or concerns over the quality of something in this study guide, please send us an email so that we may improve.

As you continue forward in life, we would like to remain alongside you with other books and study guides in our library, such as:

ACCUPLACER: amazon.com/dp/1637751346

We are continually producing and updating study guides in several different subjects. If you are looking for something in particular, all of our products are available on Amazon. You may also send us an email!

Sincerely,
APEX Test Prep
info@apexprep.com

Free Study Tips Videos/DVD

In addition to this guide, we have created a FREE set of videos with helpful study tips. **These FREE videos provide you with top-notch tips to conquer your exam and reach your goals.**

Our simple request is that you give us feedback about the book in exchange for these strategy-packed videos. We would love to hear what you thought about the book, whether positive, negative, or neutral. It is our #1 goal to provide you with quality products and customer service.

To receive your **FREE Study Tips Videos**, scan the QR code or email freevideos@apexprep.com. Please put "FREE Videos" in the subject line and include the following in the email:

a. The title of the book

b. Your rating of the book on a scale of 1-5, with 5 being the highest score

c. Any thoughts or feedback about the book

Thank you!

Made in the USA
Coppell, TX
25 June 2024